THE
Screwing
OF THE
Average Man

David Hapgood

THE
Screwing
OF THE
Average Man

Doubleday & Company, Inc.
Garden City, New York
1974

Library of Congress Cataloging in Publication Data

Hapgood, David.
    The screwing of the average man.

    1. Consumer protection—United States. 2. Consumers—United States.
I. Title.
HC110.C63H36   381
ISBN 0-385-00589-x
Library of Congress Catalog Card Number 74–4872

Acknowledgments

THIS BOOK is the fruit of a collaboration with the editors of *The Washington Monthly*. Charles Peters, editor-in-chief, helped shape the original idea and has been an active participant all along the way. Most of the material used here was collected by the magazine's staff and contributors: John Rothchild, Taylor Branch, Walter Shapiro, James Fallows, Paul Dickson, Urban Lehner, Charles Mueller, Eliza Paul, Milton Friedman, and Philip Stern. Carol Trueblood held us all together. I am also indebted to Mary Adelaide Mendelson for much of the information on which chapter 10 is based, and I have drawn often on the ideas of Jethro K. Lieberman. My thanks to Ronald and Beatrice Gross and to Pierre Tonachel for their critical comments on the draft.

A word about the title. We like it fine, but the complaint has been heard that the use of the word "man" obscures the fact that women suffer more than their 52 per cent share of the abuses described in these pages. I usually respond by quoting the woman who protested a magazine piece titled 'A Female Chauvinist Sow Confesses' on the grounds that "pig" refers to both sexes; she appealed to women not to let males take away the word "pig" the way they did "man." Our critics remain unconvinced, or unamused, or both. Doubtless they're right, but the available solutions (person?) seem worse than the problem. One day the language will get itself straightened out. Meanwhile, here we are.

Contents

THE
Screwing
OF THE
Average Man

1

The Screwing
of the Average Man

MOST OF US SENSE, as we go about our lives, that we usually come out on the short end of our daily transactions, but we can't say for sure because the nature of those transactions is so cloudy that we cannot spell out just what is happening. This cloudiness, this inability to count our chips in a game that we vaguely realize is going against us, is the unique aspect of the screwing of the average man as it is practiced today. The fact that he is screwed is no news; what is novel, and indeed peculiar to our times, is the way in which it is done.

The average man has of course always been a loser, at least since the invention of agriculture made it profitable for one person to exploit another. Throughout history, the average man has sweated out the desires of his superiors, and they have erected on his back a majestic series of monuments to gods, to conquest, and to themselves. The average man has paid tribute to the ideals of his time by suffering and sacrifice, while the privileged classes have sanctified the same ideals by luxury and the good life. The average man built the pyramids, but history remembers only the Pharaoh's name, and it was the

Pharaoh who was scheduled to ride to the afterlife on the solar boat buried with him in the pyramid, not the workmen who actually built the boat, so that the screwing of the average Egyptian extended past the grave. As recently as a couple of generations ago, it was easy to figure out who was who by fixing people's position in relation to the railroad track: people on one side exploited those on the other. Over those endless centuries, it was clear to the average man that he was a loser, and there was no doubt about who was doing it to him.

Only yesterday it seemed that the average man's destiny was at last taking a turn for the better. Those were the years that were fat. Starting with the Second World War, which ended in a victory that enriched as well as ennobled us, the nation enjoyed a prosperity so great that even the average man was granted a share in it. Most of us were doing better with each passing year. Although the poor were still with us in substantial numbers, no one else was noticing their continued existence. For the person raised during the Depression, or if he was younger, told about it by his parents, it was close to the best of all possible worlds. He moved upward from tenement to suburb, from blue collar to white, and from the bus to his own car; the majority of Americans came to think of themselves as members of the middle class. Of course, the rich were moving ahead a lot faster, for every time the average man gained an inch, the rich took a mile, and the concentration of wealth, a process briefly interrupted during the Depression, picked up momentum again, so that soon a greater share of the nation's possessions was concentrated in fewer hands than it had been since the twenties. It didn't matter, because the pie kept growing so that no matter how large the chunk carved by the rich, an extra slice was there for the average man too.

The famous trickle-down theory—pour enough in the bowls of the rich, and some of it is bound to spill over to those below—seemed at last to be working for the benefit of the common man. Indeed, he himself was becoming part of the system, so the great institutions told him. A few years back, for example, a Prudential ad showed the average policyholder taking his western vacation on a million-acre ranch which, though in the company's name, by implication "belonged" to the policyholder. Down on Wall Street, the average man was offered an opportunity to become a capitalist, and, according to the government, if he bought savings bonds he would acquire a "share in America." We were all stockholders in the American enterprise, and the value of our shares was rising steadily in an endless bull market.

The bad old days were gone forever. The robber barons, those great predators who in the late nineteenth century swallowed up the proceeds of the average man's labor, were no more than extinct monsters. Their descendants, though still wealthy, were so housebroken that they spent their time sitting around foundation boardrooms plotting good works. Capitalism had been tamed to the point that, in at least one view, it should be rebaptized. In a 1951 article titled "Wanted: A New Name for Capitalism," William I. Nichols, editor of *This Week* magazine, wrote of "this system . . . where men move forward together, working together, building together, producing always more and more, and sharing together the rewards of their increased production." A year later Frederick Lewis Allen published *The Big Change,* a view of the United States in the first half of the twentieth century. The big change in those fifty years, Allen believed, was that the economic system had been democratized, that the corporation had been tamed by government and the public, and that the gap between rich and non-rich was narrowing. Businessmen were coming to act more like professionals, Allen said; he thought that was a desirable change. Allen's chief worry was the "poor taste of newly prosperous Americans." Optimism was everywhere, and it lasted a little more than twenty years.

Then the great surge upward stopped. Sometime in the late sixties, the average man's domestic economy stalled. He was drawing higher pay each year, but it was all eaten away by inflation and taxes, and the extra cash did not seem to buy him a better life. The setback was supposed to be temporary, but instead of getting better, the situation got worse, and by the early seventies the majority of Americans other than the rich were actually losing ground. The pie was growing by less each year, until finally it stopped growing entirely. But the rich had not lost their appetite and, as they continued to add to their share, the average man suddenly found himself squeezed out: his slice had to shrink in order to accommodate the hunger of those above him. Trickle down became trickle up. Soon the ancient call to sacrifice was heard, and the average man was once more the first to be summoned. The nation was in trouble, and his superiors called on him to suffer for them, as his ancestors had been called out to work without pay on the pyramid, and hurry up before old Pharaoh dies. As ever, the average man was granted a monopoly on sacrifice. When "controls" were imposed because of inflation, the average man was denied the wage increase that would have enabled him to stay even, but profits were uncontrolled and prices kept on going up. The nation ran short of fuel in 1973 and 1974, and though the blame could hardly be laid at the average man's door, the consequences were charged to him: his car went without gas and his home without fuel or the prices doubled, while the oil companies registered huge increases in their profits. Businessmen "passed through" their added costs to the public, but the average man, like the last person on the bucket brigade, had no one to whom he could pass through the extra bill he received. In 1974 a group of congressmen led by John McFall of California estimated that wealth was being transferred to the richest one fifth of the population from those below them at the rate of $10 billion a year. If the poor were getting hungrier, so too were the rich: things were back to normal.

As we emerged from the dream of endless progress and a bigger share for everyone, it became obvious that today's screwing of the average man was far different from the straightforward exploitation of the past. It has, in fact, become hard to tell the difference between victim and hustler, to identify ourselves with either the average man or his oppressors. We find, instead, that most people are on both sides—taking some, giving some—and are themselves not sure whether they are ahead of the game or behind. This problem, which never bothered the average man in the past, we shall call *net screwing*. It is peculiarly characteristic of our times. Indeed, the presence of net screwing, plus that of plastic, is the surest way of telling that we are in the twentieth century. In the course of this book we shall explore many aspects of net screwing, and in chapter 13 we offer a table from which the average man can calculate whether he is winning or losing in one major aspect of net screwing, the income tax.

The picture of the average man has become blurred. As we use the term here, "average man" does not refer to a person's brains, looks, age, height or social graces; it does not even—the language is having its problems these days—define one's sex. Paul Samuelson, the economist, once wrote: "If we made an income pyramid out of a child's blocks, with each layer portraying $1,000 of income, the peak would be far higher than the Eiffel Tower, but almost all of us would be within a yard of the ground." The average man lives within a yard of the ground. *Fortune* magazine, in 1968, observed that "Something thoroughly satisfying happens to people when they cross an income threshold of around $25,000 a year." The average man has not had that thoroughly satisfying experience. Gordon Burnside, writing in the *New York Times Book Review*, concluded that "perhaps the most important social division in contemporary America is between people who feel rather swamped by a variety of possible modes of being, and people with a choice of two": those two are hanging on to what you have, or spending it before someone swindles it away from you. Following the same line of thought, religion professor John C. Raines finds the average man to be that half of the American people making between $10,000 and $25,-000 and living in a "financial nightmare." Above all, the average man gets all or almost all of his income from work; otherwise, as we shall see in chapter 13, he would be able to beat the tax system and come out ahead of the game.

In some respects, however, income is not as useful as assets in drawing the line between the screwed and the winners. The person who holds a job paying $50,000 is far ahead of the pack, and yet he is subject to virtually all of the screwings described in this book. By contrast, the person with assets of $300,000 is a clear winner, though his income may be below $25,000. His wealth makes him immune to such screwings as pension plans, and the tax system will treat him far more kindly than the $50,000-a-year worker.

The average man is caught in the middle. He's not among the poor: the poor are excluded from the system, below it, old-fashioned losers like the average man of the past; a migrant farm worker, for example, needs no compass to tell him which side of the tracks he's on. Nor, obviously, is the average man among the rich, that handful at the top who are above the system. Nor is the average man, less obviously perhaps, a member of what has come to be called the New Class: the people who, though not born to wealth, were able during the years that were fat to climb to the point where they can play the game and come out ahead. Most of them are professionals, and we will have a lot to say about their role in screwing the average man. The average man is the rest of us: net losers in the system, yet never sure just why the game always comes out that way or who just stuck his hand in our pockets.

It seems ironic that America, the haven to which the average man fled from the pharaohs of the old world, should have turned out to be such a jungle of hustles for the very person we celebrate in our mythology. We Americans consider our society to be the first to recognize equality as our birthright and evenhanded treatment of all as our ideal (no matter how often that ideal has been violated in practice). The ideals of democracy, however, proved to be a challenge to human ingenuity, and man rose to the occasion. In other societies the average man was denied his rights by the rules of the game; whether by divine right or sheer power, his superiors were entitled to exploit him at will for their greater glory and comfort. In America some other way had to be found to keep the average man unequal. The solution was the swindle: it combines the ideal of equality with the opportunity for greed, for it holds that while every man has a right to his share, he won't be protected from those who would sucker it out of him. This divine right of hustlers flourished from the earliest days in America: our history is redolent with salesmen of goldbricks and snake oil. Yet in many ways the average man of a century ago was better able to cope with the swindlers around him. His world was both simpler and smaller, and he had a better grasp of his daily transactions. If his wagon broke down, he knew what was wrong with it, and when the cartwright had fixed it, he could evaluate whether the work was worth what he was being charged. He might buy a goldbrick once but probably not twice, at least not from the same person. In a small town the average man knew the reputation of the people he did business with. He might not know exactly how the pharmacist or the toolmaker plied his trade, but if they were swindling their customers, he would soon get wind of it. He was taken now and then, of course, but because he soon learned how it had happened, he could expect to do better the next time around.

All that has changed. The size of the community, the frequency with which we move, and the multiplying complexity and specialization of our transactions have deprived us of our old feel for what is going on around us. With the spread of education, we know a lot more about Brazil and a lot less about what the life insurance policy really means. We know nothing about the people we deal with in a city department store or a suburban shopping center. We no longer know what we're putting in our stomachs. Not long ago David Brinkley read off the listed ingredients of the white substance that passes for cream on an airline tray; of the ten or so chemical components of that "cream," the only ones that were intelligible to the average person were the artificial flavor and color. Still less, of course, do we understand the machines. Our ancestors understood their wagons, our grandfathers may have at least partly grasped what happens inside a Model T Ford, but the contemporary automobile is beyond the comprehension of all but those who make their living from it. We turn to strangers to keep the machinery of our lives functioning, and when they hand us the bill, we have no way of telling what we got for our money.

Many services have also been turned over to strangers that once were taken care of within the family. We need life insurance because the family is no longer a unit in which the survivors are supported by their relatives, and, when we are old, we need pensions and nursing homes for people who used to finish their lives within the family. (Except the wealthy, who can take care of themselves with their own money.) Once again, the average man knows little about what he is getting when he pays for services he used to find in the intimacy of his own family. For all these reasons, the average man is a far easier mark than he used to be.

Marks are made to be scored on, and a new breed of hustler soon seized the opportunities offered by the complexity of modern life. They are the experts. The expert is far harder to cope with than yesterday's snake oil salesman, for he comes clothed in the respectability of the lawyer, the administrator, the insurance agent, and he is there to minister to the needs of the average man. Complexity is the essence of his hustle: if the subject is basically simple, like life insurance, the expert will make it complex enough to require his services; and if it is already complicated, he will make it more so, and more of his services will be needed. Thus, in the world of machines, the computer man outranks the car dealer. The client loses out in a car deal because he has only a vague idea what goes on inside that machine, but he knows still less about the computer, and the opportunity is correspondingly greater. The computer man sells his client a machine of a given capacity; then, when the client's business grows, he will offer to convert his computer to a higher capacity. Now, the higher capacity already exists inside the computer; all that is needed is to connect a couple of wires. But the client knows nothing about what happens inside a computer, and so he will pay as if massive surgery had been performed on his machine. It's like selling a car with only two of six cylinders functioning, then charging for a second car in return for hooking up the extra cylinders. An automobile dealer, hearing about this maneuver from a computer salesman, paid his friend the ultimate hustler's compliment: "There's a lot we can learn from you!" Similarly, among the professions, opportunity is greatest at the apex of complication, among the doctors and lawyers, less among the simpler forms of expert like plumbers and car mechanics.

The average man finds control over his life slipping out of his hands and into those of the growing army of experts. In everything from his teeth to his picture tube, the average man's common sense has given way to the pronouncements of an expert who tells him what he needs, what it will cost, and how well the job was done. Following the pioneering example of the doctors, the other professions established the principle that it is up to the expert himself to determine how well he is performing the service he sells. The customer is not allowed to argue with the expert, if indeed he can ever understand what the expert is saying, for each caste of experts has designed a jargon, a professional esperanto, that is more or less unintelligible to those outside the caste. The usefulness of this jargon for concealing from the customer what the expert is doing was described in the case of law by Fred Rodell in his *Woe Unto You Lawyers!*: "Law deals almost exclusively with the ordinary facts and occurrences of everyday business and government and living. But it deals with them in a jargon which completely baffles and befoozles the ordinary literate man. . . ."

The experts have created new forms of monopoly to enforce their views on the public. (See chapter 11 for more on guilds and other monopolies.) With the co-operation of government, itself a monopoly of a different kind, the experts band together in professional guilds licensed by the states. The next step, inevitably, is to raise prices. One way is to cut down on the number of people in the guild. Another is to prevent the membership from engaging in unseemly capitalist competition; guilds force their members to charge minimum prices because, as they explain it, lower prices would threaten the quality of their services. The experts are then free to define the scope of their work, and soon the average man finds himself being protected against dangers he had not previously been aware of and buying benefits he had not known he wanted. Some of the professions have even invented special terms to describe this kind of swindle: when a lawyer invents legal needs, it is called "breeding litigation"; when a broker buys and sells to run up his commissions, he is "churning"; and when your life insurance agent sells you a new policy in place of the adequate one you already have, he is "twisting" you. (Of course not all experts are hustlers, but the public is defenseless against those who are.) The result is that the average man finds that, though his income seems to be going up, much of it is siphoned off to buy these new services from experts whose income is rising a lot faster than his.

Experts seldom compete with each other in their working over of the average man. As his body is divided up by medical specialists, like that diagram of a steer in the butcher shop, so is the average man's income allocated to the various professions for exploitation. Occasionally the experts quarrel, as in the current struggle between lawyers and insurance men over no-fault car insurance, but usually they respect each other's territorial rights: each gets his cut of the steer. However, this does not mean that the experts do not screw each other, for each is a mark when he's not practicing his own trade. The lawyer took the automobile dealer to the cleaners, but some day the lawyer will need a new car, and the dealer will have his chance to get even.

This is *transfer screwing:* the experts doing onto each other as they do onto the public. It can best be seen in action in the small town Rotary Club. Rotary by tradition only takes one member from each occupation, so that when they meet every Wednesday to lunch and deal, no one is competing for his territory; each Rotarian gets a clear field to practice his hustle on his fellow members. The atmosphere of good fellowship is financed by those outside Rotary who feed a steady flow of cash into the system so that everyone inside, while being screwed moderately by the other members, comes out ahead in his balance of payments.

How experts make out in the system of transfer screwing depends on their place in the hierarchy of professions. Those at the top, like doctors and lawyers, are comfortably in the black. The tribute they pay to other experts is so small in relation to their own take that it can be considered a charitable contribution to keep the system going, a bit like the doctor who sent the Internal Revenue Service a check for $2,500 because his conscience was bothering him; if his conscience still was troubling him the next day, the doctor added, he'd send in the rest of the money. Alongside the traditional high professions there has sprung up recently an expert class that thinks and administers for governments and foundations; the word "analyst" frequently appears in their titles. Though they make less money than, say, doctors, these experts enjoy an even greater freedom from the marketplace; they are paid for by the public indirectly, through taxation or whatever swindle produced the foundation's wealth, and so the average man never gets a chance to refuse the experts' services. Down at the other end of the scale, among the expert proletariat, the picture is badly muddled. This is where we find the egg graders and certified shorthand reporters, those occupations that are in constant danger of being called jobs rather than professions. Their take comes in small amounts compared to the high professionals, and they are always going to lose out to the doctors and the lawyers. So the low expert, though he may be selling people unneeded services at monopoly prices, is likely to be paying out more to the experts who are taking him. Here the expert shades off into the average man as he figures out that, in the balance of screwings, he is in the red just like his clients.

What happens when a group of experts converge on one person can be seen in that remarkable ritual known as the "closing." It is the major event that marks the sale of a house. Once upon a time the major skill involved in creating a home was that of the carpenter who built it. Now, however, the construction has been standardized, and the carpenter's skill has been transferred to the experts who manage the papers by which ownership is transferred from one person to another. That transfer provides employment, as John Rothchild noted, for "a growing industry of scribes, heraldic researchers, and protocol officers—people who have been idle since the decline of the family tree business." They are busy now, flanked by secretaries and typewriters, at the job of protecting us from a host of new perils that they have discovered. Their ministrations are costly; between them, the buyer and seller will pay out from 9 to 12 per cent of the value of the house during the bloodshed at the closing.

The title insurance man stands out at the closing because he has moved a full lap ahead of the pack of experts. Despite the general protection of the doctrine of self-evaluation, which holds that the expert himself decides how well he does his work, experts occasionally get laid low by a dissatisfied customer: an ingrate who wants his money back, and will even go to court to get it. These professionals are inhibited by the fear, no matter how remote, that incompetence may get them into trouble. The title expert has solved the problem by the remarkable tactic of selling the client insurance on his own performance. Title insurance, described in more detail in chapter 4, works like this. An expert searches the records to see if the seller really has clear title to the house. He charges the buyer for his service. Then he sells the buyer an insurance policy that will protect him in the event his search failed to turn up a flaw in the title.

In effect, then, the expert makes the buyer pay for his work and pay again, in advance, for protection in the event the expert botched the job. Title insurance may well be the most important advance in professional thinking since the American Medical Association discovered how to apply occupational birth control to the number of doctors. It is easy to foresee what will happen once the precedent catches on among the other experts: the agent will sell you life insurance, then a second policy to cover the chance that his company will fail to pay off your survivors; the surgeon, after scheduling the operation, will suggest you stop at the desk and insure yourself against the possibility that he will remove the wrong organ; the accountant will do your books, then insure you for your lawyer bills if his work results in your indictment, while the lawyer in turn will sell you insurance to support your family in the event he fails to keep you out of jail . . . The opportunities are limitless: a people that can sell title insurance can sell anything.

Sometimes, when the world is tilting badly against him, the average man gets caught in a *carom screwing*. A carom occurs when one screwing either causes or reinforces a second, so that the very fact of being screwed once guarantees that there is more and worse to come. As described in detail in chapter 8, the automobile and its related hustles are particularly rich in carom screwings. For example, the fact that cars are designed to travel ever fewer miles per gallon multiplies the tribute that the average motorist must pay to the oil monopoly, and, in what may be a uniquely long chain reaction, the flimsy construction of cars provides carom effects on the sale of spare parts, the volume of repairs, the size of insurance premiums, and lawyers' fees. If the average man gets caught in too many carom screwings, he has little hope of coming out ahead of the game.

While the average man's pocket is being picked, his attention is distracted by some other strategies which help to give hustling in our time its distinctive flavor. Foremost among these strategies is *the third-party payment system*. *Third-partying* consists of taking the losers' money and dumping it into a large trough, from where it is ladled out to the winners—thus interposing the pooling of the money between the average man and his beneficiaries. Taxation is the most familiar third-party payment system. As government's share of the national income increases, the average man's share in deciding what is done with his money diminishes. It is impossible for most of us to have more than the haziest notion of what happens to our tax money. Though most people doubtless sense that some of it goes to those who already have too much, some to purposes we approve, and some for things we don't like, there is in practice nothing we can do about it: elections are not held on whether the merchant marine, say, should get a federal subsidy. The average taxpayer cannot earmark his share. Some of his taxes will go to Lockheed Aircraft Corp., some to welfare, some to the banks in excess interest on the national debt, some for schools—all of it is so intermingled in the pool that the average person can feel neither outrage nor satisfaction, but rather impotence.

Another form of government third-partying, in which no cash changes hands, is called *fail-to-collect*. Rather than dish out subsidies to its friends, government simply avoids collecting from them: examples are the income tax loopholes, tax-exempt property, and interest-free government bank deposits. Here the trail is especially muddy, for, even if the taxpayer were permitted to stand by the trough and observe who comes to feed, he still would not see the beneficiaries of fail-to-collect: J. Paul Getty does not have to come to the trough in order to collect on the tax laws governing oil money, nor does David Rockefeller have to be there for the Chase Manhattan Bank to earn its money on its free government deposits. The average taxpayer has had to put in a little more so that they could put in a lot less, but he will never see their faces.

Two other major users of the third-party system are the health industry and commercial television and radio. How the health industry third-parties is described in chapter 6. Television and radio are free, as everyone knows, which means that no one can escape paying for them. (A handful of stations, like public television and the Pacifica radio chain, are financed entirely or in part by their audiences; but their fans also have to support the free part of the industry.) The costs of television and radio are passed on, through advertising budgets, to the consumers of every product ever plugged on the tube or over the air. The consumer cannot choose not to support the networks just because he never watches or listens;

nor can the audience vote with its dollars for the programs it likes. If, by contrast, sets were coin-operated, with the money going to the program watched, producers would earn as much or as little as consumers wanted to pay for their programs; the costs of broadcasting would be the same, but they would be paid differently, according to who watched what, and the buyer of hair spray and deodorant would decide separately whether he also wanted to support *Lassie*. Thus third-partying in television and radio, like the self-regulation and price fixing of the experts, prevents the consumer from butting into decisions about what they should be fed over the airwaves. (Newspapers and magazines are third-partied to the extent that they live on advertising, but the public can decide whether or not to pay the cost of a subscription. Books are not third-partied at all: anyone not buying this book will not share in its cost, distressing as that thought may be to the publisher and the author.)

Youtooism is more advanced a strategy than third-party payments. Where third-party aims to confuse the average man about the identity of those screwing him, youtooism goes a step further and attempts to convince him that he isn't being taken at all—that in fact he's among the winners in the exchange of net screwing. It is a strategy peculiarly suited to hustling under democratic auspices. Under the youtoo principle, when a privilege is extended to the rich, it is also seemingly extended to the non-rich, but the wheel is so fixed that the rich win and the rest lose; if the system works right, the losers leave the table thinking they came out ahead. The most obvious youtooism is found in the tax system (discussed in detail in chapter 13). Many of the tax loopholes have a tail that hangs down within the reach of the average taxpayer. For example, any taxpayer can deduct interest, so it would seem that anyone who owes money will come out ahead. The joker is that while the average man takes his deductions by the thimbleful, the rich are taking them by the carload, and the government loses so much on the big deductions that to keep its revenue constant it has to raise taxes on the average man by more than he saved on his deduction. If, for instance, a real estate operator borrows $10 million and deducts his interest of, say, $800,000, while a homeowner is taking off $500 on his mortgage interest, the homeowner is going to end up worse off than if neither of them had the deduction. Somehow a lot of people seem to miss this point, and youtooism makes them supporters of their own screwing. Aside from its fast shuffling of the numbers—one for you, fifty for him, everybody wins—youtooism makes accomplices of people; that little tail they are holding makes many think of themselves as insiders, doing what the big boys do, if only on a smaller scale: they too can talk about tax shelters. This may be what accounted for the willingness of small investors in the stock market to keep coming back after the beatings they regularly took. Youtooism, more than anything else, prevents people from seeing that they are net losers.

In reality, most people must lose because of the limits placed on youtoo by *Catch-85*. Under Catch-85, the number of people who benefit from a special privilege is limited to no more than 15 per cent of the population; the rest must lose so that their money is available to pay the winners' share.* Thus the homeowner must lose on

* The figure 85 is arbitrary, for the percentage of losers will vary according to the nature of the screwing. Optimists may put the average somewhat lower, though anyone placing the percentage of losers below

his interest deduction if the real estate operator is to win. So far, however, the dream of youtoo has prevailed over the grim arithmetic of Catch-85.

Wordnoise, like youtooism, is a necessary part of swindling in a democracy. The basic idea of wordnoise— that swindlers cover their acts with the sound of language —is of course not unique to our times; as long ago as the eleventh century, a band of European buccaneers were able to convince history to call their Middle Eastern raids the "Crusades." Still, democracy causes this particular weed to flourish because the egalitarian ideal requires a great deal of hypocrisy to camouflage the screwing of the average man. Hypocrisy was far less in demand, except perhaps on religious occasions, in societies where exploitation was the accepted rule. We can safely assume, for example, that the average American has never heard from those hustling him any statement as clear as those made by a Roman slave owner to his property. A generation ago George Orwell told us that we can read people's intentions by their use of the language: if the words are so long and fuzzy that we cannot understand what is being said, or if we surmise that they are saying nothing at all, we can be fairly sure that the speaker is trying to swindle us.

The language that reaches the public has gotten still more suspect since Orwell's time. Arthur Herzog, in his 1973 book *The B.S. Factor*, drew the essential distinction between lying and faking. A lie is something you can get caught at, while a fake is fail-safe. "America," Herzog wrote, "will be the first civilization to eliminate lies." The

---

half deserves investigation. Pessimists will put the number of losers higher, and members of the wilder schools of thought may well press on to the ultimate zero—Catch-100, where everybody loses.

lie, that is, will be replaced by the more secure fake: a statement that, while designed to deceive, is too mushy and impenetrable to get you into trouble; no one can disprove a fake (your car warranty, for example) because no one can figure out exactly what it is saying. Fakery reaches the average man in the form of an increasing volume of wordnoise so great as to drown out other voices and, occasionally, even his own thoughts. Examples of wordnoise are embarrassingly common: almost any governmental or commercial message will do. Much of today's wordnoise is broadcast by experts who are manufacturing complexity in order to mystify their clients, and, in later chapters, we will touch on the use of wordnoise to hustle the average man in insurance, the Internal Revenue Code, pension plans, and the high professions of law and medicine.

It should be noted here that Herzog's distinction between lying and faking has its analogy in the modern attitude toward crime, at least of the non-violent variety. Just as America is replacing the lie with the fake, we are eliminating crime by making all the really good hustles legal. It is old-fashioned to steal, for example, when much more money can be made safely in real estate or government contracting. As a result, the Mafia is increasingly being forced to go legitimate in order to survive as a business enterprise. Sutton's law is in need of revision. Willie Sutton, when asked why he robbed banks, said, "Because that's where the money is." Willie Sutton was a professional in his day, but now robbing a bank is the act of an amateur: a professional would, say, loot a mutual fund, shove his winnings through a tax loophole, and never risk going to jail. A similar legitimacy has been in part extended to the more modest forms of white-collar crime. Regulators of consumer frauds, for example, are typically content, when they catch a scoundrel in the act, just to make him give the money back, thus providing him with no valid reason not to swindle the next person who comes in the store. If the same principle were applied to street crime—give the money back if you're caught, and no hard feelings—it would give the occupation of mugger some much-needed social status.

Our concentration here on modern forms of screwing does not mean that the older hustles have disappeared. Monopoly is still around, even if it wears a blander face these days. Since the earliest times, ambitious swindlers have been trying to eliminate competition and charge the average man more for less. The robber barons, viewed nowadays as wicked old capitalists, could better be described as early adherents of the currently fashionable philosophy of socialism for the rich. Building a better mousetrap was the last thought they had in mind; they wanted to corner the market and sell a trap that couldn't even catch flies. Their fortunes were made not on capitalist competition but on the opposite: John D. Rockefeller did not make his money by producing oil more efficiently but by wiping out everyone else in the business, and J. P. Morgan did the same in railroads, steel and telephones. Today, as we shall see in chapter 11, monopoly is an important part of the screwing of the public, though its nature has changed since the robber baron days. Professional monopolies have added their weight to that of the old industrialists: the AMA vies with General Motors for the public dollar. So have monopolies based on government connections. When *Fortune* in 1968 measured the really big fortunes, those of $150 million and up, it found that more than half of them were fertile old money that had kept on breeding: names like Dupont, Ford, Mellon, and Rockefeller. Most of the new money, *Fortune* found, was made in government-protected enterprises like defense and the old reliable, oil. The fastest comer of them all, H. Ross Perot, made his serving the poor and the sick on government contracts. All these fortunes have one characteristic in common: none of them was earned in the competitive free market that, according to high-level wordnoise, is the bedrock of the American economic system. Free enterprise is for the average man. The rich know better.

Still other swindles that we meet in our daily rounds will not be described here because they are merely modern versions of traditional maneuvers. The undertaker, for example, is a type of hustler who immediately comes to mind. But he has been around almost as long as death itself, and besides, as we note in chapter 5, dying nowadays is more profitable to the lawyer than it is to the funeral parlor. Credit is a major area of screwing that we shall not cover here. Few swindles affect so many Americans as credit; the evidence is in the monstrous growth of consumer debt and bankruptcy. The way Americans are lured into buying beyond their means, then lured into refinancing their debts at ever increasing amounts of interest, then foreclosed or repossessed when they have been bled dry, is a tragically old story to many families. But screwing by credit is nothing new: the moneylender has been with us since time out of mind, and his basic method remains unchanged. Consumer fraud is another major screwing we will not be covering (at least not in its most familiar form; though expertism is a form of consumer fraud). Every time the average man ventures into the market, he is in danger of being taken by slack packing, watered meat, collapsible construction, and all the thousand and one other afflictions of the consumer. If he buys on time, he will be caught in the carom effect: screwed on the goods he bought, screwed again by the finance company. But consumer fraud, like credit, is not distinctive to our times: the goldbrick has been on sale for a long time, though today it is likely to be a piece of swamp or desert sold to land-hungry city slickers as a real estate investment.

Doubtless there are other screwings that could have been included if books were accordions. Congressman Edward Koch of New York City, when told the title of what was then a work in progress, stretched his arms wide to indicate the scope of a bookshelf and asked politely, "So you're writing an encyclopedia?" Not an encyclopedia. Our aim is to identify those major ways in which the average man is exploited, and made to hold still for it, that are distinctive to our times: the hustles, that is, that have been invented in response to the present condition. Some, like school, are experienced primarily by the young; others, like pensions and nursing homes, have the old as their victims; the majority, however, pursue us impartially throughout our lives. We shall, in the chapters that follow, illustrate those hustles as the average man meets them in a series of encounters that, taken together, go far towards defining the quality of life in this place at this time.

2

The Genteel Way
of the Banker

DURING THE FIRST THIRD OF THE CENTURY bankers were often synonymous with robber barons. For example, J. P. Morgan, besides his immortal observation that if you have to ask how much a yacht costs you can't afford it, also left us such industrial giants as U. S. Steel and AT&T. Morgan created these and other corporate gold mines by using his capital to destroy competition and bring one industry after another under the control of one, or at most a handful of companies.

The wave of bank failures that marked the twenties and the rigors of the Depression did little to enhance the image of the banking profession. Bankers were regarded as heartless men who went around evicting widows and orphans, and if the Third National Bank of Armadillo went bust because some trusted cashier had slipped off to Argentina with most of the liquid assets, you—and anyone else with deposits there—were just out of luck.

Bankers have come a long way in the last forty years. Not only do they no longer rate as villains, they have become one of our most revered professions. A recent Harris

Poll, which detailed the decline of trust throughout American life, showed that bankers were a conspicuous exception. Almost 60 per cent of those polled said they had faith in banks. In part, this new look is due to the role that bankers have come to play as the faithful guardians of the national economy, with such urges as their profit motive kept discreetly under wraps. As John Kenneth Galbraith remarked, "If anybody else is lobbying for a higher price, we take for granted that they want more dough, but if a banker is lobbying for higher interest rates, this is pure unadulterated righteousness. Everybody else says they want more money, but let David Rockefeller speak for higher interest rates and, boy, that's statesmanship."

During an era when library "Quiet" signs have about as much impact as UN resolutions, banks and cathedrals are virtually the only buildings we still enter with any sense of awe. Banks are past masters at making you feel guilty about coming in and taking home your own money. Most of us have experienced some occasional moments of panic as we have stood at the teller's window waiting for approval in order to cash a perfectly good seventy-five-dollar check. And remember the first time you went in to see your friendly banker about a loan? On one hand you felt quite awkward admitting that you needed the money, but on the other hand, if you had managed your financial affairs so prudently that you'd never before had to borrow, you were quickly chastised by the inevitable question, "Have you had any loan experience with us in the past?"

Banks trade on this embarrassment, coupled with our almost total ignorance of things financial, to pull off some of the most outrageous, but always genteel, screwings of them all. The genius of these bank heists is that they never tamper with the principal, they just keep developing new and better ways to avoid paying interest on it. Although in recent years they have been reformed in response to consumer pressure, Christmas Clubs provide the classic example of the genre. Remember how grateful we used to be that our bank was holding onto our two dollars a week interest-free, rather than forcing us to use a piggy bank? Banks, of course, welcomed those holiday clubs as an ingenious way of acquiring interest-free capital. Some banks are still reluctant to pay interest on Christmas Clubs. A West Virginia bank recently ran ads urging savers "to join the club that fights drug abuse." The bank's angle was simple—instead of paying interest, they were donating one dollar per holiday account to a local anti-drug agency. Now, one dollar represents a year's interest at 5 per cent on only twenty dollars. Assuming that the average holiday account is much larger than that, it is clear that the bank was asking its Christmas Clubbers to donate a lot more to the struggle against lower bank profits than to the battle against drug abuse.

These days checking accounts are probably the bank swindle that touches us the most directly. Although many of us take pride in the way we triple-check our monthly statements from the bank to make sure that no sticky-fingered computer operator is rifling our checking accounts, it is a rare soul who finds anything odd in the way he is paying the bank ten cents a check so the bank can lend out his money at 10 per cent interest. And those of us who thought we were outsmarting the game in signing up for free checking by maintaining a minimum balance, say $500, are in equally bad straits. Unless you are the sort who tries to buy candy from vending machines by writing a check, you are foregoing far more in lost interest on the $500 than you could possibly save on the free checking.

Although the amount of an individual's loss is still not breathtaking, interest-free checking accounts are perhaps the biggest things banks have going for them. On any given day, commercial banks—the only ones allowed to handle checking accounts—are holding $200 billion in checking account money. This amounts to 40 per cent of these banks' assets and they don't have to pay a penny of interest to use it. At 10 per cent, the bank customers are losing a total of $20 billion a year; any individual can, with a little effort, figure out his share of the total fleecing. Admittedly, a few of the more competitive banks have begun offering free checking. But even in these bastions of relatively enlightened banking, free checking is quite different from actually paying interest on these checking deposits.

In the theoretical free market, competition would soon force all banks to pay interest, or lose their checking accounts to the more aggressive fellow across the street. But here's where the federal government, that guardian of the free enterprise system, comes in. Banks are protected from the rigors of competition by a series of federal laws which produce monopoly behavior without the inconvenience of actually creating a monopoly. Checking accounts remain the private preserve of commercial banks because the government refuses to allow savings and loan associations or credit unions to get a piece of the action. A 1933 statute is even more blunt—it simply forbids paying interest on checking accounts. Originally designed to help the banking industry weather the dark days of the Depression, today all it does is brighten the lives of bank stockholders by creating an additional $20 billion in profits. Despite the size of the screwing, there is no effective pressure on Congress to repeal this 1933 statute. When the idea came up briefly in 1973, the American Bankers Association quickly pointed out that paying interest on checking accounts would affect "the stability and competitive balance of the financial system." Part of the reason nothing happens is that laws like this preserve the illusion of fairness: I may not be getting any interest on my checking account, but neither is the guy at the next window. The government's role in the operation is also a perfect way to deflect criticism from the banks, who are reaping the benefits of this windfall. If you complained to your local banker, he would patiently explain that the decision was not made by him and then politely suggest that you write your Congressman. Since most legislators are as bewildered about banking as you are, and many of those on the committees that handle bank legislation have banking interests of their own, this sort of approach is useless unless you enjoy receiving form letters that begin, "Representative Blank appreciates your letting him know your views on this important subject."

Although the thrill of the daring daylight bank robbery has appealed to the American psyche since the heyday of Jesse James, most bank-inflicted screwings have all the drama of a TV dinner. Gentility is the watchword and most bank hustles are impeccably legal, abstract and rather boring—like the bankers themselves. Banks are particularly adept at leaving the unsavory dirty work to others, while they continue to reap the profits. Each year countless Americans are sandbagged by credit in one form or another, but typically the early morning phone calls and the threatening letters come from a finance com-

pany, a collection agency or a store. Each of these operators is totally dependent on money borrowed from a bank,
but the banker is the last person who would be coming
around when it was time to repossess. The swindles directly affecting the customer are little noticed because the
loss to the individual is small (like the no-interest checking accounts) and, because of their complexity, they are
hard to detect. The big swindles, which invariably involve
the government, do not arouse public indignation because, though the swindle is obvious, it is far from clear
who is being taken or by whom—this is the third-party
payment principle. The banks are still in the business of
promoting monopoly and its product, higher prices. Morgan Guaranty, for example, has working control of four
of the five largest copper producers, but should you get
exercised over the price of copper, you are hardly likely
to finger the bank as the villain.

An example of a two-bit swindle is the 360-day year.
If you borrow money for twelve months, your loan is due
in 360 days, but you have to pay interest for the entire
365 days. Four fifths of the banks use some form of this
short year. Possibly they are trying to promote calendar
reform; the 360-day year means twelve months of thirty
days each, and we would no longer have to remember
that bit of doggerel "Thirty days hath September . . ."
Still, it hardly seems fair to leave the bank's interest calendar ticking during these five bonus days (six in leap
year). From the individual borrower's point of view, the
loss is small—in six years, he will lose only a month's interest. But multiplied by the number of borrowers, it
adds up to quite a bit for the banks. A recent Illinois
court decision illustrates how profitable the 360-day year
can be for the banks. A class action suit against the proc-

ess led to a court order for one bank to refund between $30 and $50 million extracted from loans over a sixteen-year period.

Another small screwing, this one for homeowners, is the escrow account. Many mortgage agreements require the customer to pay his annual taxes and insurance, in advance, into an escrow account at the bank. Thus the bank has the use of his money, interest-free, until the taxes and insurance actually come due.* Again the cost to the customer is small. A homeowner with a $600 tax bill would get $8.88 if he were paid 5 per cent interest on his escrow account. The banks make about $100 million a year on interest-free escrow money. The bankers' defense of escrowing is twofold. First, they don't really make money on escrow because of administrative costs, which raises the question why they insist on doing it. Second, if they didn't escrow the homeowner, the tax authorities might have trouble collecting from him; while it is nice to see the bankers show such unsolicited concern for the problems of government, their defense loses some of its punch when one realizes that many banks themselves come in late with their escrow tax payments. Taking the broad view, it does seem heartless to deny the banks those millions just to save us $8.88 apiece.

The escrow also provides a fine example of the carom effect: a screwing that provides the opportunity for taking the client a second time. Once the banks had instituted escrowing, the client clearly needed someone to help him with the paperwork, and thus was born still another expert, the escrow agent. Little known in the East, the escrow agent is a familiar burden on the West Coast; his score at closings at last report averaged $148 in

* A few states now require banks to pay interest on escrow accounts.

Los Angeles and $135 in Seattle. The Department of Housing and Urban Development concluded rather politely that "the addition of escrow agents adds substantially to the cost of conveyancing without significantly adding to the level and quality of services."

These two hustles have the virtue of being easy to understand. The going gets tougher when you try to find out where you are likely to get the best interest rates for your savings. This is another area where the government restricts competition by setting tight ceilings on the interest rates that banks or savings and loan associations can pay. Interestingly enough, there is no limit, this side of usury laws, on how much banks can charge borrowers for the privilege of using the money you deposit in your savings account. Banks' profits come from this spread— the difference between what they have to pay you to get your savings and what they collect on loans.

One thing is pretty clear—you do better putting your money in a savings and loan rather than a commercial bank. The savings and loans cannot write checks and generally are restricted to writing home mortgage loans, but because the government believes in boosting homeownership (for them that can afford it), savings and loans are allowed to pay a fraction of a point more on savings than commercial banks.

This is where it begins to get muddy. What matters is how much interest you actually receive, rather than the stated interest rate. According to the American Bankers Association, there are fifty-four methods of computing interest in common use; in his article "How Your Banker Does It" (*The Washington Monthly*, July–August 1973), Paul Dickson put the number at over 100. Not surprisingly, different methods produce considerably different results. Jackie Pinson, a graduate student at Kansas State, figured out that two accounts paying the same stated rate of interest can differ by as much as 171 per cent in earnings in just six months. Most of the differences derive from the frequency of compounding; as a rule, the more often it happens, the more your money earns. Needless to say, even the most dedicated comparison shopper is soon lost in these complexities. So, for that matter, are the bank's employees. The Ralph Nader study of New York's First National City Bank found that only 40 per cent of the platform employees (the people sitting at desks one step above the tellers) understood the costs of the bank's various types of checking accounts. Although they are astonishingly adept at helping you decide whether you want a mauve or ochre checkbook cover, they are not the sort of people who can unravel the intricacies of compound interest.

Competition among banks, like automobile sales, revolves around a lot of intangibles like checkbook covers, rather than such basic concepts as price. From free giveaways for opening up a savings account (they never tell you that the federal government sets a $2.50 limit per $1,000 deposited on the value of your free dishes) to such folksy pitches as the short-lived "call us Irving" campaign of New York Irving Trust Company, the stress in bank ads is on frills rather than substance. Most banks are far more likely to allow you (for a slight service charge, of course) to have Karl Marx's picture or the hammer and sickle superimposed on your checks, than they are to give you an accurate reading of exactly how much interest you will be receiving on your savings.

It used to be equally difficult to tell how much interest you were paying when you borrowed money from the bank. Then came the truth-in-lending law, passed in 1969 over vigorous opposition, including the head of the National Retail Merchants Association, who said: "Few laymen can accept the fact that interest rates in excess of 6 percent a year are the rule rather than the exception. It would be unwise to educate them at the cost of a serious setback in the economy." The banks' response to the new law was to charge home buyers seeking a mortgage for the truth-in-lending statement that explains how much the borrower will actually pay. Evidently the banks felt truth was too precious to give away free. There is no charge for lying-in-lending.

The perils of competition are held at bay by the difficulty of getting into the banking business. Although opening a medium-sized bank often requires less capital than starting a chain of pizza parlors, you need considerably more to become a banker than the requisite capital and a yen to close down operations at 3 P.M. every afternoon. The sine qua non to go into banking is a charter, issued either by your state banking commissioner or the U. S. Comptroller of the Currency. This is just another area where the government shelters banking from the normal rigors of a competitive economy. According to free enterprise theory such decisions as starting a business are made by the investors, those with money to lose, but when it comes to banking these decisions are placed in the hands of the government regulators.

The criteria for getting a charter are pretty foggy, but political clout generally helps on the state level. For the more prestigious federal charters, the major criterion is a guarantee that your bank won't hurt any existing banks. You not only have to prove that your banking won't cause any other bank to fail (which is the rationale for the existence of bank regulators), but also that you won't even cause a dip in their profit margins. Your clients will all be new ones: those who have just moved into the area, or possibly those who have just learned of the existence of banking and have impetuously decided to take their money out of the mattress. Reduced to its simplest, this means that in an era of zero population growth there would be no new banks.

The key phrase in all of this is "overbanking." Although never precisely defined, it appears to refer to a competitive situation where banks are forced to start offering free checking and a few of the more aggressive units start grumbling loudly that they want to pay interest on checking accounts, as well, to attract even more deposits. Needless to say, this is a situation that bank regulators strive to avoid at all costs. One bank examiner, for example, wrote in regard to a pending application that "a concentration of banks in or near the [shopping] center, however, would certainly be unfortunate, and the competition, to the degree that it would probably develop, would be unhealthy." Unhealthy competition was also on the regulatory mind when an application for a bank charter on Key Biscayne island, where the only bank is run by Charles G. (Bebe) Rebozo, was denied by the U. S. Comptroller.

Regulators also screen banking personnel, not the $115-a-week tellers, but the Ivy League vice-presidents, looking for those most likely to launder money for the mob. Of course, laundering money in the name of public service elicits quite a different response from banking regulators. Some of the Mexican money that paid for the Watergate burglary originally came from a Minneapolis businessman, Dwayne Andreas, who shortly thereafter received a federal charter to be the only banker in a giant new shopping center in Minnetonka, Minnesota. Most applicants for a bank charter are supposed to exude qualities like "character" and "integrity." What this means in practice is not easy to define, but the effect seems to be to make banking a kind of old-boy world in which the more crudely competitive types (who turn out to be Irish Catholics, blacks, Jews, women, and anyone else who did not attend prep school) are carefully blackballed. With these potential boat-rockers removed from the banking game, banks can continue, but only in the most genteel fashion, to play screw the customer.

Once you have gained entry to the banking business, the water's fine. As in any monopoly, the profits are high, the stress is low, and the risk of loss is minimal. In 1971, less than 1 per cent of all banks lost money, and even those banks whose earnings were in the lowest tenth still managed to make a 6 per cent return on their capital. One bank regulator commented that "short of rampant dishonesty or incompetence on a scale almost defying imagination, it is virtually impossible for an established bank to lose money." It is also getting harder for the average man to get the fruits of those profits through the corporate income tax, for the banks, while making more money, have managed to reduce the amount they have to pay in taxes—their effective tax rate, 38 per cent in 1961, was down to 17 per cent by 1972.

Government helps the banks help themselves in other ways as well. Take the government's habit of leaving federal funds in interest-free bank accounts. According to congressional critics of this practice, the government has on any given day almost $6 billion in these no-interest accounts. (One student, Martin Price, pegs the sum at a much higher level—$50 billion.) If the government could get the same kind of interest on this money that it pays out to big investors on short-term Treasury bills, it could add about $400 million to the federal Treasury. Although this practice costs each American about two dollars in reduced government services, this classic third-party screwing is too abstract to become the kind of political issue that many voters can understand, let alone become aroused over.

Following the laws of physics, these deposits gravitate to those banks that already weigh the most. A 1972 House Banking Committee study found that just 102 big banks hold 43 per cent of these no-interest funds. And the largest account is, not surprisingly, at David Rockefeller's Chase Manhattan, followed by another Rockefeller bank, First National City. Rather than feeling any gratitude for its free money, the Chase also duns Uncle Sam for an additional $1 million a year to compensate it for operating branch banks on military installations overseas.

One form of these government accounts will be of particular interest to taxpayers: the tax and loan accounts in which the Internal Revenue keeps the money it has collected. Especially if the taxpayer has just been charged $16.73 interest for sending his return in late, it is worth pondering that the government does not deign to collect interest from the bank where it puts his payment. If the bank were forced to pay interest, of course, the IRS could pay the taxpayer a refund instead of charging him interest. The average man may be particularly puzzled by the fact that some of these government accounts are time deposits: the government must give thirty days' notice to withdraw. Even the ordinary depositor can get interest on such accounts but somehow the United States Government cannot. This may make the average man feel he is a smarter depositor than the Treasury, unless it also occurs to him that ultimately he is footing the bill for the Treasury's reluctance to collect interest on his interest.

Granting banks free money is not a habit limited to the federal government. State governments often are found doing the same thing. In Maryland, a few years back, the state Treasurer, John A. Luetkemeyer, placed $6 million a year of interest-free in Equitable Trust Co. of Baltimore, of which he happened to be chief executive officer. Alabama keeps interest-free money in a bank in George Wallace's hometown, and New York does the same in a bank in which Governor Malcolm Wilson has stock. Even the private sector does it. In 1973, Ronald Kessler of the Washington *Post* disclosed that bankers on the board of trustees of Sibley Memorial Hospital had put more than $1 million of the hospital's money in interest-free accounts at their own banks: the lost interest works out to $1.50 on the average patient bill.

Although the government does not mind foregoing interest on our money, it feels that the same fate should not befall a bank, especially a big bank. That is what happened a couple of years ago with the First National City Bank of New York. By the bank's own error, it paid the government twice for $38.8 million in government securities. The bank's bookkeepers found the error two and a half months later. The bank asked for, and got, its money back. That's not all it got. The Treasury also agreed to give the bank the interest-free use of $38.8 million for another two and a half months, to make up for the amount the bank had lost—through its own error, not the government's. The precedent is an interesting one:

presumably taxpayers who accidentally overpay their taxes can ask not only a refund but interest on their money for the time the IRS held it.

The banks put the government's money to good use—with the government itself. Banks invest much of that $6 billion in interest-free federal deposits in U. S. Treasury bills, on which the government was paying, at this writing, about 8 per cent. Thus, incredibly, the government is paying the bank 8 per cent in order to borrow back the government's own money. From the bank's point of view, it is collecting 8 per cent for passing the money from one government pocket to another.

When the banks put the money in Treasury bills, they make out much better than the average man does when he patriotically buys U.S. savings bonds. His savings bond, if he keeps it to maturity, will net him about one quarter less than the Treasury bill; if he sells it before maturity, he will net only a bit more than half what the bank made. To give some idea of the gall that the banks bring to this business, one of the services that banks cite to justify the bonanza they are reaping from the tax and loan accounts is that they sell savings bonds to a grateful public. Faced with this knowledge, the average man might be tempted to say the hell with the office savings bond drive (assuming that this bit of financial independence won't cost him his next promotion) and go down and buy himself a Treasury bill. A few years ago, a lot of people did just that. At the time the minimum denomination on a Treasury bill was $1,000. The Treasury quickly upped the minimum to $10,000, driving the ribbon clerks out of the game.

In 1974, the Treasury locked a side door through which the ribbon clerks had been sneaking back into the game.

As it had with the T-bills, the Treasury raised from $1,000 to $10,000 the minimum on its notes (borrowings for periods of one to seven years). The action was taken at a time when notes were earning the highest interest since the Civil War—8.75 per cent. The effect was to force the average man back into the arms of the banks, which are conveniently limited by law to paying 5 to 7.5 per cent for similar loans. Of course, if he had enough money the investor would have no problem: there is no limit on what banks can pay on notes of over $100,000, and at this writing loans of that size were earning around 11 per cent. But if the investor had that kind of money, he wouldn't be a ribbon clerk.

The ribbon clerks got one last chance in 1973 to grab for the high interest rates available to the fat cats who could afford the $10,000 Treasury bills. For a tantalizingly brief five-month period, the average saver could purchase $1,000 four-year "wild card" certificates of deposit. What made these wild cards unique was that their interest rates were set entirely by market forces, rather than government regulators. Soon the floating interest rate on the $1,000 wild cards was going as high as 8, 9, and even 10 per cent.

Then the bubble burst. The savings and loan associations were frightened by possible competition for the wild card savers from the commercial banks and orchestrated a massive lobbying campaign against these consumer-sized certificates. The S&L lobbyists were so glib that they even got such congressional defenders of the little man as Hubert Humphrey and Wright Patman to lead the fight against the wild cards. The anti-wild card legislation was shuffled by Congress so fast that no hearings were held and the bill passed by a voice, rather than a roll-call, vote. Now the small saver with $1,000 to tie up for four years has to content himself with a maximum interest rate of 7¼ per cent. Although banks generally nickel and dime you to death, the loss dealt the small saver by this bit of hasty congressional action should not be minimized. Over a four-year period on an investment of $5,000 (half the money needed to buy a Treasury note) a 2 per cent interest differential could cost a saver as much as $400—or the price of a color television.

Since thanks to that government action you may be unable to watch "Hollywood Squares" in living color, it is not surprising that Uncle Sam is rather reticent about his banking policies. Almost all government files on the granting of bank charters, for example, are off limits because, in the words of a former acting Comptroller General, "We don't want anyone to come in here on a fishing trip." And when Martin Price was studying the government's no-interest accounts in the days when John B. Connally was Secretary of the Treasury, he was told that the government accounts were so scattered that the only way they could be tabulated was if Price was willing to pay government workers twelve dollars an hour to do the job. Although banks are earning more than $400 million a year from the tax and loan accounts, the General Accounting Office has recently estimated that the cost of processing these accounts is a scant $25 million—leaving the banks a net of $375 million (or, if you prefer, an annual return of 700 per cent on their investment). The banks claim that they provide the government with another $100 million in free services and use this to justify the no-interest tax and loan accounts. However, some of these services, like the pushing of savings bonds, are of dubious value to the average saver. And other practices, such as reporting large or unusual currency transactions, are clearly in the banks' best interest.

The national debt, as it is now managed by the government, is another vast bonanza for the banks, and an equally large disaster for the average man. Since 1953, the government has allowed banks to buy a piece of the national debt. In 1973 government provided 27 per cent of the demand for credit in the nation's credit markets. Without this huge demand by government, interest rates for the average man would drop to more reasonable levels. In the fourteen years before 1953, 4½ per cent mortgages were common, and the government itself was borrowing, through the Federal Reserve, at an average of 2.3 per cent. Congressman Wright Patman, chairman of the House Banking and Currency Committee, believes that letting the banks in on the national debt has cost the public from $350 to $500 billion since 1953. Part of this is billed indirectly to the average man, in higher taxes to finance the higher interest rates his government has to pay. Part of it hits him directly—in mortgages at 8½ per cent, as of this writing, almost twice the pre-1953 rate, and in higher interest on all his other forms of borrowing. The monstrous total of $500 billion estimated by Patman may be too high, but there is little dispute over the basic point. The government has managed the national debt in such a way as to maximize bank profits and add to the interest costs to the general public—at the rate of, using Patman's lower figure, some $200 per year per taxpayer.

Hardly anyone protests, or even notices, the handling of the national debt, though the impact on the public is obvious. ITT makes headlines when it raids the government, while the banks go on quietly picking up much larger booty. This is the genius of banking: the bankers take us in ways that are discreet, complicated, legal and boring. It is a screwing by gentleman's agreement.

The national debt swindle is far too abstract, too lacking in drama or obvious villains, to stick in most people's minds. The government's subsidizing of banks with interest-free accounts is a model of discretion. No taxpayer's money is actually delivered to the banks; there is no budget item reading "bank subsidy." The government merely fails to collect from the banks, and nowhere in its accounts is there a listing for "failed to collect from banks: $400 million." The hustling of the client is done by rules —like the ban on paying interest on checking accounts— so well established that they are rarely questioned. The treatment is administered in a spirit of sober responsibility; there are no used car dealers in this business. If you don't mind being considered dull, banking may be the best way to do it.

3

Stock Market: The Slaughter
of the Innocents

IT SEEMED A GOOD IDEA at the time. During the first two decades after the Second World War, millions of working-class Americans had enjoyed steadily rising incomes. The average man was edging into the middle class. As a family's income passed $10,000, its members found they could live better than ever before and still have a bit left over. Here was a nest egg that, properly managed, could make the down payment on a home, put children through college, assure a comfortable retirement. What to do with the nest egg? Savings accounts paid meager interest—the egg wouldn't grow much in that nest. Real estate took too much capital and too much knowledge; seldom could you buy your way into a land venture with that $5,000.

That left the stock market. A lot of privileged people made their money on the market—maybe it was possible for the little guy (as he is known on Wall Street) to hitch a ride with them. Everyone heard the if-only stories based on the Market's performance in the 1950s: if only I'd bought IBM or Xerox ten years ago, now I'd have ten-fifty times my capital. Some risk, of course, but memories of 1929 had faded. Besides, we weren't going to have any more of those big depressions, the experts explained, and we had new institutions like the SEC to protect the investor. The stock market had something else, less tangible, going for it. Buying shares was a form of youtooism: it got the average man in on the action, reading the stock tables, learning a bit of the lingo, one step closer to the big boys in the inside. It was gambling, but unlike the horses it was moral, even patriotic, for your money was helping America Grow.

Wall Street was willing. Stockbrokers on the Street picked up the scent of those millions out there who wanted to bring them their modest offerings. The welcome banners were hung across the Street: "Own Your Share of American Business," "Wall Street Comes to Main Street," and the richly ironic "People's Capitalism." Merrill Lynch, bullish on suckers, opened offices all over the landscape. To ensure proper service, the exchanges raised fees on the small investor, so that he was paying almost twice as much per share as the big boys. Mutual funds, with much higher fees still, were operated as a group venture by a fund manager for people who wanted to diversify on small stakes and make the kind of killing that takes a big muscle.

They came by the millions. On all the Main Streets of America, the little guy brought his nest egg to the newly opened branch office and entrusted it to those experts who would guide him through the delightful mysteries of playing the market. The number of Americans who owned stocks rose from five million in 1950 to twenty million in 1965 and thirty-one million by 1970. They never rushed in faster than in the year 1968. During a remarkable year marked by the assassinations of Martin

Luther King and Robert Kennedy, the riots at the Democratic Convention and the My Lai massacre, the withdrawal of Lyndon Johnson and the election of Richard Nixon, Wall Street was making its own history by raking in the average man's chips faster than ever before or since. In the first five months of that year, Merrill Lynch alone opened 181,000 new accounts. As John Brooks put it in *The Go-Go Years*, "one American in every eleven hundred—counting men, women and children—opened a new brokerage account with a single firm."

The new investor arrived, of course, just in time to be in on the crash. The value of his nest egg began to go down in 1969, and by 1970, depending on what his broker had gotten him into, he had lost all or most or some of his savings. The glamor stocks favored by the brokers selling to the newcomers dropped by 81 per cent in those two years. The new investors in American business suffered losses far greater than those endured by those who went through the 1929 crash. In the earlier crash, investors lost some thirty billion—but in the crash of 1969–70, they lost ten times as much, more than three hundred billion dollars. It was a record screwing, and the little guy, who knew the least about what was going on, was hit hardest of all. What happened?

He entered the market in a spirit of innocent greed. He should never have been allowed out alone on Wall Street, and as soon as he ventured out on that sidewalk he got mugged. He didn't know the basic realities of life on the Street. One was the familiar principle of Catch-85, which holds that the little guy has to lose so others can win. Yes, there was money to be made in the market, but the insiders, those already on the Street when he came strolling along, knew they could take his nest egg without cutting him in on the profits, and that is what they did. The little guy didn't understand that the primary purpose of the stock market is to manufacture capital gains (sometimes losses) so people in the upper brackets can avoid paying taxes. (The purpose he had been told, helping America Grow, is insignificant: only about 5 per cent of new capital comes from the market; the great bulk of it comes from banks and corporate earnings and, for new ventures, from private deals.) Capital gains is a game played by experts with big chips. The broker knew the game, but he played it with his big clients; he had no time for penny ante with the small investor. It might have helped the little guy if he had studied those Internal Revenue Service tables showing how each income class makes out on its capital gains. He would have seen, as economist Gelvin Stevenson pointed out in an interview, that the rich are much less likely to lose in their capital transactions than people in his income class. For people down around $10,000 a year, the ratio of capital losses to gains is about two hundred times as high as it is for those in the $500,000-plus category.

The new investor missed the irony in the slogan "People's Capitalism." The slogan meant exactly what it said: the people were being offered a chance to take the risks of free enterprise. The people, yes, but not the insiders of the Street. They preferred their brand of socialism-for-the-rich. Sheltered from the winds of competition and the prying of public regulators, they played their game with his money—he took the risk, they took the gain. Too bad the average investor didn't hear what they were saying about him. Indeed, before deciding to invest, he would have done well to disguise himself as a conglomerate and eavesdrop on Wall Street gossip about the little guy. This is what he would have heard:

On his chances of winning: "Where are the customers' yachts?"

On his shrewdness: "Watch the little guy and do the opposite. He's always wrong."

On his role on the Street: "What would we do without them? They buy when we're ready to dump, and they sell when we figure the market has bottomed out and is ready to turn around."

The new investor had walked chin-up into a one-two punch: if one didn't deck him, the other would. The two actors here are an odd couple, what with the younger ones being the spiritual grandfathers of the older ones, yet both playing their roles on the stage at the same time. They are, in the order in which the investor was to become acquainted with them, the broker who sold him his stock and the swindler who juggled the money out of that stock and into his own pocket.

Stockbrokering is a genteel monopoly. It is one of the supreme ironies of our times that the stock exchange, nerve center of world capitalism, the place the socialists point at when they're mad, is run on principles more reminiscent of socialism than of capitalist free enterprise. Brokers enjoy the kind of protection from competition that we accord to the professional guilds. Stocks traded on an exchange can only be sold to the public by brokers who belong to that exchange. Nor do the members have to engage in the vulgarities of price competition; the exchange dictates the prices its members must charge the public. Like most monopolies, it is an easygoing sort of business. With competition excluded, it is possible to earn a handsome living without undue effort or any great talent. The brokerage business has become a club that shelters the more lackadaisical descendants of the old robber barons.

Such were the businessmen who greeted the average man when he ventured into the market. Not the broker himself—whoever met Merrill, Lynch, or any of the rest of those names?—but that employee known as the stock salesman or customer's man. He was the expert who would guide the fledgling investor through the intricacies of "speculation" (as it is always called on the Street, never "gambling"). Paul Dickson, the writer who was once a Merrill Lynch trainee, tells us in his *Washington Monthly* article on "The Wall Street Treatment" (November 1971) just how much expertise the investor can expect from his customer's man.

The salesman gets his job after passing "a multiple-choice exam which is ever so easy, predictable, often available in advance, and really serves as more of a test to see if the prospective broker can handle the terms of the industry—so he can sound like a broker—rather than to see if he comprehends what is going on." The salesman knows little or nothing about the companies whose stocks he buys and sells for his clients, which is not surprising, as Dickson points out, since there are some 25,000 stocks around. "When we call our brokers and ask them about some obscure Canadian oil stock, they have two alternatives: (1) to say they don't know or (2) intone something about Canadian oils looking good for the next six months. During my days as a Wall Street trainee, the prime message was, never say you don't know." Should the salesman prove to be competent, his employer will put him on the big accounts—"leaving the proven dumbos and the try-outs to service the 100-share transactions" of the little guy.

The salesman depends for most of his information on his firm's "security analyst." The analyst operates under constant pressure from industrial public relations firms trying to inflate their clients' stocks—and under no pressure to tell the investor the truth. As a result, as Christopher Elias observes in *Fleecing the Lambs,* "most of Wall Street's research, with the exception of that provided for the institutional investor, resembles nothing so much as tip sheets written by touts." Much of what the analyst tells the salesman, who, in turn, tells the investor, is simply yesterday's news copied out of *The Wall Street Journal.*

Inside information does, of course, exist. On any given day, some denizens of the Street know something that, if put to proper use, can help the investor either make money or, more often, avoid losing his shirt. These are the "tips" the little guy hungers for—and never gets. He is bound to be, like the aggrieved spouse, the last to know. Information, when widely shared, becomes valueless— what counts is who knows first. If the broker has a big client who can make a million on the tip, and a hundred little guys who could make ten thousand apiece, it is pretty clear who is going to get the news first, and who will hear it, if at all, only after the train has left the station. More likely, especially in the great garbage market of the late 1960s, the small investor will be touted on to the stock that the insiders want to get rid of. Paul Dickson again: "Back when I was a trainee with the nation's largest brokerage firm, it was unloading Howard Hughes' TWA holdings and a line that the boys liked to use when calling their little clients was, 'I've saved some of Mr.

Hughes' stock for you.'" In these circumstances, the investor would do better picking his stocks at random out of the stock tables.

The brokerage system contains a built-in incentive to screw the investor, because brokers earn their money only on their commissions on sales. The broker gains nothing if the client's stock goes up, nor, needless to say, does he share the loss if it goes down—except, that is, when he plays the market on his own with his clients' funds. (Clients are advised to leave their money between transactions with the broker in a "credit account"—interest-free, of course, like the accounts government keeps in favored banks. In 1970, brokers' clients were losing the interest on $2.5 billion in such accounts.) Generally all that matters to the broker is how often the stock is traded. He has no incentive to put the clients' money in a good stock and leave it there; if he did, he'd have no business. So he keeps his accounts "active," which is legal, or he "churns" them, which is the same thing but illegal. Since it is usually impossible to tell the difference between "activity" and "churning," and since that is the way the broker makes his living, a huge number of stock transactions have as their only reason the broker's desire to earn more commissions. Occasionally a broker churns the client a bit too hard, and the sucker strikes back. Here is a case described by Christopher Elias in *Fleecing the Lambs:*

> Not long ago a New York resident, Guy R. Pierce, opened an account with C. B. Richard, Ellis & Company. Pierce's investment funds were modest in size—$3,000 in all. But in one month, as it was later described by a judge of New York's civil court, "Fifteen purchases of a single security were made in the plaintiff's account aggregating

over $31,000, and sales of the same security were made during the same period of time aggregating more than $26,000." For churning the account, the brokerage house charged Pierce commissions of $1,022, and it reduced his $3,000 stake to $110.98 in cash and securities worth $50! At one point his broker bought and sold short the *same stock in the same day* and managed to lose money both ways. As put by the judge, who returned Pierce's money to him, "Horses would have given the plaintiff a fairer opportunity to realize on his investment."

Sheer incompetence was the cause of much of the little guy's suffering on the Street. Like other monopolists, brokers value the leisurely life they lead at least as much as the extra money that the monopoly permits them to extract from the public. That, after all, is why they're in the business; unlike granddaddy, who worked weekends stealing his millions, the broker's modest goal is a good income and an easy life. So Wall Street never really got ready for the arrival of hordes of small investors. Their old-fashioned methods were geared to trading on an elite scale. Most brokerage houses, with the exception of Lehman Brothers and a few others that had instituted computerized filing, still moved the actual stock certificates from one broker to the other each time a transaction was made—a system that could not handle large-scale trading. When the little guys stormed the brokers' offices, climbing the doors and shoving their money through the transom, the industry was bewildered. They tried lackadaisically to rake it all in, but it was more than they could handle with their limited energy. Soon the clients' stock certificates were lying all over the Street, like ticker tape after the parade, and the rate of failed transactions rose to levels remarkable even by the Street's easygoing standards. A "fail" is a transaction between two brokers in which the client's stock certificates fail to get from the seller to the buyer. With paper all over the place, the stocks were going astray, lost or stolen, at an increasing rate; clients were receiving the wrong stocks or none at all. Finally the Mafia had to move in to bring some order to the stealing, though mostly the certificates were stolen by underpaid young back office workers who, though they may not be justified for stealing just because they were working under sweatshop conditions, nevertheless can hardly be blamed for making off with certificates they found jammed behind toilets and stuffed into wastepaper baskets. The Street took the relaxed view that all was well if the fail rate was no more than a billion dollars—if, that is, at any given time, no more than a billion of the clients' money was missing. But even that easy target was more than our genteel monopolists could manage, and by 1969 the fail rate had passed four billion dollars—leaving the little guy with the single consolation that by then chances were good that the stock his broker had lost for him was near to worthless anyhow.

His stock was most likely to be worthless if he had bought shares in a company promoted by one of that great generation of swindlers who emerged during the 1960s. These were the men who made the stocks go up—and down. Unlike the easygoing broker, the promoter was no genteel descendant of the robber barons—he was a throwback to the original model, a Daniel Drew in modern dress. He had come to Wall Street to kill, not to survive, and he needed the average man's help. He needed a lot of true believers, people to have faith in his promotions, and the little guy in his innocence was a natural for the part. He would put his money in a name—those exciting names of the glamor stocks, which, if combined in one monstrous conglomerate, would read something like Chicken Fried Nursing Home Software Performance Systems. The names had to be good, for in most cases that was all the promoter was selling—he wasn't building any better mousetraps.

The basic promotion was a paper version of the old goldbrick. Form a company with an intriguing name, then go public. Sell shares to the public at one price, to yourself at a much lower price. (If you bought Metrocare stock when it went public, you paid twelve dollars a share, while promoter Frank Gabriel was getting his shares at fifteen cents apiece. When Wells Rich Greene went public in 1968, Mary Wells Lawrence sold shares that cost her $7,525 to the investing public for $1,226,575.) Now start pumping hot air into your creation. This requires some flackery from, say, the public relations firm of Hill & Knowlton, some touting by a broker who wants to ride the stock up for a while, and some juggling by the accountant to make it look as if the company is making money. Encouraged by his broker, the small investor rushes in to buy, and the stock soars; the higher it soars, the more attractive it becomes. The rising price has endowed the promoter with a lot of paper wealth. He uses this paper to merge with a company that has some real money, making sure he retains control. He pumps more hot air into his two-humped camel, part real and part paper, uses the new paper wealth to acquire more companies, and so on . . . for a while. Eventually the perception will grow on at least some people that the balloon is held up only by hot air. The accountants' creativity may not be up to manufacturing ever rising profits, or the stock may get caught in a downdraft. This is the moment of truth. The most skillful of promoters will see the end coming and will bail out in time. He will sell his own stock, as unobtrusively as possible, while the price is still high. (Jack L. Clark of Four Seasons bailed out via a secret account at his brokers, Walston & Co.) As the hot air begins to leak out, the balloon sags downward; the more knowledgeable investors will see what's happening and bail out also. The small investor will, of course, be the last to know, and he will be left holding the empty balloon after it has hit the ground. His nest egg has turned into thin air. As for the promoter, he has gotten out with a huge profit, and, best of all, it is in capital gains, and therefore pays half or less the tax imposed on the despised income from work that provided the small investor with the money he has just lost.

The great garbage market of the 1960s spawned a galaxy of star promoters. There was Roy Ash of Litton Industries, who went on to be President Nixon's Director of Management and Budget, and James Ling of the Ling-Temco-Vought conglomerate. Bernard Cornfeld took the action to Europe with his Investors Overseas Services. Gerald Tsai, Jr., born in Shanghai, had the distinction of being the first oriental promoter to make a killing in the market. The public loved Tsai. He started a mutual fund called Manhattan Fund in 1966, with little more in assets than his earlier reputation for reading the market. When he went public, Tsai hoped the public would give him $25 million to play with—and the public responded by putting $247 million into Tsai's fund. Despite that grand opening, the fund performed poorly, and within three years Tsai himself read the signs: he sold out for $30 million in 1968, having gotten rich himself while failing to perform for his investors. (The Manhattan Fund dropped only 7 per cent in 1968, the year Tsai got out, then 10 per cent in 1969 and 37 per cent in 1970.) The adventures of two other promoters, Cortes Wesley Randell and Phillip Steinberg, illustrate what was happening in the great go-go market.

Cortes Wesley Randell targeted what, in retrospect, seems the most obvious of hustles—the youth market. Everyone, in the early sixties, was talking about the fact that the American young had a great deal of cash to spend, and let's get our share of it. Randell, aged thirty, founded the National Student Marketing Corporation in 1964. In *The Go-Go Years*, John Brooks describes Randell as a strapping six-footer with a glib tongue and an easy smile. He sold himself as a purveyor of counter culture knickknacks and student services—though in truth he cared so little about his market that he failed to develop the resources he had. His interest was the stock market. He went public in 1968 with well-known accountants (Arthur Andersen) and lawyers (Covington & Burling). With that solid backing and the glamor of the youth market, his stock just had to fly. On the first day of sale, it went from six to fourteen, and two months later it was selling at thirty. The investors had made Randell a millionaire. With his paper wealth, he acquired six other companies, and by the end of 1968 National Student stock was selling at eighty-two; now Randell was a millionaire several times over. His original lawyers and accountants had both dropped out without explanation, but no one paid any attention to that. Randell was going around predicting that next year he would triple his earnings, and enough people believed him—not just the innocents, but big institutions like Morgan Guaranty and the General Electric Pension Fund—so that in 1969 his stock reached 120, twenty times its opening price only the year before. But already the first signs could be observed of hot air leaking from the balloon. As John Brooks explains it, "Having predicted tripled earnings for a given year, Randell found himself forced to resort to creative accounting to make the prediction come true; then, having written artificially high earnings for that year, he was compelled by his game's inner dynamics to predict that those earnings would triple again in the following year—and then somehow goad his accountants to Parnassian heights of creativity to fulfill the new promise." Once the insiders became suspicious of National Student Marketing, the balloon sank even faster than it had risen: from 140 in December 1969 to three and a half in July of 1970. But Randell and his associates were too smart to believe their own hot air. Their timing was perfect. In December, at the peak of the market, they unloaded 300,000 shares of their company, and watched it go down, dragging the unwary investor with it, from their vantage point on top of a great pile of capital gains. Randell and some of his associates, including an accountant, were indicted for stock fraud in early 1974. National Student stock was then selling for twenty-five cents a share.

Phillip Steinberg was another of the young upstarts of the sixties. His contribution was to prove that, while it was all right to gobble up some kinds of companies, and certainly acceptable to join the old-timers in screwing the small investor, an interloper who challenged the great bull elephants of the Street was going to get a tusk between his ribs. Steinberg made his first score, in his twenties, with a computer-leasing firm called Leasco Data Processing Equipment Corporation. When he went public with Leasco, Steinberg picked up three quarters of a million dollars, and only two years and three mergers later, his assets were $74 million. In 1967, after a carefully prepared secret campaign, Steinberg won control of a much larger company, Reliance Insurance Company. Reliance, which had cash reserves in the area of $100 million, was a conservative Philadelphia company which in comparison to Leasco's hare could well be defined as a financial tortoise. Leasco's fast market profiteering appealed to Reliance stockholders, while the much tinier Leasco coveted control of all that ready cash. Steinberg, still only twenty-nine, was worth fifty million now, and *Forbes* announced that he had made more money than any other American under thirty. That's enough to go to anyone's head—as Steinberg promptly demonstrated. He picked as his next target the nine-billion-dollar Chemical Bank of New York. Now, the Chemical Bank is closely allied, by stockholdings and interlocking directorships, with the Rockefeller interests. It is possible that Steinberg did not at first know just whom he was taking on—the Rockefeller connection is not widely known, and is not mentioned even in John Brooks's careful account of the affair. In any case, he soon found out. Chemical Bank mobilized to fight back, and soon Steinberg found himself under heavy fire on several fronts. Down in Washington, Senator John J. Sparkman, chairman of the Senate Banking and Currency Committee, was preparing to introduce a bill making bank takeovers more difficult; the bill had, in the Senator's words, been "sent in" by the lawyer for Chemical. The New York State Legislature was being urged to adopt a similar bill by the governor—Nelson A. Rockefeller. Steinberg got calls from two of his bankers saying they would not participate in the effort to take over Chemical. Most serious, the price of Leasco stock—

the financial base for Steinberg's attempt—began mysteriously to drop; no one was able to prove how that was done. The young promoter may have sensed that They were all around him: when his company held its annual meeting, it was in a Rockefeller bank (Chase Manhattan) and when Steinberg took a few days' vacation in the midst of the battle, it was at a Rockefeller hotel (Dorado Beach in Puerto Rico). Steinberg counted the artillery arrayed against him and he gave up the assault on the Chemical Bank. Reflecting later on his experience, Steinberg got off a line that could serve as the epitaph of every hustler who made the wrong enemies: "I always knew there was an Establishment—I just used to think I was part of it."

The small investor whose nest egg ended up as an omelet on one of these promoters' tables may well have wondered what happened to those people who were supposed to protect him against the swindles of what he thought were the bad old days. Where, for example, were the accountants? These were the good gray men, boring perhaps but clearly honest, who added up the figures and told the investor—in the annual report, in the prospectus approved by the SEC—how the company was doing. Unfortunately, the accountants themselves got caught up in the hysteria of the go-go years, and when the end came, their reputations plunged as far and as fast as the stocks of the companies they had been auditing. Their black-and-white world of statistics had suddenly been colored with the bright hues of impressionism —accounting had gone creative, and, all unknowing, the average investor had become a patron of the arts.

Accountants in the boom years were as creative as the promoters who hired them. Their art consisted of making the books say what needed to be said—usually that the company was making money when it wasn't—or of affixing their auditors' approval to the hot air the promoter was pumping into his balloon. Once they had the idea, the accountants found it was possible to make the books dance to whatever tune was popular at the moment. Earnings came out just as the management desired. Many promoters favored a neat stepladder of earnings rising regularly year by year, and, as "Adam Smith" observed, "some of them kept the neat stepladder right up to the day they filed for bankruptcy." The accountants of Randell's National Student Marketing Corporation, in order to fulfill the promoter's glowing prophecies, executed in a single year such maneuvers as: putting off to future years development costs of $535,000, even though the money had already been spent; including as income $2.8 billion in "unbilled receivables," which, John Brooks pointed out, is "money that had not been received because it had not even been asked for"; and including as income the earnings of subsidiaries that had not yet been acquired. By such magic, a loss was made into a profit of $3.5 billion. Only the sharpest of eyes could have detected the sleight of hand in the annual report. The small investor, struggling through the columns, would have no chance of seeing what was going on—no reason to unload his National Student stock.

All the creative accomplishments of accountancy found shelter under the broad tent of "generally accepted accounting principles," the phrase that appears in the auditor's statement. The accountants had little choice if they were to stay in business, for it was the promoter, not the investor, who was paying their wages, and if one accountant was not artistic enough, the promoter would look for another who was: this is known as "shopping for accounting principles." The major accounting firms were selling other services—public opinion surveys, testing, even product development—to their clients. It was hardly likely they would jeopardize all this to protect the little guy, who wouldn't know enough to be grateful, much less pay them a fee. Reflecting on the meaning, if any, of "accounting principles," Leonard Spacek, former chairman of Arthur Andersen (the firm involved in the Four Seasons swindle), had this to say:

> How my profession can tolerate such fiction and look the public in the eye is beyond my understanding. I suppose the answer lies in the fact that if your living depends on playing poker, you can easily develop a poker face. My profession appears to regard a set of financial statements as a roulette wheel to the public investor—and it is his tough luck if he doesn't understand the risks that we inject into the accounting reports.

The accountants are a professional monopoly, and like the other guilds they believe in self-regulation. They did not want anyone else auditing their work, and they looked with compassion on any transgressions within the guild: they did not propose to kick themselves off the gravy train. Nor was the SEC, which had the power to regulate accountancy, interested in exercising that power in the investor's defense. Indeed, by the late sixties, the SEC appeared to have lost virtually all interest in any kind of regulation.

The SEC was the other institution that the small investor might have looked to for police protection when he walked alone on the Street. Created in the 1930s to keep the stock market from repeating its misdeeds of the 1920s, the SEC had done excellent work in its vigorous youth. Then, like other regulatory agencies, it had gradually declined, ending up in the lap of the people it was supposed to be policing. The accountants don't want to be regulated; fine, let them go regulate themselves. The Street in general did not want an energetic cop on the beat; brokers also believed in self-regulation. That was all right with Washington also, especially after 1968. During the election campaign, Richard M. Nixon said that the SEC's "heavy-handed regulatory schemes" might "seriously impair the nation's ability to continue to raise the capital needed for its future economic growth." After the election, the new head of the SEC not only practiced self-regulation—letting the industry do what it wanted— but made that doctrine its stated policy. The SEC had taken itself off the beat just before the investors were to undergo their record mugging on the Street.

Without benefit of accountant or SEC, the little guy kept plunging deeper into the market. The fact that his broker was touting him on to hot-air stocks was not his only problem—the broker himself was now getting into financial trouble, and for a most peculiar reason: too much success. The brokers' guild was eager, in its genteel way, to pick up all the money the small investor was dropping on the Street, but the guild's energy did not extend to finding ways to process that new business; there are, after all, limits to what a gentleman should do for money. One brokerage house after another, drowning in paperwork it couldn't handle, floundered towards bankruptcy. Still others had extended themselves beyond the limits permitted by their amount of capital. When the crash came, a number of houses, including such big ones as Hayden Stone and Francis I. duPont, were on the edge of collapse. For the investor, this meant that, having already lost much of the value of his shares in the crash, he was now going to lose the shares themselves in his broker's impending bankruptcy.

The crisis of the brokers shocked the Street out of its customary lethargy. It was one thing for investors to lose their shirts—those were the risks of the game—but for members of the club to go under with them was unthinkable. Such lurid events would, the Exchange explained, shake the public's confidence in the system—a confidence presumably unshaken by the recent disappearance of so much of the money the public had invested in stocks sold by the Exchange's members. Rescue operations were mounted to salvage the troubled brokers. DuPont was saved, not by the rich relatives in Delaware, but by none other than H. Ross Perot, the Texas hustler who, as noted in chapter 6, had made more money in less time than anyone else in history; Perot put up $55 million to bail out duPont. The firm finally went out of business in 1974. (During the crash, Perot set another record of sorts. In one day, he lost more money on paper—half a billion—than old J. P. Morgan was worth on the day of his death, and he still had at least a billion left. It is doubtful that the loss had any effect on Perot's life-style. Certainly it meant less to him than the loss of $5,000 would to a person with assets of $10,000.)

More assurance was needed, the industry felt, if the small investor was to continue financing the Street's operations. His confidence would be strengthened if he could be insured against losing his shares through a broker's bankruptcy (though not against losses on the shares themselves). But who would pay for such insurance? The Street turned to the same person who finances its tax avoidance schemes—the taxpayer. Congress was in-

duced to finance insurance of up to $50,000 on any one
person's brokerage account, over the objections of people
like small investor advocate H. R. Reinisch, who asked
why the Street should not pay for insurance against its
own incompetence. Charging the insurance to the public
meant that the little guy, even if he dropped out of the
market, would still have an opportunity through his taxes
to go on paying for his broker's mistakes.

To further reassure the public, the President said—
while the market was sinking daily—that if he had any
spare cash he would be buying shares. (The advice he
got was evidently better than what he gave the public,
since at that time the President was putting his own cash
into real estate. But the public didn't learn that till three
years later.)

The public was at first reluctant, despite the President's
advice, to return so quickly for another round. "Adam
Smith" was warning the small investor that the game was
getting tougher for him to win; others, like John Brooks
and Christopher Elias, were telling him he was playing
with someone else's marked deck. In 1972, the number of
shareholders dropped by 800,000, the first such decline on
record; people were taking more money out of mutual
funds than they were putting in. Despite the crash, the
rules of the game had not been changed in the small investor's favor; the crash had demonstrated that, as John
Brooks observed, the SEC's rules gave "the small investor
the semblance of protection without the substance."
Now, if anything, the cards were more stacked against
him than before. Certainly the ante had been increased:
in the early seventies, the commission rates on individual
investors were increased by 50 per cent, while the
brokers decreased substantially the rates they charged

institutional investors. The big investors like pension funds were coming to dominate the market, and, since they tended to think and act alike, this meant the market was liable to sudden swings as the big investors moved their huge funds around. The small investor, lacking their knowledge, was likely to be crushed in such swings. If they decided to move out of a stock, it would plummet before he could act; if they moved into a stock, it would shoot up—again, before he could act. By 1973, the small investor could even get in on a hustle that had been dormant for more than ten years—the "special offering." This is a stock that someone wants to unload in big quantities, but which none of the big institutional buyers will touch. The broker is in essence bribed to handle the stock by being given a "credit" worth two to three times his normal commission; the public is told they can buy the stock without paying a brokerage fee, which is what supposedly makes it "special." What is actually special about the stock, of course, is that nobody in the know wants it, as the small investor soon learns by watching his investment sink gradually toward the bottom of the market. It is such investment opportunities that give flavor to one of the Street's better jokes on the little guy:

> On his broker's advice, the little guy repeatedly bought Stock X. There came a time when the little guy needed cash, so he asked his broker to sell his shares of Stock X. And the broker said: "Sell? Who to?"

Despite these dismal prospects, Wall Street was cordially inviting the little guy to deal himself in again, and financial columnist Sylvia Porter even raved that it was his patriotic duty: "you, the public investor, are the backbone of our country's capital-raising mechanism and you are one of the few advantages we still retain in world competition which we dare not risk losing." The smell of blood attracted newcomers to feast on the little guy's prospective return. In late 1973, for example, the Chase Manhattan Bank took full-page ads to announce a payroll deduction stock-buying scheme for the investor who could put up as little as twenty dollars a month. There would, the ad acknowledged, be a brokerage fee, and also a "service charge" of "no more" than two dollars a month per stock. This meant the little guy, if he put all twenty dollars a month in one stock would be paying out, on top of the brokerage fee, up to 10 per cent of his investment per month for "service." But all this was all right because, as the Chase ad proclaimed: "It's so darned automatic!"

The president of the New York Stock Exchange, Bernard J. Lasker, thought in 1972 that the game would be played out again just as it had the last time around. Sounding less than starry-eyed about his industry, Lasker had this to say: "I can feel it coming, SEC or not, a whole new round of disastrous speculation, with all the familiar stages in order—blue-chip boom, then a fad for secondary issues, then an over-the-counter play, then another garbage market in new issues, and, finally, the inevitable crash."

Lasker may be proved right eventually, but as of this writing, small investors seem to be staying out of the game in which they were so badly burned. Perhaps the little guy is not always wrong after all.

4

Insurance: The High Cost
of Protection

IN THE GARDEN OF EDEN, before the first expert slithered under the gate, there was one basic type of life insurance. The description of the policy covered two thirds of one page, and was written, in the spare prose style of the period, by Herbert Denenberg. Hardly anyone could fail to understand what the policy promised and what it would cost. Health insurance did not exist in those days, because health care was free, and neither did title insurance, because the need for it had not yet been invented. (Auto insurance, which raises quite different issues, is described in chapter 8.)

That was before the rise of the experts. By mid-twentieth century in America, the experts were in full control, and insurance had become one of the nation's biggest and least comprehensible industries. Never is the average man more bewildered than when he confronts an insurance agent across his kitchen table ("more sales are made at the kitchen table than anywhere else!" says an agents' training manual). The agent has convinced him that he would be causing a problem to his family if he were, as one industry euphemism goes, "removed from the scene." ("If, God forbid, you should pass away" is another one.) Now the agent is offering him a wide variety of ways in which the company can help him solve his family's problem, all at a price well within what the agent has determined to be the man's means. The client doesn't understand any one of the policies he is being offered, much less the differences among them, but this is hardly surprising, since the agent doesn't understand much about them either, other than his commission rates (except for that small minority of specially trained agents known as Chartered Life Underwriters). The agent, after all, is not the expert, only the expert's salesman, and most agents are, like their clients, losers in the net screwing system. The winner is not at that kitchen table.

Whether he understands it or not, the average man buys. Everybody buys life insurance—nine of ten American families have some form of insurance on their lives, and it is generally accepted as something we should all do. The rich could take care of their survivors with their own resources; they buy life insurance as a tax dodge because its proceeds are exempt from the estate tax. In 1971, Americans signed up for new life insurance policies worth $189 billion, compared to paying only $33 billion for new cars. That brought the total life insurance in force to $1.5 trillion, more than twice what it had been only ten years earlier. Even critics of the American way of buying cannot resist the industry's pitch. In his article on "Life Insurance Today" (*The Washington Monthly*, April 1973), Urban Lehner tells about the young artist who will allow only one appliance—a pop-up toaster—in his one-room apartment, but who also owns a $50,000 cash-value life insurance policy. Indeed, even Herbert Denenberg himself, who as Pennsylvania Commissioner of

Insurance from 1971 to 1974 established himself as the industry's foremost scourge, pays $2,000 a year in premiums for policies worth close to $200,000.

The rapid growth of life insurance in recent years is of course based on something more than the agent's ability to get his message across the kitchen table. Two deepseated changes in our society in particular have made life insurance far more important than it used to be. One is the disintegration of the extended family. When the several generations of the family lived together as one domestic unit, there was no great need for insurance. When the head of the family died, his widow was taken care of by the children; when anyone else who was bringing in money died, there were enough other members of the family to take up the slack. The family insured itself. All that has ended, the survivors can no longer turn to their relatives, and the insurance agent has moved in to fill the gap. (Life insurance, it should be noted, is not the only screwing of the average man to result from the death of the family. Others discussed in this book are the Social Security tax, chapter 13, nursing homes, chapter 10, and private pensions, chapter 9.)

Credit is the other great ally of life insurance. As we all know, Americans have gotten themselves deeper into debt than any other people in history. A few generations ago, the only extra cost of dying was the $300 needed to pay the undertaker for his fifty-dollar coffin; most insurance policies then amounted really to burial insurance. Now, however, if the average man dies while he is still in his working years, his survivors are saddled with his obligations to the credit industry: the remaining years on the mortgage, the home improvement loan, thirteen more payments on the car, which is already falling apart, the color television, and most recently the unpaid balance on the credit card. The bank and the finance company will expect the checks to keep coming in after he is no longer in a position to write them; some banks, in fact, require life insurance as a condition for a mortgage. All this is made clear across the kitchen table. The husband, barely able to keep his head out of water, is well aware that without his salary the whole shaky edifice of credit would collapse. His fear makes him easy prey when the agent, who has calculated roughly how much blood is left in this particular turnip, explains that the debts he will bequeath to his survivors can be taken care of for as little as twenty dollars a month. . . . This is another example of carom screwing: the more the average man has been taken by the credit industry, the greater his need for the insurance man. Again, the wealthy are exempt, since they need not get enmeshed in credit in order to be active consumers.

The basic principle of life insurance, once the expert camouflage is removed, is simple. It is a gamble between you and the insurance company (and, in fact, the word policy, derived from the Italian *polizza*, is one of the names by which the numbers business is called). The company bets that, before you die, it will take in enough from you, in premiums and the income it earns on those premiums, to pay off your survivors and have a profit left over. The client's self-interest is more than a little muddled, since premature death is the only way to come out ahead financially; if he lives long enough for the company to make a profit, then he would have been better off investing the money he put into premiums. The gamble involved in life insurance was made explicit in the wager policies that existed in the eighteenth and nineteenth centuries. Under these policies, you could insure someone else's life without his knowledge; according to Lehner, the wager policy had to be outlawed when people discovered the obvious way of beating the company. The "tontine" was another kind of wager policy. Everyone bought into the tontine, but those who dropped out lost their premiums, which were then divided among the survivors. These and other hustles led Elizur Wright, insurance commissioner of Massachusetts in the mid-nineteenth century, to observe: "I became persuaded that life insurance was the most available, convenient, and permanent breeding place for rogues that civilization had ever presented." Wright's opinion was sustained in 1973 when officers of Equity Funding Corporation, in a scheme reminiscent of Gogol's *Dead Souls,* invented 62,400 non-existent clients and sold their "policies" to other companies.

Today the wager between company and client appears in two basic forms. One, the oldest and simplest, is called term insurance. As the name indicates, term is sold for a limited number of years, usually five, but never for life. After the term expires, the insurance must be renewed. Then the client must face the dismal fact that he's not as good a risk as he used to be, because he's that many years closer to dying. If he wants to renew his policy, one of two things will happen: if he keeps the same face value, the premium will go up, or if he pays the same premium, the face value will go down. This will happen each time he renews his term insurance until the end: each time he will pay more to get less. The $100,000 term insurance he bought at age twenty-five will, forty years later, either cost him five times as much or, if he pays the same premium, only be worth $20,000 to his survivors.

Term insurance mirrors reality. To avoid confronting the client with the raw fact of his increasingly probable failure to survive, the industry in the nineteenth century developed the second major kind of insurance. It is called cash-value, and about three quarters of life insurance today falls in this category. Cash-value solves the problem of term insurance by averaging premiums over a lifetime: you pay a constant premium for a constant face value because you overpay in the early years of the policy. The overpayment is considerable: in the early adult years, cash-value will cost three to six times as much as term for the same amount of coverage. The reward is that the premium will never go up, as indeed it shouldn't at those rates. Clearly, the company is far ahead in the gamble on the client's survival in the early years of cash-value insurance. The surplus is invested, producing income for the years when the company's gamble is a poor one—though by then the company is too far ahead to lose. Cash-value also amounts to a form of forced savings, a low-grade bank account. The difference between the premium you pay and what it costs the company to insure you, plus its profit, is the "cash-value" part of the policy. This is, as the agent will point out early in the conversation, the kind of policy on which you can borrow, and if you ever drop the policy, the company will give you back some of your money. Furthermore, if the company is making enough money, it will share its winnings: these are the dividends that are deducted from the premium on cash-value policies.

Despite its apparent disadvantages, the case for term insurance is persuasive. It begins with a reminder of the real need for life insurance: enabling the survivors to weather the loss of a salary and paying off the credit economy. These needs are greatest in the middle years of life, when the average family has children to raise and all those debts to support. These also are the years when term insurance is the best buy. Later on the need for insurance diminishes. The children are grown and off on their own. The house is paid off, or the couple has sold it and moved to an apartment. After retirement, the death of the one who used to be the wage earner means relatively little to the household's economy. Even if the survivor needs some insurance money, she—it is usually she—will not need much and she won't need it for many years. These are the years when term insurance is a poor buy, but also the years when there is little or no need for insurance beyond what it takes to get past the undertaker. The person who, at thirty-five, needed $100,000 in insurance may, at sixty-five, only need $10,000 or so: that is also the pattern of term insurance. The person who did it that way will have paid much less for insurance than his counterpart who bought cash-value insurance; he was free to devote the difference to investment, to riotous living, or just to paying cash for what the other fellow was buying on time. By contrast, the person who holds a fixed amount of cash-value insurance is likely to be underinsured in his earlier years and overinsured later on. (It should be emphasized that term is not always the better deal. A young widow may have a marketable skill that enables her to support the children and the mortgage; an older widow who cannot find work and has no pension will need considerable insurance money to see her through her last years. In both those cases, cash-value may be preferable. The important point is to understand the difference between the two rather than simply listening to the agent's blatherings.)

The insurance industry hates that kind of talk. Term, the agent is fond of admonishing the man across the table, "melts away like a block of ice, leaving a big puddle of nothing." The industry's anger boiled over after *Consumer Reports* published in 1967 a series of articles making the case for term insurance. The articles (issued in revised form as a pamphlet in 1972) compared the consequences at age sixty-five of having bought term or cash-value starting at age twenty-five or thirty-five, and assuming that the savings on buying term were invested. If the person buying term earned only 4 per cent on his investment, he would come out ahead; if he earned 6 per cent, he would come out considerably to the good. An insurance trade magazine, *The National Underwriter*, responded with a broadside that managed a sideswipe at the insurance man's competitors for the average man's dollar:

> What does "can afford" really mean? Too often it means a pitifully small amount for premiums after expenditures for a too-costly car, too-lavish home, too-quickly replaced furniture, and too-fancy expenditures have left so little that the head of the family excuses himself from buying a decent amount of life insurance on the ground that he can't afford it. But he can "afford" creature comforts and status symbols that put him in hock up to his neck. Advice like that in the Consumer Reports article gives many readers an excuse for not buying the permanent life insurance they need and could afford with a little self-discipline. They'll take the term insurance advice, but we doubt many will even start on the investment program that goes with it. And of the few that do start, still fewer will carry it to completion, for it's too easy to sabotage such an account for a new power boat or a summer home.

Now, aside from the gratuitous remarks about the competition—what's wrong with powerboat salesmen and finance companies?—it is clear from the above that the insurance industry doesn't like term insurance. The agent will sell the average man term if that's all he'll buy, but if he can sell him anything else, he will. From the agent's side of the table, that is because his commission is considerably lower on term, but it is the company, not the agent, that rigged the commission rates. Term insurance is in disfavor because, unlike cash-value, it does not produce a big surplus for the company to invest for its own benefit. Secondly, term is too simple to meet the requirements of expert competition. Clients who buy term can easily figure out what they are getting and what it is costing them, and, if term were the prevailing form of insurance, fewer people would make less money in the insurance business. The point was made by Edward B. Bates, president of Connecticut Mutual Life, in a speech to the New York City Life Supervisors Association: "No agent, general agent, or agency system can live very well on the commissions from only term insurance."

The industry is quite right in arguing that cash-value insurance is a form of involuntary saving, and that many of us need to be forced to do what doesn't come naturally. The trouble is that it's a lousy way to save, for the rate of return on investment via life insurance is extremely low. The average man who saves by buying cash-value insurance is screwed just as he is if he puts his money into a savings account or U.S. savings bonds, while his superiors earn a much higher return on their Treasury bills, municipal bonds, and other forms of investment to which only the wealthy have access.

Expert competition in insurance, as in the professions,

requires that the nature of the product be fogged over beyond the understanding of most mortals. One way to accomplish this goal is to multiply the number of seemingly different policies available till the sum reaches close to infinity, much as the auto manufacturers now offer an infinite number of variations on the same basic car. Another is the familiar tactic of wordnoise: couching the description of the policy in language that does not convey to the reader any sense of what is going on. When Denenberg measured the readability of insurance language on a scale of 100 (for the most easily understood), he found that the industry's contracts scored from 10 to minus 2 —compared to 67 for the revised Bible and 18 for Einstein's Theory of Relativity. The result is that the average man buys not what is written in the policy, but what the agent tells him at the kitchen table—and what the agent says does not appear in the contract. After the agent leaves, the client has little idea what he bought or whether he really needed it. The insurance companies, each with its army of agents, compete fiercely for the average man's dollar, but—as we see also in the cases of cars and doctors—that competition does not include truly competitive pricing. Herbert Denenberg calculated that the price of the same coverage varies up to 170 per cent from one company to another, and he estimated the total overcharge at $5 billion a year. For an extreme example, the client who buys a certain policy from the Teachers Insurance Annuity Association will be charged $49 in costs, while the identical policy will carry $2,724 in costs if bought from the Alexander Hamilton Life Insurance Company. The complexity of the policy assures that the average man will not be able to judge the price, if only because he doesn't really know what he's buying, and the agent can easily convince him that his policy, though more expensive, is far superior to the one the other fellow is peddling. Thus the average man is doubly screwed: he buys more than he needs, and he pays more than it's worth.

A massive industry is built on this foundation. The industry includes 1,700 companies, although 90 per cent of the business is done by the 200 biggest ones, and all told it holds around $250 billion in assets collected from policyholders. The power to invest those assets, which, according to James Gollin in his *Pay Now, Die Later*, is held by about a thousand executives, makes insurance companies a major force in deciding who does and who does not get a share of the nation's available capital. One investment that insurance companies like is finance companies, which, as Gollin notes, is somewhat ironic, since the insurance company is plugging thrift—as in the call to self-discipline quoted earlier—while the finance company is selling the opposite. Thus the customer may find that his friendly finance company is lending him back his own money via the insurance company.

The industry does, however, avoid the most embarrassing kinds of investment. "You couldn't expect people to understand why we'd want to lend their money to a casket company," one insurance executive said. Still, it's not always easy to know where to put it. As far back as the late 1800s, the president of Mutual Life complained that "we had a lot of money coming in that we did not know what to do with." More recently, an insurance executive told Gollin: "We've got money lying around all over the place. If you really want to know the truth, our problem is figuring out what to do with all that money." Giving it back to the public in lower premiums does not seem to be one of the options under consideration. In 1964, the industry paid out in death benefits only one seventh of its income, and, according to a study cited by Gollin, the companies by then had collected $45 billion more than they could ever need to pay off the policies then in force. That $45 billion will never get back to the policyholders; the companies will keep the change. Not that the companies are overtly cheating the policyholders. In Gollin's words: "Any sane man who has considered the nature of life insurance will realize that from the viewpoint of industry management, there's no reason to cheat. It's . . . much more lucrative to be honest."

The agent is the intermediary between the average man and the industry's management. He is an anachronistic figure who, but for the needs of expert competition, would doubtless have disappeared with the end of the days when insurance premiums were collected weekly at the home. If policies were as simple as the basic facts of insurance, agents would be surplus, and people would buy their insurance by mail or by telephone or by stopping in at the office. But, with insurance policies made complex beyond comprehension, the companies required someone to explain his needs to the average man and talk him into buying. As a result, close to half a million agents prowl the land in search of Americans who can be convinced that they need more or different life insurance.

The distinctive life-style of the agent may convince the casual observer that he has an easy job. He rivals the bored housewife in his dedication to good causes. On Tuesday afternoon, when his clients are working, he is driving a Little League bus, and Thursday noon is likely to find him at a United Fund lunch. Often he runs for political office, especially those part-time local and state offices that few people holding down the normal job can afford. But the rest of us need not envy the insurance man his free-form existence, and not just because even working is preferable to attending United Fund lunches. Beneath his affable exterior, the insurance agent is a driven man. He's not running around like that because he cares whether the fund drive goes over the top. He's just trying to make the contacts that will lead him to the few remaining pigeons among the most heavily insured people on earth. It's not an easy task.

The agent is driven by the terms of his contract with the company. Once upon a time he answered an employment ad that began: "SALES CAREER—outstanding opty for . . ." After a test which, by all reports, is impossible to fail, and a couple of interviews, he was asked to sign a contract. It sounded pretty good: a salary plus commission on his sales. So he signed, and he was just as aware of what he was doing as his clients are, later on, when they sign the contracts he offers them. In Gollin's words about the agent signing his contract: "Needless to add, he won't read a word of it; and even if he did, he wouldn't understand it." Eventually he will come to realize that, first, he is not an employee of the company but is self-employed, and, second, that he isn't drawing a salary at all: it's just an advance against commissions, and if he gets too far behind he'll have to try another line of work. Most of his fellow recruits did just that; according to Gollin, nearly 90 per cent of those hired as agents drop out within three months. But our man hung on, and as he shuttles around from event to event, displaying his charm and responsibility, offering discreetly to drop by and check your "insurance program," he is trying to pass along to his clients the treatment he got from the company.

The commission system imposes its own imperatives on the agent. His cut usually is what the trade calls "fifty-five and nine fives," meaning 55 per cent of your first year's premium and 5 per cent of each of the succeeding nine years'. This means more than half the agent's self-interest is exhausted if you keep the policy he just sold you for a single year; after ten years, he doesn't care what you do with it. Not surprisingly, about a quarter of all new policies are dropped within thirteen months, and only one in five is kept up till maturity. Many of those abandoned policies are the result of "twisting," which is what the agent does when he talks you into exchanging your present policy for the one he is offering you; if there is cash value in the policy you are giving up, the agent will point out that the cash can pay the first premiums on your new policy, including his 55 per cent. Twisting, greatly deplored by the company whose customer is being twisted away by another company's agent, is inevitable under the commission system the companies have created. It is inevitable also for a more basic reason. Since virtually all Americans who want insurance already have it, and in many cases more than they need, the only way the agent can live and the company prosper is if a lot of those people can be convinced to buy more and different kinds of insurance. Here again complexity and gimmickery play an important role: it is easier to sell the customer if he cannot understand either the policy he is giving up or the one he is getting in its place or the difference, if any, between the two.

Complexity served also, at least until recently, to defeat the efforts of critics to arouse the public to the high cost of life insurance. Few of us were willing to keep our minds on the subject long enough to grasp the nature of the screwing. The attack on the industry that has seemed to draw the most blood is that of Herbert Denenberg: he has attracted more unwelcome attention to the subject than all his predecessors. Besides being a dissident expert —he taught insurance ·before becoming Pennsylvania Commissioner of it in 1971—Denenberg has the gift of saying things simply and getting headlines. Judging from the outcry for his scalp, Denenberg made some headway. (His most endearing habit, by the way, was handing out form letters to the governor demanding his firing, to save his critics the trouble of composing their own messages.)

Denenberg's most hostile act to date has been the shopper's guides he has issued rating life insurance companies' policies.* (He has issued guides for other forms of insurance, and even one on how to avoid unnecessary surgery; Denenberg is as unpopular in the health industry as he is among insurance men.) The guides explain what the buyer is getting with various policies, and thereby attempt to undermine the years of patient labor by the experts who write the policies. Denenberg's intent is to reintroduce the notion of price competition in place of expert competition, which Denenberg calls "competition by confusion." The guides evaluate the policies offered by the 480 largest companies selling insurance in Pennsylvania, and they include lists of the ten best and the ten worst buys in both cash-value and term insurance. They even take up the subject, never discussed by insurers, of

---

* The 1972 Consumers Union *Report on Life Insurance* is an excellent general guide to the subject. *Consumer Reports* rates individual policies in a series of articles beginning in January 1974. *The Great American Insurance Hoax,* by Richard Guarino and Richard Trubo, is a good guide to insurance in general.

how much the same amount of money would have yielded had it been invested in something other than insurance.

Though it is impossible, without falling into the trap of complexity, to evaluate all the myriad gimmicks offered in life insurance, Denenberg's shopper's guides do give the consumer a rough idea of what he is getting. A good enough idea, at least, to get a rise out of the industry. When the guides first appeared, the Pennsylvania companies set up a toll-free "Consumer Information Service" number to get their message across. When Rose De-Wolf, a columnist at the Philadelphia *Bulletin*, called the number she got the inevitable response: life insurance is a very complicated subject; if you get in touch with an agent, he'll tell you all about it. The most conventional defense of the industry came from other state commissioners of insurance in response to a questionnaire by Ralph Nader. Denenberg's colleagues, who with few exceptions share the usual regulator's love of their industry, were unenthusiastic about the shopper's guides. (Many of the commissioners came from the industry or will go there after they leave government.) In their answers to Nader, they trotted out the familiar arguments for expert competition. The subject was too complex; an adequate explanation, said the man from Kansas, would not be comprehended by the "average insurance consumer." Others took the position—standard with professional guilds—that price comparison is misleading because it ignores differences in "service" among the companies. (This argument makes especially little sense with respect to insurance, where the major consideration of service is how promptly the company pays the death benefits.) One commissioner suggested worriedly that Denenberg's ratings might be used in selling insurance. Four of the thirty-two commissioners who replied to Nader said they had never heard of the guides.

The long-range effect of Denenberg's guides on the insurance marketplace is unclear as yet. Denenberg himself, with characteristic modesty, believes that he has single-handedly transformed the industry, despite the absence of legislation. Since nothing opposed by the industry is likely to be adopted by state legislatures infested with insurance agents, Denenberg has testified in favor of action by the federal government. What he claims Washington should do (although he may have intended this more as a threat to the insurance industry than a serious legislative proposal) is to limit life insurance to a couple of simple, standardized policies—in order to protect the average man from the consequences of expert competition. Though the idea is horrifying to those who profess to believe in the free market—and is not in any case likely to come to pass in the foreseeable future —it is worth taking a moment to peer into Denenberg's Garden of Eden:

The savings to the public would be enormous. First, and most obviously, in money: Denenberg estimates the present annual overcharge at $5 billion, which is more than one fifth of what we pay in premiums in each year. That would be only the beginning. With policies simplified to the point that the reader could understand them, the agent would become surplus, and the buyer would save a large part of what now goes into commissions. Most important, we would in all probability spend a lot less on life insurance, once we knew what we were buying and once we were being hustled only by television ads and not by a real live agent. (Banks, of all places, already do sell it cheaper by eliminating the agent —but banks are only allowed to sell insurance in three states, Connecticut, Massachusetts, and New York, and even there the amount a bank can sell to one person is limited.) In addition to money, we would also save all the time and frustration we now spend at the kitchen table, groping through fifty-word sentences and listening to the agent recite his litany of net-costing, special riders and premium waivers. These would be happy developments for everyone except the industry itself and those who indirectly depend on it: who will run the fund drive once the insurance man has gone the way of the dodo?

If life insurance, shorn of woolly complexity, is a basically simple proposition, health insurance is not. The first deals with a single, inevitable, standardized event—death —while the second insures against events that may or may not happen and whose costs may run from the trivial to the astronomical. Complexity is used in opposite ways in the two branches of the industry. Where the life insurers manufacture complexity to screw the customer, the commercial health insurer uses his superior knowledge of a basically complex subject to make the product deceptively simple. ("Commercial" in this case means profit-making, and excludes Blue Cross and Blue Shield, which are described in chapter 6.) The difference can be seen in their respective attitudes toward mail-order selling. Life insurers shun mail order, though it is a feasible way to sell simple policies, in order to preserve the agent system of face-to-face hustling. Health insurers, on the other hand, find mail order an excellent vehicle for their simple presentation: the client learns its complexity much later, when he tries to collect.

Health insurance is the used car lot of the industry. You do not find the agent loitering at the Little League game, discreetly soliciting an invitation to explain the mysteries of his product. Instead, the health insurer is bellowing out his message, as in this ad for National Home's hospitalization policy:

> One out of two families will have someone in the hospital this year. It could be you—or some beloved member of your family—today—next week—next month. Sad to say, very few families have anywhere near enough coverage to meet today's soaring hospital costs.

Hardly anyone can avoid getting the message. If you missed the ad in the paper, you are likely to get a letter giving you the same advice: buy before it's too late. The letter may be signed by Art Linkletter and start off like this: *Dear Friend: You know me. I wouldn't recommend anything I didn't honestly believe in . . .*

In his *The Health Insurance Racket and How to Beat It*, John Gregg† gives the example of the Melvin G. Crandells of Jekyll Island, Georgia, who received the following eight solicitations from health insurers in a single week:

1) A Safe Drivers Hospital Plan for one dollar for the first month.

2) A Cash Refund Token to apply on a savings account $100-a-week hospital plan.

3) A Big Check Information Certificate to return for free information on a $100-a-week "money-back hospital plan GR 77C."

---

† Gregg is a reformed health insurance agent who left the industry to become chairman of Policyholders Protective Association International, a consumer group headquartered in Georgia.

4) The American Association of Retired Persons $100-a-week Hospital Plan B.

5) A Med-O-Matic plan exclusively offered to senior citizens.

6) The Updated Plan of the Engineering Society of Detroit.

7) Globe Life's Auto Driver's Accident and Hospital policy.

8) The American Ordnance Association's Double Security Program.

The Crandell family seem to have been joiners. Organizations, and especially fraternal orders and labor unions, are useful channels for the health insurer to reach the public. Joining, say, the Elks may make you, like the Crandells, a hunted species. The health insurer sells the organization's leaders on something it has invented called a "franchise group": all this means is that the insurer has gotten the mailing list, and soon the membership will be getting his message in the name of the organization. The members of the Grand Lodge of the New Hampshire Independent Order of Odd Fellows, for example, got a letter beginning, "Dear Sister and Brother . . ." and going on to describe a plan "fitted to our membership needs . . . designed for us by Health Underwriters Agency, Inc. . . . This plan is underwritten by Union Fidelity Life Insurance Company . . ." At the same time Union Fidelity was selling a plan "designed especially for residents of Mississippi": it was the same plan that had been fitted to the Odd Fellows. Indeed, the needs of the Odd Fellows of New Hampshire evidently were the needs of everyman, for the company was also selling the same package as a special plan "for people of all ages." According to John Gregg, the same Union

Fidelity plan, while tailored to New Hampshire Odd Fellows, Mississippians, and people of all ages, was being sold by another company to Tennessee union members as "designed to fit the special needs of organized labor and their families." Union members are particularly sought after by the health insurers, and, by Gregg's estimate, many of them end up buying "specially designed" health insurance for 25 to 100 per cent more than the same policy would have cost them on the open market.

Whether it comes through the Odd Fellows or a newspaper ad or an agent, the health policy will be deceptively simple rather than deceptively complex. In order to promise the largest coverage for the lowest premium, the company must minimize the amount it will have to pay out. It does this by unobtrusively excluding from coverage those risks that are likeliest to run into money. A good example is the common $100-a-week hospitalization policy. The company knows that the average hospital stay is 8.3 days, so many of those policies only start paying after an "elimination period" of seven days, leaving the company liable for just 1.3 days of the average stay. Using 1969 figures, Gregg figured that such a policy would pay just $14.28 on a $580.42 hospital bill (average stay at average cost). The rest is up to the customer. The same principle of excluding what's likeliest to happen, applied to individual policies, results in the rider excluding any disease the person has had or is known to be prone to. The argument for riders is that otherwise those people wouldn't be able to get health insurance at all. But the companies, while reducing their coverage, do not reduce the price; a policy with riders costs the customer as much as one without them. According to Gregg, the industry's response is that "rate adjustments would complicate their billing and accounting procedures."

Such swindles are in the modern manner: they are legal, and they work because the companies' statisticians know more about the probabilities of illness and hospitalization than the average man is likely ever to learn, at least before it's too late. Some other practices found occasionally in the health insurance industry are, for all their ingenuity, no more than old-fashioned shell games. One is the "dual application." The agent will say, after he has filled out the form, that he's done a sloppy job, and would the client mind signing a second, blank application, which the agent will fill in from the first form—later. The false information inserted into the blank form will permit the company later on to deny a claim that it would otherwise have had to pay.

Other hustles are the "better policy" and the "lump sum settlement." The better policy game resembles the twisting of the life insurance agent, except that in this case the client is twisted right out the door. This is what can happen to a person who holds a guaranteed-renewable policy and has suffered an illness—a heart attack, say—that makes the company wish he were doing business somewhere else. The agent will tell him that because . . . —whatever pretext the agent can dream up —he would be better off with a new policy, in fact he will get more coverage for the same premium. He applies for that new policy, and his heart condition is carefully recorded on the application. He may be told, but will not grasp the implication, that his old policy will lapse when the company receives the new application. His new application is then denied, and he has voluntarily given up the old policy. The company is "off the risk," as they say in the trade, and the client is out in the cold. Lump-summing is the practice of offering a client with a long-term claim against the company—usually someone who has been disabled—a cash settlement now instead of continuing coverage. For someone who is in financial trouble because of his disability, the offer to trade the future for the present may be too tempting to resist, and the company will have gotten off that risk at considerable saving. As John Gregg points out, the best reason for refusing a lump sum offer is the fact that it was made: the company must be figuring that it will win, and therefore the client will lose.

Commercial health insurers, in contrast to Blue Cross and Blue Shield, are notoriously reluctant to pay off claims unless the client is persistent and not easily bamboozled. Many of us are familiar with the telephone call in which the person at the other end points out that there are certain flaws in the claim, the head office might reject it entirely, so why don't we settle for fifty cents on the dollar? The commercials and the Blues differ in their behavior because their self-interest is different. As noted in chapter 6, the Blues are controlled by hospitals and doctors, and therefore are happy to pay their bills, passing on the cost to subscribers or the general public. But the commercials are in business for themselves, not the health industry, and that is why they feel no great desire to foot the bill if they can avoid it. The commercial companies are evidently alert to the difference, for many of them insure their employees with the Blues instead of with their own companies, leading Gregg to observe that they must think that their product is "good enough to sell but not good enough to buy."‡

Life and health insurance as businesses must cope with the fact that the risks they insure against are real: certain in one case, likely in the other. Everyone dies, and many get sick. Title insurance avoids this problem by insuring against a risk that, with exceedingly rare exceptions, does not exist at all. It is the perfect kind of insurance to sell. It is also, as noted in chapter 1, the expert's dream: he charges for his services, then he charges a second time for insurance against his possible incompetence.

The average man confronts title insurance only rarely —which helps account for the industry's survival. Their only encounter occurs when the average man buys a home and thereby submits himself to that remarkable ceremony known as the closing. As the buyer is led to the closing table for the ritual sacrifice, he sees half a dozen experts eyeing him with friendly appetite as they finger their carving knives. He may identify the title expert, but as they all fall upon him to slice off their respective hunks of closing costs, he is hardly likely to remember among all his other losses the cut of his flesh that went to title insurance. Probably he will lump them all together in his mind and console himself that it won't happen again soon, if ever.

Title insurance derives from the title search.* The purpose of the search is to find out whether the seller really

‡ Herbert Denenberg, who rated health insurers operating in Pennsylvania in early 1974, concluded that fifteen of the twenty-five largest companies do not offer good buys to the consumer.

* I am indebted for most of the information in this section to an unpublished paper by John Keys.

owns the property free and clear of any claims against it. Someone has to go and leaf through the records down at the county courthouse. In theory, the search may go back to the original colonial charter or land grant (precolonial owners' rights not being recognized) in order to ward off the insurer's favorite nightmare: the person who bursts through your door, waving a valid title dating from 1756, and shouts: "Get off my property!" Now that just about never happens, although Vincent Price did once claim about half the Southwest on a phony Spanish land grant—but that was in a movie, *Baron of Arizona*, and even on film Price wasn't able to make his claim stick. In the real world, the title search is usually limited to recent years, and often goes back no further than the last time the property was sold, when of course the title was also searched. Already at this stage, even before title insurance has appeared, the search can generate considerable make-work for the experts. Take, for example, the developer who buys a hundred acres, pays to have its title searched, and eventually sells it off in 400 quarter-acre lots. Each of the 400 buyers will have to pay for his own title search, though all their lots are part of the property that was just searched, and, if the referral system is working properly, all 400 will be steered to the same experts who did the original search—and who now can charge for it 400 times over.

The job of title searching can be tedious in some cases because the records are scattered around in a disorder guaranteed to keep a few more county employees on the payroll. (A centralized standard record-keeping system could easily be installed and would wipe out the entire title industry.) Still, the skill required is not great; you can learn the basics of title searching in a day or two. But experts have to eat too, and so the business is monopolized by lawyers and title companies. The companies often keep their own set of efficient property records, but they still charge from $100 to $500 as if they were groping around the original land grants down at the courthouse.

The work is easy and the searchers are experts—but evidently their product cannot be counted upon. That's why the buyer also needs title insurance to protect him in case there's something wrong with his title. Of course, the buyer thought he had paid the title searchers to do just that. But now he finds out he has to buy more protection, often from the same people who did the search: the kind of double exaction that is frowned on by the more ethical members of the Mafia. He may say, if he has faith in experts or if he figures he can sue the title searchers if something goes wrong, that he doesn't want the insurance, he'll take his chances on just the search. But no: the bank says if he wants a mortgage he has to buy the title insurance. The reason given is that the insurance is required to enable the bank to resell the mortgage on the national market, where—here we close another circle—it will most likely be bought by a life insurance company. If the buyer says, since he has to take the insurance he doesn't want to buy the title search, and if he can make that stick, then he will be issued a policy that exempts from coverage any title defect that would have been uncovered by a search—a policy, in other words, that fails to cover the only danger for which the insurance was needed in the first place.

The buyer may believe that, having paid twice for the same protection, he can now relax in certain ownership of his home and forget about Vincent Price and his phony land grant. Not quite. Since the bank demanded the insurance, many policies cover only the bank's share of the deal, not the owner's equity. Should the title go sour, the insurance will pay off the bank, but will not recompense the owner for what he has put into the purchase. All Price has to do is wait till the mortgage is paid off and then make his move. The insurance company is willing to sell the new homeowner a policy that covers him too—but that of course will cost extra. Safe at last? Not necessarily. Some policies provide that if the insurer has to pay out an amount equal to the face value of the policy—if, that is, there proves to be some reason for the insurance—the insurer has the right to take over the property, fix up what's wrong with the title, and resell it to recoup his loss. And that makes the buyer a former homeowner.

All these flaws in title insurance should not unduly disturb the average man as long as he bears in mind that the danger to his title is only a scarecrow waved at him by the experts. If there's no danger, the holes in the insurance have no real meaning to him. This does not mean that defective titles never occur—they do, but they are exceedingly rare and almost all of them can be fixed at little cost without endangering the buyer's ownership. Indeed, the buyer runs a far greater risk of losing his property because he cannot keep up with all the tributes demanded by the experts than he does of losing it because of the title.

The amount of the title insurance screwing can be calculated from the industry's figures. The average cost of title insurance, a one-shot payment, is $129. Title insurers pay out 2.5 per cent of their income in claims. That gives us $3.22 as the average value of that $129 policy. The rest, just short of $126, minus a bit for overhead, is expert make-work. Although not a major screwing for the average man because it happens so seldom, from the industry's point of view it comes fairly close to the ideal of selling a service and providing nothing at all in return. Yet the industry is not as profitable as it might appear: its net in recent years has averaged just under 10 per cent, which with 2.5 per cent to the clients and something for overhead, leaves a lot of money unaccounted for. The explanation is that the title insurers are forced to share the take with the rest of the real estate industry. While the insurers are well protected against their policyholders, their colleagues in real estate know their guilty secret, and so the title insurer has to buy his business by paying commissions to real estate brokers, lawyers and developers. The developer mentioned earlier might, for example, exact a commission in return for steering those 400 buyers to the right title company. The desire to keep as much money as possible flowing around the real estate circuit precludes price competition in this as in so many expert-run businesses; in the industry's eyes, it makes more sense to keep prices up and then negotiate who gets what share of the take, than it does to let the money escape to the average man in the form of lower prices. For the same reason, the industry shows no interest in installing a central title record system of the kind that exists in England, where the government keeps the records and certifies titles for a small fee, which goes into a public insurance fund that pays off any mistakes that occur.

In the excitement of buying a home, the average man is hardly likely to see through the title insurance swindle. He is hearing the pitch for the first time, it comes from respectable experts who are helping him get his home, and besides he has a lot else on his mind: the moving, the furniture, and can he really afford the mortgage? He pays the $129. Should he choose to resist, he has little chance of winning, even if he is an expert himself. Take the case of Martin Lobel. Lobel is legislative assistant to Senator William Proxmire; he is also a lawyer and a one-time professor of property law who has taught a course in land title research. When he bought a home in Washington, he took over the previous owner's mortgage, which carried title insurance. Lobel said he would do the title search himself. He was told he couldn't do the search and that he would also have to buy his own title insurance —if he didn't want to buy the insurance, then he didn't have to buy the house. If Lobel could not do it, the average man surely cannot either.

As he hands over his $129, the home buyer may pause for a moment to reflect on the imagination of the title insurers who created the danger against which they are now protecting him. Immortality, should it ever come to pass, would present a similar challenge to the life insurance industry.

5

Lawyers: The Experts' Experts

ON ANY MAP of the screwing of the average man, the lawyer appears all over the landscape. The lawyer is a member of a professional monopoly, and he is also the expert hired by the other experts. Hardly a hustle worthy of the name can be conducted without a lawyer among the conspirators. Mystifying the public by manufactured complexity, the essential strategy of the experts, is normally achieved by hiring a lawyer to write the fine print in which is hidden the barbed wire that protects the hustle from the citizenry. In fact, whenever some new complexity is added to his world, the average man can be fairly sure of two things: first, a new way to hustle him has just been born, and, second, the lawyers will do more business—one lawyer representing the hustlers and another offering his services to the victims.

The role of the lawyer in keeping the public ignorant was evident twenty centuries ago, when Jesus said, as reported by St. Luke: "Woe on to you, lawyers, for ye have taken away the key of knowledge: ye entered not in yourselves, and them that were entering in ye hindered." In the modern era, the boom in expertism has vastly increased the need for lawyers. London lawyers used to charge by the word, and the principle, if not the practice, appears to be still in force, for the great majority of documents that the average man cannot penetrate—from his life insurance contract to the obscurities of the tax codes—was written by lawyers. Whenever a rich man is figuring out how to pay less taxes, so the rest of us can pay more, a lawyer is helping him, and of course the great third-party screwings by government are lawyer-administered: lawyers are by far the most numerous professionals at every level and branch of government; as they used to say in Tammany Hall, more lawyers live on politics than flies on a dead camel.

The lawyer even appears at times as the good guy. He is Perry Mason saving an unpopular defendant, the public interest law firm successfully suing to prevent a polluter from crapping up the river, the loner beating the system. The ultimate good guy, Ralph Nader, is himself a lawyer. But cases where lawyers help the average man are, as governments always say about war crimes, no more than isolated instances, for the administration of law is profoundly rigged against the average man. Anatole France said it nicely: "The law, in its majestic equality, forbids all men to sleep under bridges, to beg in the streets, and to steal bread—the rich as well as the poor." You can get equal treatment under the law, that is, if your money happens to be equal, but of course the average man's money is never equal to that of those who are hustling him. When the average man is up against a rich opponent in court, each will get what he pays for—the average man, the minimum time of a cheap attorney; the wealthy man, the full resources of a skilled law firm. The rich man's lawyers will prepare his case more thoroughly and argue it better, and, if the judge merely arbitrates the points of law, that's who is usually going to win. Similarly, rich defendants in criminal cases do better than the average man not because the fix is in, but because they can afford to buy an adequate defense. Fair refereeing does not mean much if what is being refereed is a boxing match between Joe Louis and your grandmother.

Furthermore, the price of admission to equality before the law is rising as the legal guild, like the other monopolies, raises its prices to improve its members' incomes. In the big law firms of New York and Washington, starting salaries by 1973 were around $18,000. A newcomer could look forward to annual raises of two to three thousand dollars, and eventually a partnership that could catapult him into six figures. Doubtless it is the prospect of such earnings, rather than the idealism so often and so unfairly attributed to the young, that has caused the recent boom in law school applications.

To produce these salaries, leading partners in the big-city firms are now billing their clients at $150 an hour and sometimes even more. Even the time of a young associate is being charged at $50 an hour. In a smaller firm in a medium-sized community, the going rate is $40 an hour for an experienced associate and $30 an hour for one fresh out of law school.

These rates present something of a problem for the average man in need of legal help. Say he's cheated on a $300 refrigerator and wants a lawyer to sue the seller. The lawyer will have to explain that his fee would be larger than the amount that would be recovered in the suit. In an interview for this book, Ralph Nader said, "The legal system has priced itself out of the range of most of its potential consumers. The law has never gone in for economies of scale. It's as if you couldn't buy a car for less than $20,000." Nader went on to point out that what is bad news for the average man is also bad news for the average business, "which can have all the legal problems of a giant corporation plus one more—they can't afford to pay a good lawyer for the time it would take him to handle the work."

In modern America, the need for a lawyer is even more certain than the need for an automobile. When you die, when you get a divorce, when you buy a house, when you have an auto accident, not to mention the hundreds of times during your lifetime when you are fleeced in your role as a consumer, a lawyer either must or should be involved. Where a doctor only gets you when you're ill, the lawyer gets you in sickness and in health. The law's delays and its endless forms fall especially hard on the average man. A Rockefeller will not panic if his lawyer has to wait a couple of days in the courtroom for the judge to get to his case. The average man knows that his lawyer's meter is ticking at anywhere from fifty cents to five dollars per minute.

There are of course some legal matters that do not require much of a lawyer's time and which the average man should be able to afford even at today's inflated hourly rates. But here the legal profession meets the challenge with the minimum fee, the standard device by which professional monopolies ward off the specter of free enterprise. Sometimes these are informal. Thus a Washington divorce lawyer says his firm will not ordinarily take a divorce for less than $2,500. Often, however, these minimum fees have been formally adopted by a state or local bar association. More than half the states have statewide fee schedules, and so do many county bar associations. For example, the Fairfax County (Virginia) Bar Association established minimum fees for those title searches which, as noted in chapter 4, are one of the ways in which the experts come down on the average man should he happen to buy a house. The minimum fee is 1 per cent of the first $50,000 of the purchase price, and 0.5 per cent above that. Searching that title typically takes about fifteen minutes of the lawyer's time (unless one of his employees does it). On a $50,000 house, that's $500—perhaps one case in a hundred is complex enough to be worth that fee. Evidently the local bar felt it would be unethical for the profession to earn less than $500 for fifteen minutes' work.

The bar associations are vigilant in hunting down lawyers who sell their service to the public at below the monopoly price. Thus the California State Bar Association has instituted proceedings against a firm called The Legal Clinic of Jacoby and Meyers. Two young lawyers, Leonard D. Jacoby and Stephen D. Meyers, have been accused by the bar of "moral turpitude and dishonesty." Their offense is having set up an office designed to deliver low-cost legal help through the use of young paraprofessionals and the development of time-saving manuals covering procedures in typical cases. Their fee for an uncontested divorce, for example, is only $100. The bar in their area of California charges a minimum fee of $400 for the same service.

The minimum fees recently have come under attack. In 1974 the Department of Justice filed a price-fixing suit against the Oregon Bar Association, and earlier a Nader lawyer had convinced a district judge to outlaw the Fairfax County minimum fees. But the Fairfax Bar Association, on appeal, was able to get the kind of decision that guild members should have a right to expect from their fellow practitioners on the bench. The appeals court overruled the district court and upheld the bar association's right to fix the price of its members' services. The court also explained that this was in the public interest: "We have no doubt that the primary aim [of the minimum fees] was to benefit the public." Other lawyers were able to see a different kind of primary aim. Here is Graham Bartlett, president of the Tennessee bar, explaining why lawyers in his state decided to give up the minimums: "We felt that they had served the purpose, because through surveys we have taken, we knew that the income of the lawyers had been raised tremendously."

Setting minimum prices is only one of the ways in which lawyers behave like other professional monopolies. In standard guild fashion, the lawyers have established control over an area of service, access to the law, and forbidden competition by outsiders as "unauthorized practice of law." That provides the lawyers' monopoly turf. The way to expand the territory is to make people resort on as many occasions as possible to services that only a lawyer is allowed to deliver: inserting the lawyer, that is, between the public and what the public either wants or can be made to want. In a narrow sense, that of fanning a legal spark into flames, the trade calls this "breeding litigation." In a broader sense, the way in which the lawyer expands his market might better be called "breeding paranoia," for, if paranoia is the mental condition of our times, the lawyer is its Typhoid Mary. He encourages us to think of the world as a jungle infested with enemies waiting to leap upon us if we are not armed with the proper legal papers. Some of those monsters do in fact exist; others, however, are as common as unicorns. The lawyer is eager to protect us against both. Even an ethical lawyer views himself as protecting you against all possible risks; he can make you as paranoid as a hustler can. When Washington lawyers were interviewed for this book, many said they had become the first person to whom their clients turned for counsel on business, and even personal problems—the high priests of corporate life. The average man absorbs his paranoia on a humbler level. One way is title insurance: in chapter 4, we identified this as the Vincent Price syndrome. Another example is the drawing of a will. Many of us are familiar with the experience of seeing our one-paragraph draft balloon in a lawyer's typewriter into twenty pages of exotic verbiage protecting us—or so we are told, for the language is now far beyond us—against perils we had not previously known existed. (And the courts will see to it that the complex version is more acceptable than the simple one.) Now, while our heirs are more likely to be mugged by Martians than actually to confront some of those perils, others are worth buying protection against—if we're rich. Guarding against a one-in-a-hundred danger, for example, is worth $10,000 to the person leaving a million-dollar estate, but the same protection is worth only ten dollars on the average man's estate of $10,000. As the price of the protection goes up—the cost of drawing a will has risen by 50 per cent in the last five years—the value of its protection for the average man diminishes accordingly.

The major ways in which money flows unnecessarily to lawyers from the average man are determined more by institutional arrangements than by the face-to-face laying on of paranoia. Number one, in law as in society, is the automobile. The fault system, described in chapter 8, guarantees that cars fill 57 per cent of court time, and the automobile with all its consequences provides from one quarter to one third of lawyers' incomes. Divorce is another big money-maker. Although you don't need a lawyer to get married, you do need one to get a divorce, even the simplest of uncontested partings that raises no legal issues. Here paranoia re-enters the picture, for, when two people are separating on less than the best of terms, it is easy for the two lawyers to breed in them the kind of fears that will motivate each to pay for added protection against the other's possible malevolence. Back in 1967, the cost of the two lawyers in a divorce was estimated at $1,000 to $5,000 for people in the $10,000 to $20,000 income brackets: nowadays even an uncontested divorce will cost each partner $250 to $500 and sometimes more. A large part of that bill is of course expert make-work.

Earlier we speculated that the most successful screwings are those which occur seldom, so the victim has no chance to learn from experience. Add to this the thought that the victim is less likely to protest if the proceeds come out of new money rather than out of his current income. Probate satisfies both our conditions: it happens just once in a lifetime (actually after a lifetime), and the money that is hustled comes out of the estate, which is all gravy to the heirs anyhow. And so we find in probate the most glaring of legal hustles—what Nader calls "the screwing of the average corpse."

Probate is society's way of making sure the dead person's will, if any, is valid, that his debts and taxes are paid, and that his estate will go to the people named in the will or the people named in the law if he left no will. Probate is a professional monopoly: you cannot settle an estate without paying a lawyer somewhere along the line. It is also a profitable industry employing, along with lawyers, judges, clerks, subexperts like property appraisers, all of them living off the dead person's remains. Most of the cost of settling an estate goes to the lawyers, and most of it is either unnecessary or could be done by a nonlawyer at far less cost. The probate or surrogate court is where the action takes place. All estates have to pass through that court, where the judge approves the lawyers' fees; in many cases the judge has the power to appoint a lawyer as "special guardian," paid by the estate to protect the rights of children or the mentally incompetent. The resulting flow of money makes the probate court one of the most prized plums in the orchard of local politics. Fiorello La Guardia, New York City's reform mayor, once called the Manhattan Surrogate Court—which handles close to $1 billion in estates a year—"the most expensive undertaking establishment in the world." La Guardia was right, for, though undertakers' services are notoriously overpriced, the lawyers are laps ahead of them. In a year in which 100,000 Americans died leaving estates of $60,000 or more, the settling of those estates cost $800 million compared to funeral costs of $150 million. The lawyers' papers cost more than five times as much as the undertakers' casket and embalming fluid. If the lawyers are able to squeeze so much more blood out of the average corpse than their rivals, it is because the undertakers' hustle is an old-fashioned one that more and more people are able to understand and resist, while the probate system, protected by the expert mystery of the law, is immune to attack by the average man.* And if there is more complaining about funeral costs than about probate costs, it is doubtless because the undertaker is paid in cash, while the lawyer's bill is subtracted from the estate.

Murray Teigh Bloom, whose *The Trouble with Lawyers* is the best recent book on the profession, first got interested in probate through the experience of a friend. Here is how Bloom tells the story:

> Harry left a modest estate to Julia and their two young sons. A family friend and lawyer who was handling the estate warned her she would be up against a peculiar and slightly expensive problem: a special guardian.
>
> As she explained it to me, the surrogate court had to appoint a special guardian "to make sure the rights of our sons weren't being compromised. Me, they won't trust. They have to bring in some outside lawyer. Then I started hearing stories of how much these courthouse characters can ask for. And you've got to pay them or the estate never gets settled."
>
> Her indignation and vehemence must have brought crinkled skepticism to my face. "Wild, isn't it?" she said. "I didn't believe it, either, first time."
>
> Now her brother-in-law, who knew his way around politics in the county, entered the picture. He said he could save Julia some money here. As he explained it to her, every surrogate kept a patronage list of lawyers he appointed as special guardians. The more influential ones, the men he owed bigger favors, of course got the larger

---

* Sadly, it seems the average man is less able than others to resist the undertaker. That, at least, has been the experience of an economy cremation firm in New York City, which in early 1974 was selling its product for $265 with no hidden extras. One of the firm's directors said that after three years in business, only one of its several hundred clients could be described as working class; the rest were professionals and rich people.

estates and correspondingly larger fees. But to some extent, on these smaller estates the patronage list was controlled by a certain court clerk. Now her brother-in-law had a lawyer friend who was on this list, and although the normal fees for an estate the size of Harry's would be about $500, the lawyer friend, as a favor, would do it for a token $100. But the court clerk had to be paid, too. For $150—cash, please—he would see to it that the lawyer friend would get the special guardianship in the estate. . . .

The clerk was paid and the friendly special guardian came to Julia's home one Saturday afternoon. He called Harry's sons in and said:

"Boys, I know you want to be playing outside, so I won't waste your time. Tell me: when your father made out his will in December, 1965, was he sane?"

"Of course he was," the older boy burst out. "What's the matter with you?"

The special guardian said: "Don't get excited, boys. That's all I have to know."

He later phoned two witnesses to the will and filed a brief report in which he concluded that the will was valid. Perhaps two hours of work in all for the $100. But then it had been a big favor. With the $150 to the court clerk, Julia and her sons had paid out, in effect, $125 an hour for "work" that any fairly intelligent legal stenographer could have done at $3 an hour.

The moral of Bloom's tale is twofold. First, obviously, is the swindle of probate itself: the unnecessary special guardian and his outlandish fee. The second moral is that in this instance corruption serves the average man better than legality. By bribing the clerk, Julia got her clerical work done for only $125 an hour; had she gone the legal route, it would have cost her $250 an hour. This makes probate a hustle in the modern manner: crime doesn't pay as well as obeying the law. Scandals in the probate courts are understandably rare now that the stealing has all been legitimized. From the point of view of the average man trying to settle a relative's estate, if he can find a crook in the probate court he may be able to minimize the extent of the screwing.

The spectacular probate coups are against the estates of the rich. Bloom tells the story of the Minneapolis lawyers who, through a special guardianship, bled $245,000 out of an estate originally worth less than $1 million. In his *How to Avoid Probate* (the answer, unfortunately, is that it's not easy), Norman F. Dacey tells of a bipartisan estate hustle.† A Democratic probate judge was helping his friends milk the estate of a wealthy heiress. A Republican running against him used the milking as an election issue, won the office—and began milking the estate in his turn. Yet, although the probate lawyers would obviously rather screw a rich corpse than a poor one, the average man is far from immune. Indeed, he pays tribute to probate at a rate higher than that of the rich: estates of $10,000 to $20,000 lose an average of 20 per cent to probate, while an estate of $100,000 will only lose 10 per cent of its value, and above that amount, the percentage lost is lower still.

Most of the money spent on probate goes, by widespread agreement, to support expert make-work. Judge William Haworth of Oklahoma, interviewed on the CBS television program "Sixty Minutes," estimated that 90 per cent of probate legal work is unnecessary; he added that what work had to be done could usually be done better

† When Dacey's book was first published, lawyers succeeded temporarily in getting it banned from New York bookstores as unauthorized practice of law—a good example of guild members defending their turf.

as well as more cheaply by a legal secretary. No matter how simple the work, however, the average survivor had better not try to do it himself. John Baker, a Wisconsin businessman, found that out a few years ago when he tried to go it alone. As Murray Teigh Bloom tells it, Baker, executor of his mother's estate, was outraged when he discovered that his lawyer, by figuring his fee on a percentage rather than hourly basis, was going to charge him ten times as much for the estate as for the rest of Baker's legal work. Baker started studying what was involved in being his own lawyer on the estate, and he soon learned the secret: the work is easy. He went to court and—but the word had gotten out and the entire legal fraternity mobilized like white blood cells to combat the threat that all the widows and orphans, following Baker's example, would handle their estates without benefit of lawyers. The judge ruled he couldn't appear without a lawyer. Baker, still on his own, appealed to the Wisconsin Supreme Court, relying on a provision in the state constitution reading: "Any suitor, in any court of this state, shall have the right to prosecute or defend his suit either in his own proper person, or by an attorney or agent of his choice." The court ruled unanimously against Baker. Whatever the constitution might be thought to say, he couldn't probate that estate without a lawyer, the court held, and, furthermore, Baker must be wrong in thinking the fee his lawyer asked was too high because it was the fee established by the state bar association. The system was saved. On a nationwide level, the probate system has not come under serious attack. For one thing, probate reform is politically unpopular, for it would impoverish local political organizations, forcing them to turn to other sources of income. In private conversation, lawyers will often admit the evils of probate. But, as they also say, it's only dead man's money, and the heirs didn't earn it either. For the average man seeking to avoid probate, the only plausible counsel is that of columnist Thomas Collins: "My best advice on the matter is just not to die."

The average man, then, is charged far too much, often for work that doesn't need doing, when he is forced to employ a lawyer. On the other hand, when he really needs help with the law—that $300 swindle—he finds that the lawyer will cost him far more than the amount at stake. Sometimes he finds himself caught in a carom screwing, as when he has to go to a lawyer to help him through the fine print written by another lawyer. There are, it is true, a few ways in which one can sometimes get low-cost legal help. The poor can theoretically get lawyers from Legal Aid or the Neighborhood Legal Services program. But the need is many times greater than the resources of those offices, and the average man, who isn't poor, is ineligible.

The contingent fee—a case where the lawyer collects a fraction of what he recovers for you, nothing if he loses —is a way the average man can afford a lawyer. Contingent fees are common in auto accident cases; the lawyer usually gets at least one third of the winnings. While most accident victims would be better off under no-fault insurance, the person lucky enough to be seriously injured by a well-insured motorist can get a good lawyer, and make a good score, on a contingent basis: the goal is to get enough for "pain and suffering" to cover what the accident cost you, plus the lawyer's share, with some left over for you. If you have a particularly interesting case, you can sometimes find a lawyer who will take it at little cost just for its intellectual challenge. Some lawyers, also, will take a case they think will make a splash in the press, bringing them more business. The American Civil Liberties Union will take cases that raise important Bill of Rights issues. But, if the question is, which of these lawyers will take the average man's $300 swindle? the answer has to be "none of the above."

For a time it seemed the average man stood a chance of getting a lawyer through the workings of what is called "pro bono publico": unpaid legal good works. The late sixties witnessed a flowering of "pro bono" practice, with young law graduates demanding that their prospective employers give them time off for good works. However, according to Ralph Nader, "The minute there was a slight recession in the legal job market in 1971, the law students got chicken. In 1970, they were sending the law firms questionnaires about pro bono. Now they're too busy putting on their vests." An interviewer for Covington and Burling, one of Washington's most prestigious law firms, reported that when he visited the University of Virginia Law School in 1969, he had twenty-five applicants, most of whom expressed an interest in pro bono practice. In 1973 Covington had 140 applicants from Virginia, not one of whom mentioned pro bono. "It's an amazing shift and it's generally true at the twenty or so schools where we recruit." Other firms have reported a similar decline of interest in pro bono.

The court of small claims is one place the average man can go and try to get his $300 back. In these courts, which exist in one form or another in every state, you can sue without a lawyer, the filing fee is no more than fifteen dollars and usually less, and the judge, if he is doing his job right, will help you present your case rather than overawing you with the majestic complexities of the law. (Douglas Matthews' 1973 book, *Sue the Bastards: The Victim's Handbook*, is a good guide to working the small-claims machinery.) Since the maximum claim is typically around $500, the small claims court should be the ideal place for the average man to get even on that refrigerator. It should be, but too often it isn't, for small claims has fallen far short of its sponsors' expectations. For one thing, businesses have been quicker than people to see the use of these courts, with the result that most of the small claims action consists of debt collection. If, that is, the average man stopped making his payments when he found his refrigerator didn't work, he is likely to be on the receiving end in small claims. In some courts, lawyers are permitted, and the judges tend to play by their guild rules, leaving the non-lawyer nonplussed. Experienced businesses are skilled at getting postponements, forcing the consumer each time to miss a day's pay. Some courts permit appeals, so the businessman can simply move the action to a regular court, where the stakes are too high for the average man—now he needs a lawyer, after all— and he is forced to drop out; as they say around the courthouse, if justice triumphs, take an appeal. Nor is winning in court enough: often it proves impossible to collect the judgment. However, despite these liabilities, a Consumers Union survey found that a majority of consumers who took the trouble to go to small claims got at least some of their money back.

Until it was cut off at the knees by the Supreme Court, the class action seemed a way that a lot of screwed customers could recoup their losses. The class action is a kind of collective lawsuit which, even if brought by only one person, can result in a judgment in favor of everyone who has undergone the same swindle. It can solve the $300 problem, that is, if a lot of people are in the same leaky boat. If you can get enough $300 losers together, you can afford a lawyer and a class action in which a lot of strangers will also benefit, at considerable cost to the business that sold you all that same lemon. This is often the case with a defective product, though seldom with a service: your television repairman may be screwing a lot of customers, but you can't bring a class action unless all of them are being taken in exactly the same way. Legal services and public interest lawyers also have used class actions to force governments to give whole categories of people services to which they are entitled; governments have tried to prevent these actions, evidently on the grounds that just because they got caught screwing one citizen is no reason they should stop screwing others who are in the same fix.

One example of a successful consumer class action occurred in 1967, when Montgomery Ward offered by mail to sell life insurance to its charge customers. Although the letter asked people to check a box if they wanted the insurance, the company billed insurance charges to people who had not checked the box. Only a few dollars per person was involved, but a lot of people. One customer, Robert Holstein of Chicago, filed a class action on behalf of everybody, and the result was that Montgomery Ward had to refund $595,884 to 111,465 people. In chapter 2, we noted the class action suit against a bank that recovered millions for clients who had suffered the small-scale screwing of the 360-day year, and another bankers' hustle, the escrowing of homeowners, was menaced by a class action until the courts came to the rescue. The class action can be lucrative to the lawyers involved, as when the lawyers who recouped $17 million in a class action against Illinois Bell Telephone collected a fee of $1 million.

The courts eventually moved in to shield business and government from the threat of troops of threadbare citizens waving their flawed merchandise and broken promises. First, the federal courts have ruled that anyone bringing a class action and asking damages must notify, at his own expense, all the potential beneficiaries—a requirement that is financially, and in some cases physically, impossible. Then in late 1973 the U. S. Supreme Court ruled that, if there must be this kind of spectacle, we can at least set the stakes high enough to keep out the ribbon clerks. In a pollution case brought by lakefront property owners against a pulp mill, the Supreme Court ruled that in most kinds of cases you could not join a federal class action unless you could claim damages of at least $10,000. The figure of $10,000, which happens to be about the average man's annual income, seems to represent some kind of high-level consensus on who belongs in the game. When, as noted in chapter 2, the U. S. stopped selling its high-interest Treasury bills in denominations of $1,000, it set the new minimum price at $10,000. The message to the average man seems to be that class action justice, like T-bills, is a game he can join if he can afford table stakes equal to his annual income.

The legal system as practiced today is entrenched behind a series of institutional fortifications. The first of these, as in any professional monopoly, is the guild: the American Bar Association. The ABA is an essentially feudal structure in which most power rests with autonomous state and county bar associations. These associations regulate the profession: they admit lawyers to practice, discipline them, and, by setting the minimum fees, decide how much their services are worth to the public. Like other guilds, the bar association practices occupational birth control: each bar association can determine, through its administration of the bar examination, how many new lawyers will be permitted in its territory. In order to ensure obedience to the guild, some states have an "integrated" bar, which doesn't mean what you think it does, but rather that all lawyers practicing in that state must belong to the bar association. Like its sister guild, the American Medical Association, the ABA can be found at or near the end of the line in the march of human progress: it played, for example, no leading role in the great human rights struggles of the 1960s. (Individual lawyers were of course in the front lines of those battles, but not their trade association.)

Again like the doctors, the guild seems slow to read the shifting patterns of self-interest. Take, for example, the ABA attitude toward prepaid legal plans, under which a member would get all the lawyering he needs in return for a flat annual fee. The analogy to health financing (see chapter 6) is obvious. Yet, years after the doctors had discovered the socialism-for-the-rich aspect of Medicare and Medicaid, the bar association was still stubbornly opposed to prepaid legal plans, and even today the profession's acceptance of the idea is grudging. Evidently—though a non-lawyer hates to give free advice—the lawyers had not yet glimpsed the bright future of prepaid law: with the average man at last able to see a lawyer without paying forty dollars an hour, the demand for lawyers' services would shoot up; their rates would go up accordingly; when the annual premiums got uncomfortably high, some mechanism would be found, as it was in health, to third-party the cost onto the general public; and the lawyers would be able to collect bigger fees from more people who, because of the third-party effect, would not even be aware that they were footing the bill.

In the national office that expresses what is alleged to be the collective will of its membership, the ABA comes on like a textbook case of conflict of interest. A glance at the makeup of the committees (or "sections") which set ABA policy will make the point. When in 1972 the ABA created a special committee to consider no-fault automobile insurance, it turned out that all ten members were making money from the existing system; not surprisingly, the committee came out against no-fault. As Mark Green observed in an article on the ABA (*The Washington Monthly*, January 1974), "the subcommittees comprising the Natural Resources Section are headed by lawyers whose clients read like a Sierra Club enemies list. William Forman, chairman of the Hard Minerals subcommittee, represents Anaconda Copper and U. S. Gypsum; Charles Wheeler of the Oil subcommittee represents Cities Service; Terry Noble Fiske of the Public Lands and Land Use subcommittee is the lawyer for four associations of contractors and realtors, and his subcommittee's vice chairman is from a firm representing American Smelting and Refining, Johns-Manville and Standard Oil of California." Two more examples: the section on Antitrust Law, headed by Thomas M. Scanlon, IBM and Shell, and the Section on Public Utility Law, headed by F. Mark Garlinghouse, AT&T. These examples make it easy to predict where the ABA will come down in any struggle between corporate sharks and the average man.

All guilds have their lobbies, not just the ABA, but the

lawyers also enjoy a unique grip on the institution being lobbied—government. If the layman turns to the political process for relief from the exactions of the lawyers' professional monopoly, he finds that the other fellow got there first. Lawyers are numerous in the top positions in government, in the leadership of the political parties, and in the membership of Congress and the state legislatures. Lawyers do not vote as a group on most public issues, but you can usually tell your representative's occupation when a question affecting lawyers' income is on the agenda. Lawyer legislators are unenthusiastic, for example, about probate reform and no-fault divorce. The main reason no-fault auto insurance is making some headway despite the lawyers is that it is backed by a competing professional lobby: insurance men, as noted in chapter 4, are also numerous in the state legislatures. Lawyers in public office tend to maintain a discreet silence on the subject of lawyers' fees. A good example occurred during the 1973 Watergate hearings. On more than one occasion, witnesses testified about the defense funds funneled to the Watergate defendants—sums so gigantic in relation to the legal work done as to make a Park Avenue surgeon weep with envy. Yet no member of the committee or its staff asked about those fees: everyone in a position to ask a question was a lawyer.

Lawyers also find government to be a good client. One example is the legal fees they collect for preparing bond issues, a subject examined in detail in one state, New Jersey, by the Center for Analysis of Public Issues in a 1971 report titled "Local Attorney's Fees in Bond Issues: Nice Work if You Can Get It." Nice it certainly is, though in most cases it can hardly be called work. As described in the report, the job consists mainly of filling out standard forms and is more clerical than legal. For this accomplishment, those lawyers selected by the local political process charge fees based on a percentage of the amount of the bond issue. Therefore, as construction costs and the size of bond issues go up, so does the lawyer's fee; only the amount of work he does stays the same. Most county bar associations set minimums for the lawyer's percentage and warn sternly against undercutting the price. Competition is equally bad, as explained by one bar association: "Competitive bidding and responding to invitation from Boards of Education, municipal governing bodies and the like to submit a competitive bid for legal services is disapproved." Interestingly enough, the lawyer only collects his percentage if the bond issue goes through, making it a sort of political contingency fee. If it is defeated, he is paid a much smaller amount based on the time he actually put in. The reason apparently is that if the bond issue is beaten, the lawyer's fee has to be paid out of the regular budget, where its size might attract the unfavorable attention of the citizens, while if the bond issue passes, the lawyer's fee is simply lumped in with the other costs of the project and passed on to future generations to pay. Usually the amount is relatively small, except of course in relation to the work involved, though a lawyer in Keansburg Borough, New Jersey, once managed to carve a $47,000 fee out of a bond issue of only $103,500. Because the fee is added to the bond issue, the citizens also have to pay interest on it, thus inflating the already swollen cost of the lawyer by 50 per cent or more. Here one screwing connects with another, for somewhere downstream a rich man is going to buy those bonds as a way to avoid paying his income tax.

The legal monopoly is protected by its control of still

another institution, the courts. When you witness the weird imperial ritual that surrounds the judge—the black robe and the high throne, the third-person form in which he is addressed, everyone rising when he enters—you begin to wonder if it's not all designed to conceal the fact that the person in charge is after all just another lawyer. The one time the judge is almost certain not to be impartial is in cases that pit his fellow lawyers against their clients. Though the cost of dragged out cases, of last-minute postponements and rescheduling, is borne by the client in lost time and higher fees, it is no cause for surprise that institutions run by lawyers should put their own interests first. The only exception is when the judge's personal interest conflicts with that of the lawyers, for the courts are a spectacular example of a point made elsewhere in this book: waste is the surest by-product of monopoly. Left to run their courtrooms as they please, most judges do what comes naturally, and the hours they keep—the short work day, the frequent breaks, the long vacations—constitute a powerful argument in favor of the time clock. A great judge. the late Jerome N. Frank, once said of his position on the U. S. Court of Appeals: "Easiest job I ever had." It is ironic that Chief Justice Burger used overcrowding the courts as an argument for limiting class actions, since court delays are due as much to judicial indolence and inefficiency as to the number of cases— the next time you hear about crowded court dockets, take a look around your courthouse at 5 P.M. For all these reasons, if the average man is seeking faster and cheaper justice, it won't do him much good to tell it to the judge.

Any lingering doubt about his standing in court can be dispelled if the average man takes a tour on jury duty. No medieval serf wiping the mud off his face after the count and the bishop gallop by was made to feel less important in the scheme of things than is the average person doing his duty as a citizen in the system of justice. He will be both bored and insulted. Bored, because much of the time he is sitting around with nothing to do; according to a study by the Law Enforcement Assistance Administration, 37 per cent of jurors' time is devoted to waste, and many people go through their two-week stint without doing anything at all, often at considerable expense to themselves. Insulted, because his time, his convenience, his dignity, and his intelligence are all treated with equal contempt by those who operate the courts. It would be ridiculously easy to make much more efficient use of jury panels, giving those summoned the sense that they are there for some purpose, saving money for the taxpayers, speeding the process of justice. It doesn't happen (with rare exceptions like Judge David Ross's reform of the criminal courts in New York City), because an efficient jury system would interfere with the easy life of judges and the convenience of lawyers, and because the lawyers' guild, like other monopolies, is both addicted to waste and under no pressure to heed the interests of the average man.

These massive fortifications—a strong guild, influence in government, control of the courts—are an imposing barrier to any real progress in bringing equal access to justice to the average man. If the opposition could be circumvented, there are several useful reforms waiting on the shelf. Lawyers would be cheaper if their training were shortened from three years to one, followed by on-the-job specialization. Paraprofessionals could handle at much less cost a lot of the work for which we are forced now to turn to lawyers; in fact, they are already doing much of it, as when a legal secretary fills out the probate forms, but because we must go through the lawyer he can charge his rate for the secretary's work. A huge amount of the litigation that now occupies the courts and impoverishes the clients could simply be abolished by such measures as probate reform and no-fault automobile insurance and divorce. All that would help, but it is doubtful whether it would solve the problem of the $300 refrigerator. Just how far the present order is from the $300 solution can be seen from the experience of Philip G. Schrag. Schrag was chief enforcer for Bess Myerson's Department of Consumer Affairs in New York City. He was armed with a staff and one of the strongest consumer protection laws in the nation. Schrag's job was to solve the $300 cases—and he failed. The reasons were several, as Schrag tells it in his book *Counsel for the Deceived.* The courts condoned endless delays that enabled his opponents to drag cases out past the memory and endurance of his witnesses. If he caught a businessman in an act of fraud, the courts did not punish him, so there was nothing to deter the person from going on swindling the public. A special circumstance in Schrag's case was that his agency, a new one, was often sandbagged by other parts of the city bureaucracy, an organization dedicated to preventing from happening tomorrow what didn't happen yesterday. The starkest lesson of Schrag's experience is that, despite the powers of his office, he was never able to get the $300 back except at a cost of many times that amount.

Despairing of reform, some people advocate the final solution of abolishing lawyers. They cite the example of China, which gets along without lawyers by using laymen to mediate disputes. The most impressive voice favoring abolition is that of Fred Rodell, the dissident Yale law professor and author of the classic *Woe Unto You, Lawyers!* It is not at all clear how abolition would work in practice, and who would substitute for the lawyer's role as the independent professional available—if he can afford it—to the individual at odds with the institutions around him. Not only does talk of abolition distract attention from the real reforms that could be accomplished, but that kind of cure could easily prove worse than the disease, for nothing is surer than the need of the average man for an advocate, loyal to him because paid by him, who can pilot him through the shark-infested waters of modern life. That, in fact, is why we so often see the lawyer as good guy, as well as in his usual role of war counselor to those who are swindling us.

Back in 1939 Rodell saw that it is impossible to separate the problem of lawyers from the broader issue of expert control. He described the lawyer as expert-of-all-experts:

> For every age, a group of bright boys, learned in their trade and jealous of their learning, who blend technical competence with plain and fancy hocus-pocus to make themselves masters of their fellow men. For every age, a pseudo-intellectual autocracy, guarding the tricks of its trade from the uninitiated, and running, after its own pattern, the civilization of its day. It is the lawyers who run our civilization for us—our governments, our business, our private lives. . . .
>
> It is through the medium of their weird and wordy mental gymnastics that the lawyers lay down the rules under which we live. And it is only because the average man cannot play their game, and so cannot see for himself how intrinsically empty of meaning their play things are, that the lawyers continue to get away with it. . . . And perhaps if the ordinary man could see in black and

white how silly and irrelevant and unnecessary it all is, he might be persuaded, in a peaceful way, to take the control of his civilization out of the hands of these modern purveyors of streamlined voodoo and chromium-plated theology, the lawyers.

6

Health: In the Hands
of the Experts

THE AVERAGE MAN is never so helpless as in his encounters
with the health industry. Even the toughest of consumers
tends to melt when illness brings him into the industry's
jurisdiction; fighting the doctor is not at all like fighting
the landlord. It is this profoundly unequal relationship,
maintained at least as much by the patient as by the industry, that distinguishes our experience with the health
industry from the other acts of piracy we have been describing. It is this peculiar quality of the industry that
makes the much-ballyhooed "health crisis" so difficult
to resolve in favor of the customer.

Begin at the doctor's office. After a lengthy wait, the
patient will be received for the few minutes—the time
grows shorter each year—that the doctor has allotted to
his case. He will pay more per minute for the doctor's
presence, and argue about it less, than he does in any
other professional encounter. He will leave having no
way other than the doctor's word of knowing what the
visit meant to his health. If he gets well, he won't know
whether the doctor had anything to do with it; if he

doesn't, he won't know whether the doctor could have done better.

The customer is in a similar state of uncertainty about his two other main encounters with the health industry. Often he leaves the doctor's office clutching a piece of paper bearing a message he cannot make out. He takes it to a pharmacist, who, through a unique form of monopoly, can overcharge him at a record rate for his prescription; he will not know what he took, what it should have cost, or what it did to or for him, if anything. Much the same will happen if he is sent to a hospital. He will not know whether he really needed to go there or whether he was sent there mainly to keep the hospital from suffering from low revenues and unfilled beds. If he is operated on, he will never know whether the operation was well performed or even whether it was necessary. When he leaves the hospital, he will have as little chance of understanding the gigantic bill as he did the prescription he took to the pharmacist.

His ignorance is the industry's bliss. The health practitioner takes the same view of the average man that God took of Adam: the less he knows, the better. It is an ancient tradition. The patient has been mystified at least since the first witch doctor emerged from the mists of prehistory, rattling those bones only he could understand. In early times, and still today in some cultures, the witch doctor claimed jurisdiction over our health in the next life as well as this one. The first act of specialization—dividing the witch doctor into priest and doctor—did not entirely remove the halo from the medical practitioner. Indeed, with the decline of belief in the afterlife, the witch doctor's aura of the supernatural has attached itself far more to doctor than to priest. It is the doctor whom we expect to take the ultimate responsibility of life and death. Doctors, like priests, refer to the rest of us as "the laity" and in the march of human progress, the members of both professions can usually be found occupying similar positions, far from the front. The public has obligingly recognized the doctor's halo; Gallup polls in 1973 showed that "physician" was the profession most respected by the public, and that the measure of respect had increased over the last five years.

Until quite recently, there was little to hide from the patient beyond the basic fact that the medicine man himself didn't understand what the rattling bones were saying. That was still pretty much the case in those days, around the turn of the century, that are now known nostalgically as the "Golden Age of American Medicine." Here is how that time is described by Dr. George Silver, a respected critic of his industry:

> In the days of the five-cent beer with free lunch, not too much was expected of medicine or of doctors. The patients then exercised a kind of condescending restraint, in that they knew the doctor didn't know much more than they did, but it was sort of nice to have him around. The people who couldn't afford to, or didn't think it necessary or advisable to, consult the physician, didn't see any reason why there needed to be a structure within which medical care could be given so that everyone who wanted it could have ready access. Those days are therefore called the "Golden Age of American Medicine." In those golden days, doctors couldn't do very much but there were lots of them, they were distributed well throughout the country, even in the most isolated places. . . . Hospitals were scarce, but then most of medical practice was outside of hospitals: even surgery and certainly childbirth. We didn't have to worry about long-

term care, nursing homes, middle medical institutions, convalescent homes, and the like, because the extended family took care of its own.

Now, no doubt another reason we didn't have to worry about all these extra institutions was that people didn't live as long in those days; a couple of old-fashioned epidemics could put a lot of nursing homes out of business. But the gains in medical knowledge have been nowhere near enough to justify the current deification of the doctor. As Dr. Kerr L. White, Professor of Medical Care and Hospitals at the Johns Hopkins Medical School, has said, "I don't think that more than 20 per cent of what is done by doctors, nurses, etc., does any more good than harm— or use than uselessness."

The apotheosis of the physician began with the events surrounding the "Flexner Report" in 1910. This was the famous Carnegie-financed study that led to the American Medical Association's long-time role as controller of medical education and, therefore, of the supply of doctors. It was a coup comparable to the first Rockefeller's capture of the oil industry—and no Sherman Act came along to try to break it up. Most of the structure and behavior of the health industry today, both good and bad, is the result of the Flexner study.

The AMA's case, which Flexner wholeheartedly bought,* was that half the medical schools in the country were churning out quacks, and that the public would be better off if the guild were given a monopoly on the li-

* Flexner himself was neither a doctor nor a medical educator; he had been running a small private school before his moment in the spotlight. This may seem ironic for a profession that more than any other claims exclusive expert jurisdiction over its subject, until one considers that his background may have made Flexner easier to capture by the AMA experts who accompanied him on his inspection tours.

censing of medical education. The general prevalence of patent-medicine/narcotics addiction around the turn of the century, as well as the rough-and-ready tradition of frontier doctors using whiskey to treat whatever they couldn't diagnose, which was plenty, suggests that the AMA wasn't entirely inventing the problem. Also, it is not wholly unreasonable to expect a profession like medicine to come under some regulatory supervision; unlike, say, the clothing industry, where customers can be expected to experiment and then stop buying products that are shoddy or fraudulent, medicine places such a high penalty on poor selection that we need someone to screen the candidates before setting them loose on the free market.

Still, it is impressive how ably the AMA has turned the public interest to its own purposes. In pointing to the pageant of medical progress as justification for the Flexner "reforms," the AMA has benefited from two useful coincidences. Medical education has certainly improved since 1910, but this is mainly because research has produced more useful information to impart to the students; some of this research grew from the Flexner reorganizations, but a lot did not. (A curious sidelight is that acupuncture, now coming into use in this country via China, was taught in some U.S. medical schools before Flexner.) Second, the health of Americans has also improved, but this has been due far more to public health measures (which the AMA often opposed) than to more skilled care by physicians. In 1900, the three leading killers were polio, diphtheria, and tuberculosis—all of them largely eliminated now by immunization and sanitation.

Perhaps because of these pleasant developments, even

the AMA's critics have seen the scarcity of doctors which grew from the Flexner report as merely an unfortunate side effect. A revisionist view is that this side effect was in reality the main event—that reducing the number of doctors, rather than improving their education, is what it was all about. Even before Flexner began his study the AMA had written out the findings they hoped he'd come up with. As he went from school to school, often requiring as little as one afternoon to evaluate a school and accompanied all the while by the AMA representative, Flexner did not have a lot of time to disagree. His signature on the report gave the AMA what it needed, the approval of someone without an obvious self-interest in reducing the number of doctors.

Whatever his motives, Flexner helped the AMA gain the power—which has only in the last few years decreased —to dictate its terms to the rest of us. The bill has been coming in ever since. The guild's campaign for occupational birth control was successful. The number of medical schools dropped after Flexner from 162 to 69, and the nation produced 117 fewer doctors in 1940 than it had forty years earlier. (Those who failed to be born white and male were particularly affected: black medical schools were reduced from seven to two, and there were fewer women doctors in 1940 than in 1910.) The Depression led the AMA to believe it still had not cut deeply enough. In 1933, its president was saying that "one is forced to the conviction that more doctors are being turned out than society needs and can comfortably reward," and his successor felt that "a fine piece of educational work could well be done if we were to use only one-half of the 70-odd medical schools in the United States."

An even more important effect than the supply of doctors has been the kind of doctors the schools turn out. Overall the United States has a higher physician per capita ratio than most other countries, including those whose citizens are generally better satisfied with their care (England and Sweden, for example). But the American supply is not only regionally maldistributed (Washington, D.C., has 371 doctors per 100,000 people; in Mississippi and Alaska it's 78 per 100,000), it is also so overspecialized that the kind of doctor most useful to the patient—the general practitioner or family doctor or other source of "primary care"—has declined even in recent years, when the total number of doctors has increased. In 1963 there were 59 of these primary physicians for 100,000 people; by 1971 it had fallen to 41.5. A study in the *New England Journal of Medicine* suggests that we should have 133 primary physicians per 100,000 and many fewer specialists.

From the doctor's point of view, the attractions of a specialty are easy to see. Here is the AMA list of what doctors in the specialties earned in 1969, with projections for 1973:

	1969	1973
Pediatrics	$31,812	$42,484
Psychiatry	33,915	45,292
General Practice	34,734	46,385
Internal Medicine	37,630	50,235
Anesthetics	39,647	52,948
Obstetrics/Gynecology	43,690	58,348
Surgery	48,848	65,235
Others	40,283	53,796
Average	39,727	53,054

The increased riches of specialty come from somewhere, namely the patient. He pays the higher bill in several forms. Since the specialist's training is longer, he has to charge higher rates to make up for his years of lost income. Specialization also means more doctor visits—the patient who used to get his treatment in one stop at a GP is now shunted from one specialist to another. Each specialist examines his favorite organ without consideration of the surrounding material; each repeats, at the patient's expense, the tests performed by the others; each charges his own bill; and ultimately none of them is responsible to the patient. This is called "fragmentation," and is piously deplored. Probably most important, the specialists need to be kept busy, and more than most professions they are able to generate their own demand.

The doctors' bill often comes in the particularly ugly form of unneeded surgery. There is compelling evidence that a great many of the operations performed in the United States are unnecessary. The general level of health in Britain and Sweden is at least the equal of ours: but in Britain, the rate of surgery is half what it is here, and in Sweden the rate of tonsillectomy is one tenth our own. Women get more than their share of unneeded surgery. According to Dr. Richard Kunnes (in *Your Money or Your Life*), studies have shown that at least one hundred thousand unnecessary hysterectomies (around 40 per cent of the total) are performed every year. The reason for that operation you didn't need are economic: surgery pays better than other kinds of doctor work, and, although there are too few doctors, there are too many surgeons. A surgeon who also does general practice will jump at the opportunity to operate, since that pays far better than his other work. Dr. Kunnes figured that "it takes an internist treating a hospitalized coronary patient about four weeks of daily hospital visits to collect the equivalent of a surgeon's fee for a routine appendectomy, which along with postoperative visits usually accounts for no more than 3 or 4 hours of the surgeon's time." Surgeon's fees are seldom announced in advance, and still less often contested: who among us has the courage to bargain with the man who holds the knife?

Eli Ginzburg of Columbia University writes:

> Many general surgeons are not very busy and therefore a great amount of unnecessary surgery is performed. The situation is particularly shocking when hysterectomies are considered. We were told that many women undergo mastectomies when a less radical procedure would do. Many thyroidectomies are performed when psychotherapy would be preferred. There is substantial overdoctoring for a host of diseases, including in particular infections of the upper respiratory tract.

In further illustration of this point, consider:

· The AMA torpedoed Dr. John Knowles' nomination as assistant secretary of HEW for health after he said that 30 per cent too many operations were being performed. (At the time Knowles was director of the Massachusetts General Hospital.)

· When the New York State Civil Service Health Plan imposed a requirement for a second doctor's approval on operations, the operation rate dropped 20 per cent.

Statements like Dr. Knowles' especially irritate the AMA because they break the most fundamental rule: don't piss in the bed. American medicine has, under AMA control, evolved into the most classic of guilds, insulated against outside criticism and dedicated to preventing internal fouling of the nest. Doctors are, even more than the old witch doctor, a group set apart from the rest of us. Their training is not only excessively long but also needlessly severe and tedious, like a tribal initiation. It serves the same purpose: during those years of suffering (the average student must go $15-20,000 into debt to finance his education; fortunately more than a third of medical students come from families in the top 3 per cent of the income brackets) and isolation, the postulant learns that the world is divided into two tribes, doctors and laity, and that he owes unthinking loyalty to his fellow initiates; hence the remarkable unwillingness of one doctor to testify against another, even if he knows why the body was buried. Doctors during their initiation learn a language, and even a handwriting, that enables them to communicate with each other over the head of the average man. A medical student, Michael Michaelson, tells this story about doctors' language:

> When a student at my own school asked an anatomy professor why he used the expression "pathogenic of" instead of "characteristic of" he was told, "Why, son, the public might know what we were talking about." He was being funny, but he was not kidding.

Doctors are vaccinated against the public through the AMA's power to regulate the members of the profession. Doctors are disciplined by state boards of medicine; in all states but one (Kansas) all or a majority of the board members are doctors, and in many they are nominated by the state medical association. Once licensed, a doctor has little to fear from his professional colleagues. Licenses are rarely lifted, and when they are it is not for medical incompetence but for having embarrassed the guild by getting caught breaking the law. In 1967 the state boards revoked 208 licenses (out of some 300,000 M.D.s). Of those, only twenty-three revocations had to do with professional practice, and the grounds were either narcotics violations or abortion—the charge in the latter was that the doctor performed an illegal operation, not that he butchered the patient.

Evidently even the AMA believes that considerably more than twenty-three doctors are unfit to practice. Herbert Denenberg, the Pennsylvania Insurance Commissioner, cites a report by the AMA Council on Mental Health which suggested that 5 per cent of all practitioners were alcoholics, drug addicts, or mentally unstable. Denenberg met resistance in his effort to get the incompetents weeded out in his state. The head of the Pennsylvania Medical Society said the unfit 5 per cent posed no great problem, since they could easily be spotted by patients—which raises a question as to how they earn a living. And the regulator of doctors, the Pennsylvania Commissioner of Professional and Occupational Affairs, said that with his resources it would take him ten years just to find out if the 19,000 M.D.s in Pennsylvania were even alive.

In some of its new health insurance plans, the government has proposed nailing negligent doctors by establishing peer-review groups, often called "Professional Standards Review Organizations" (PSROs). Ironically the main effect of the PSROs would be to raise the AMA from its recent slump (which dates from the bad days of losing the battle against Medicare); the reviewing function would essentially be franchised out to the AMA, giving it a brand-new reason for existence and a renewed monopoly on professional censure.

The AMA sits at the apex of a hierarchy of guilds that control two thirds of the health manpower—all but the most poorly paid jobs—in the United States. Some twenty-

five health and health-related occupations are licensed
by state boards. Besides physicians, these include dentists,
the various types of nurses, pharmacists, optometrists,
and so on. With one major type of exception, each of
the licensing boards is controlled by the guild it is supposed to regulate: pharmacists regulate pharmacists,
dentists regulate dentists, etc. The exception occurs when
an occupation is controlled not by its members but by a
guild that ranks higher in the medical hierarchy. Dental
hygienists, for example, are regulated by dentists, not by
their peers. Similarly, the guilds of registered nurses hold
power over their underlings, the practical nurses. In New
York, for example, both kinds of nurses are regulated by
a board that includes eleven registered and four practical
nurses. Just to keep the status difference clear, the practicals are not allowed to vote on matters concerning only
registered nurses, although the registered majority votes
on matters concerning only the practicals.

These guilds, like the AMA, practice the economics of
scarcity: the smaller the membership, the higher the
price. The customer finds himself paying a monopoly
price not just for the doctor, but for the services of all
the other guilds he deals with during the process of trying
to stay alive and well. Always the service will be somewhat harder to get, and the price somewhat higher, than
if he were dealing with an occupation that was not regulated by its own members.

The effects of monopoly in American health manpower
are felt even beyond our borders. The one way around
the AMA's birth control policy has been for this country
to import thousands of foreign doctors each year; in 1959
some 8.6 per cent of all doctors in the United States were
foreign-trained, but ten years later the figure had risen

to 18.4 per cent. The proportion continues to rise, and in 1971 there were 14,500 foreign-trained interns and residents in American hospitals. The guild approves, as long as the foreigners stick to the less desirable jobs, like working in municipal hospitals, while the natives harvest the rich suburban practices. Nurses have also been imported: New York City once imported planeloads of Filipino R.N.s, and ads offering U.S. jobs for nurses have appeared in such out-of-the-way places as San José, Costa Rica. The effect is to drain off health manpower from countries that have less of it than we do; and also to force other countries to pay higher salaries to hold on to their remaining doctors and nurses. Contemplating these realities, the average foreigner may conclude that he is being screwed along with his American counterpart. The American who is treated by a foreign doctor may answer that he is being doubly had: he is paying the monopoly price, and he is getting a doctor who can't really understand him because he is not fluent in either the American's language or his culture. Cook County Hospital in Chicago, for example, recently shelled out $32,000 on a Berlitz course for thirty interns who flunked the English-proficiency test.

In recent years, control of the health industry has been passing from the AMA guild, dominated by small town general practitioners, to the medical complexes built around hospitals and medical schools. The patient's role in this is similar to that of the medieval serf who watched from the sidelines as one noble, the king, took control of the serf's life away from another, the local baron. Doctors are still in charge, but their type has changed, in keeping with the trend toward delivering health services in the hospital rather than in the doctor's office.

For the patient, this means mainly that he will get the treatment in a different room. In the hospital he is if anything even more helpless than in the doctor's office— where he could still flee. He will, as always, be kept in ignorance; no one but the briefly passing doctor will tell him anything about himself, and often the doctor won't either. The hospital is of course where that unnecessary surgery is committed on him. He may never have needed to be there except that it's more convenient for the doctor or because his health insurance (for reasons we shall examine later) pays for treatment in the hospital but not for the same treatment elsewhere. He is likely to be kept too long, because hospitals in many cases lose money on the days when most care is given, and must make it back on days when nothing more than the routine is provided. Many people have had the experience of being told to check into a hospital on Friday for a Monday operation: these extra days may be the hospital's margin of profit. For profit there is, even in a "non-profit" hospital. Non-profit only means it doesn't pay taxes, not that it doesn't take money. The surgeon makes money in the hospital. The medical equipment company makes money from the hospital: witness the vast amount of underused and expensive equipment hospitals have. There are in the United States 777 hospitals equipped to perform open-heart surgery, according to Dr. Kunnes. Of these, one third have performed *no* open-heart surgery, and another one third do less than one operation a month. Such padded costs find their way ultimately on to the patient's bill.

Many people profit from the hospital. How the system works in one case, that of Washington Hospital Center, was described in detail by Ronald Kessler in his 1972 series in the Washington *Post*. "Patients' bills at Washington Hospital Center are inflated," Kessler started out, "by a variety of abuses that include conflict-of-interest transactions by trustees and administrators, payments to doctors of profits of the hospital, favoritism, lack of competitive bidding and free care to the rich." Calculating only some of the hustles, Kessler figured that a patient who paid the average daily room rate of $170 was laying out $8 for educating doctors and nurses, $3 for employee and doctor cafeterias, $8 for other patients who didn't pay their bills, $5 for profit to be used in expansion, and $20 for various discounts, charity care, and free care for wealthy friends of the management. The trustees checked themselves in free at the VIP Center of the hospital, and banker-trustees turned their service to good account by depositing hospital funds in non-interest-bearing accounts in their own banks. Some of the hustles are operated on the ancient principle of mystifying the patient. Kessler quotes a hospital consultant as saying that the more mysterious the service, the more the hospital can get away with charging for it:

> Hospitals try to keep room charges down because this is a charge the patient can understand; he's been in a hotel before, it has four walls and a bed. The x-ray, on the other hand, is a big mystery. The patient doesn't bat an eye at paying $30 for a $2.50 picture.

The best hustles grow out of departments that are operated on a monopoly, profit-making basis. No one did better at the Washington Hospital Center that year than the man who held the pathology concession, one Dr. Vernon E. Martens. He was making about $200,000 a year from the hospital—for part-time work. He had a similar concession at another hospital, and he operated farms in Virginia. He ran the hospital laboratory in return for a percentage of the profits. Pathologists believe devoutly in this way of doing business. In fact, before the Justice Department made them take it out, their canon of ethics included this rule: "I shall not accept a position with a fixed stipend in any hospital"—presumably because stipends for part-time work are usually fixed well below Dr. Martens' $200,000. The pathologists need fear no competition, for the Joint Commission on Hospital Accreditation has ruled that only pathologists can hold the laboratory concession. Doctors in private practice usually get their tests done by independent commercial laboratories run by technicians; their work is certainly cheaper, and in some opinions better, than that of the hospital pathologists. But they can't bid for the hospital's business, and the results show up in a comparison between Dr. Martens' prices and a local commercial lab:

	Martens	Lab
Pregnancy test	$11	$3.50
Complete blood count	$7	$2
Routine Urinalysis	$5	$1
12-channel test	$25	$5

Dr. Martens enjoys the monopolist's dream: the clients can't go to anyone else, and he can set the price where he pleases. Until 1971, Blue Shield had specified how much it would pay for pathologists' tests. In that year it switched to letting the pathologists charge their "usual and customary" fees. Dr. Martens' "usual and customary" went up so fast that for 1971 his lab produced $873,206 more profit than had been projected at the beginning of the year. There was, of course, nothing the patient could do about it. He can't even figure out the bill.

The drugstore is the scene of the average man's third losing encounter with the health industry. When he does business here, the client is the victim of a unique form of monopoly: brand-name drugs. As most people know, many drugs come in two forms. One is generic: the drug, typically made by several manufacturers, is known (and ordered) by its chemical name. The brand-name version is the same drug marketed under a different name by each manufacturer. The two types are identical in the opinion of all experts off drug company payrolls (although brand-name drugs are sometimes padded with useless ingredients to make them appear different). But the generic type, because it is sold by all producers under the same name, is subject to price competition, while each brand-name drug has its own little monopoly. The result is a lesson in monopoly pricing. Here are two of many examples. When Seconal (brand-name) was selling for $18.30 per thousand, the price of the generic equivalent, secobarbital, was $4 per thousand. When Nembutal (brand-name) was going for $.067 a capsule, the generic, pentobarbital, was $.002 a capsule, one thirtieth the brand-name price.

If the drug industry can possibly help it, the client will not get a chance to buy the generic version. The doctor can, and often does, protect the industry's health by writing his prescription for the brand-name drug. This is not necessarily because the doctor wants the patient to pay more, unless, as happens now and then, he owns the drugstore or has a kickback arrangement with the pharmacist. The doctor may just be acting out of ignorance. (Or the doctor may honestly feel one company makes a product of higher quality, but this could as easily be the generic as the brand-name version.) Most of the doctor's post-graduate education is provided by the drug companies' "detail men," who call on him with samples of, and propaganda for, their latest trade-marked miracles; drug companies are said to spend an average of $4,000 a year per doctor on promotion, all of which has to be earned back from the customers. The detail men aren't pushing generics, and anyhow, it's not the doctor's money.

The doctor's guild could lighten his ignorance and, therefore, the patient's drug bill. It does not seem about to do so, for that would be biting the hand of an industry that feeds the AMA more than one quarter of its income ($8.6 million in 1972) in the form of drug advertising in AMA publications. The AMA retirement fund owns stock in sixteen drug and health supply companies. And in 1972 the guild abolished its own council on drugs after its members put forth some unflattering descriptions of highly profitable drugs. Nor does government seem inclined to help cut the public's drugstore bill. Back in 1970, the General Accounting Office recommended to the Department of Health, Education, and Welfare that it act to require doctors and pharmacists to use generics instead of brand-name equivalents. The office of the Secretary of HEW, who was then Elliot Richardson, came back with an interesting parry. It was, the office said, in "full agreement" on generic drugs. "However," it went on, "we feel that the inseparability of quality from price requires that we make certain that all manufacturers' versions of every drug available to American patients are in fact safe and effective." The irony is that Richardson's office saw that "inseparability of quality from price" in the one industry that has demonstrated more than any other the complete separability of the two. The fact that the same chemical is marketed under two names, one version selling for thirty times the other, does not seem to tell us much other than that we're being had. Finally, in December 1973, HEW proposed regulations which would require generic drugs for Medicare and other publicly financed programs.

The multiple contusions inflicted on the patient's finances by the guild, the hospital, and the pharmacy finally began to price most people out of the market. The industry's solution was one we have seen elsewhere in this book: third-party the business and leave everybody confused about who's picking up the check. Blue Cross was the first big venture in third-party financing in the health industry. Blue Cross was founded in the late 1920s for the explicit purpose of guaranteeing hospitals that their bills would be paid and, as the years have rolled by, it has never lost sight of that primary mission. Controlled by hospitals and doctors, Blue Cross has taken toward hospital costs the same benevolent attitude that the Pentagon takes toward defense cost overruns. The hospital, like Lockheed, decides how much it wants to spend and Blue Cross writes the check: for unneeded equipment, for that $200,000 part-time pathologist, for unnecessary patient stays, for the pervasive inefficiency of monopoly. All these costs are passed on by Blue Cross in the form of higher rates to its subscribers.

Blue Cross rates must be approved by state agencies, which perform their duties with all the vigor one can expect of regulatory authorities. Typically Blue Cross and the regulators go through a ritual dance along these lines: Blue Cross asks for twice as much as it wants; the state agency shouts loudly in the public interest and cuts the raise in half; the hospitals get their extra money while the state official has cut a fine figure in front of his constituents.

The purpose of Blue Cross is to act as a buffer that permits hospitals to raise their rates without driving away the customers. That is the genius of the third-party system: the client is unlikely to figure out that he is still paying the bill, and if he does there is nothing he can do about it. The first line of defense is to point out to anyone questioning the bill that he's not paying for it. Jane Boutwell of *The New Yorker* tells about the time she was bitten on the hand by an irate Siamese cat. She went to the hospital emergency room, where she was told to go home and soak her hand in hot water. On the way out the cashier said: "That will be forty-five dollars." When Ms. Boutwell questioned that fee for the service she had received, the cashier replied in classic fashion: "Why should you worry? Your insurance will take care of it." After this incident was published in the New York *Times*, one Margot Ran wrote in to say that her husband had paid another New York hospital $109 for room and board, though he had only been there as an outpatient for three and one-half hours, from 7 to 10:30 A.M. He'd had neither room nor board. When Mrs. Ran complained about the bill, she was told, "Why should you care, etc." and also that the room charge was made under an "arrangement" between the hospital and Blue Cross. The Thomas Memorial Hospital in South Charleston, West Virginia, provides another example. It charges $3.50 for a cervical cancer test when it's done on an outpatient basis, which the patient usually pays for herself. But when it's done to patients in the hospital, who are usually being paid for by Blue Cross or some other third party, the hospital charges ten dollars for the identical test.

It is obvious that premiums will be driven up by this kind of financing. Ms. Boutwell's forty-five-dollar cat nip is only a flea bite in the total Blue Cross bill, and yet if the same sort of thing happens to everyone, everyone will end up with a forty-five-dollar bill. But the third-party system prevents us from acting even if we grasp the nature of the game. If the patient had to pay that forty-five dollars himself, he could argue it with the hospital, and, if he won, he could carry his savings home in his pocket. But once the bill has been third-partied, arguing down the bill will not benefit the patient—unless everyone around the country is arguing their cat bites at the same time. Until that improbable day arrives, the system is safe.

Now and then there are attempts to keep the third-partying from getting out of control. In his article "It's Enough to Make You Sick," published in *Playboy* in October, 1970, Roger Rapoport has described the work of the Metropolitan Denver Foundation for Medical Care, one of eighty-nine similar groups around the country whose purpose is to knock down inflated insurance claims. Some excerpts from the account:

> "Eleven pounds of organic pork!"
> Dr. Wallace H. Livingston looked at the Boulder, Colorado, allergist's bill a second time and blinked. He turned to his secretary and asked, "Is this right? This physician is billing his bronchial-asthma patient $13.20 for 11 pounds of organic pork?" She nodded and Dr. Livingston broke out laughing . . .
> During my visit Dr. Livingston showed me some of the day's claims. One came from a GP who had performed tonsillectomies on three children from the same family in the same week. Discharge summaries indicated no history

of tonsillitis for any of the children . . . About 1,100,000 tonsillectomies are done annually and most of them are unnecessary. Between 200 and 300 children die each year because of tonsillectomy complications . . . These are some of the reasons Dr. Livingston disallowed the entire $433 bill for the tonsil triple-header. Neither the doctor nor the hospital received a penny. "This is one of our biggest problems," he told me. "One out of four tonsillectomy claims involves a second member of the family. The doctor says it's time for one kid's tonsils to come out and the mother figures she might as well have the whole brood taken care of at the same time . . ." Dr. Livingston showed me another bill from a doctor who favored a handful of diagnoses that he always stamped on claim forms. This particular bill covered a husband and wife team afflicted by "endocrine dysfunction with obesity." "Here we have a stamp doctor who treats all his patients with four bogus therapies and charges them all $367.50. We routinely knock all his claims down to $114.50 . . . Every one of these guys seems to have a favorite diagnosis. Here's one who always comes in with 'menopausal syndrome and bronchitis.' It seems like every one of his female patients comes down with these two things simultaneously. We also have a great deal of trouble with shot doctors. Look at this claim: $562 for a year-long series of 250 vitamin shots for a patient with 'cellular metabolic insufficiency.' That isn't a diagnosis, it's just a catchall, it's just garbage."

When premiums for Blue Cross (and its younger sister, Blue Shield) began to get oppressively high, the payments were third-partied once again. Employer-paid health insurance was given tax breaks that made it seem to everyone's advantage for the employer rather than the employee to pay the premiums. The Blue Cross deduction disappeared, entirely or in part, from the paycheck.

Again, the employee will ultimately pay the bill in two ways: first, in the wage increase he traded away for employer-paid insurance, and, second, in the higher taxes he pays to make up for the employer's tax break . . . but by now the trail is so winding that no one can follow it. Senator Edward Kennedy has estimated that the average wage earner works one month a year for his health insurance—even if no deduction shows up on his paycheck.

Then, in the mid-sixties, government, the greatest of all third-partiers, suddenly lurched onto the scene and—"we were only trying to help"—converted the average man's defeat into a disaster. Lyndon B. Johnson, trying to erect his Great Society with money and politics, but without foresight, pushed through Medicare for the elderly and Medicaid for the poor. The AMA, hypnotized by its own ancient war cry of "socialized medicine," vigorously opposed these greatest of bonanzas; the big medical centers, catching the scent of socialism-for-the-rich, backed the new programs. But once the legislation was in effect, even the opponents pulled themselves together and reached for their share of the flood of new money. What occurred next was as predictable as Litton Industries' latest overrun. Medicare and Medicaid created a vast new demand for the health industry's product, a demand that, because payment was third-partied, was not particularly concerned about price. What happens in such a situation? Right: the industry raised its prices to mop up all that new cash flow. In the decade of the sixties, hospital prices rose four times, and doctor prices twice, as fast as the consumer price index. Some forty to fifty million eligibles benefited from Medicare and Medicaid, but prices rose for everyone else as well. The average man, who was not old enough for Medicare or poor enough for Medicaid, found himself occupying his usual position in the scheme of things. He had to pay higher prices for his own health care, whether he paid directly or through insurance, and he had to pay higher taxes to pay the cost of Medicare and Medicaid. Because of medical inflation, even the average person over sixty-five spends more out-of-pocket on medical care now than he did *before* Medicare. Those costs soon ballooned far beyond all forecasts: according to one calculation, the cost overrun over twenty-five years will add up to an incredible $131 billion. The old witch doctor had learned how to count.

Wondrous hustles were invented in honor of the federal government. Hospitals concocted bills that on some spectacular occasions reached beyond $1,000 an hour. In the cities where the poor are found, doctors created what came to be known as Medicaid mills. Anyone wandering into those offices with any complaint was subjected to every test known to medical science—Medicaid was paying. Doctors saw patients at remarkable rates of speed, and some devoted long hours to the care of the poor: one psychiatrist put in a bill for twenty-five hours of therapy in a single day. Others pioneered new forms of treatment: one favorite is the optometrist who ordered prescription sunglasses—for a blind patient. Others may prefer the doctor who ordered a pregnancy test—for a male patient. Doctors who rose to the challenge of caring for the poor found their incomes rising correspondingly. California and New York competed for the record. In California, thirty-five doctors drew down a total of more than $3 million in a single year from Medicaid; one doctor collected $131,000. Good, but not quite in a class with the New

York doctor who collected $106,000 in the first six months of 1972—while working part time. The dentists began drilling for the Medicaid dollar. In California again, eleven of them billed Medicaid for a total of $1 million, a rate that compares favorably with that of the doctors. In New York City, the first city to make a serious attempt to control the Medicaid boom, an examination of Medicaid teeth showed that 9 per cent of the bills were for work that was never done and another 9 per cent was for work of a quality that would have flunked out a dental student; another audit showed that 25 per cent of the bills were for "overservicing"—work that the patients didn't need. The pharmacists were not left out. Their most spectacular representative was the Kentucky pharmacist who collected $328,000 from Medicaid for his service to a town of 750 people. "I think Medicaid has been good to me and I think I've been good to it," he said.

The aroma of money reached nostrils in other lines of business, and soon outsiders came tumbling in to stake out claims on the health industry's turf. In his article "A Candle for St. Greed's" (*Harper's*, December 1972), Roger Rapoport described some of the newcomers. Their speciality is building chains of proprietary (overtly profit-making) hospitals. The former head of Kentucky Fried Chicken, Jack C. Massey, is now chairman of Hospital Corporation of America, which has opened forty hospitals in twelve states. Massey said that "growth potential in hospitals is unlimited; it's even better than Kentucky Fried Chicken." The founders of Holiday Inns are also the founders of Medicenters of America. The promoters are not worried that medical progress will undercut them.

Charles Heath, administrator of Palm Harbor Hospital in Garden Grove, California, told Rapoport:

> "Sure you don't see smallpox anymore, but we've got new things going for us today. Thanks to all the smog our inhalation-therapy business is picking up beautifully. Inhalation therapy; now there's a money-maker."

Some promoters decided that the safest way to guarantee a steady flow of business, whatever the futures of smog and smallpox, is to cut the doctors in on the action. If a doctor holds stock in the hospital, the reasoning goes, he will perceive the connection between the number of patients he sends there and the health of his shares. In the Encino, California, hospital belonging to the Beverly Enterprises chain the connection is made explicit. Doctors there keep a television set tuned to a business news channel. Administrator Max Weinberg explained to Rapoport: "They like to see how their stock is doing. I usually come down every morning to find out myself." Promoters who find themselves short of customers have resorted to paying doctors a bounty for each patient they send to the promoters' hospital. Some doctors have already figured this out for themselves and bought their own hospitals. What can then happen was reported in a California investigation of Medicaid:

> One example of unnecessary services in a physician-owned hospital concerns a patient who was hospitalized for 16 days. Ten blood tests, many of them identical, were taken each day the patient was hospitalized. Of the 160 tests taken, not one revealed an abnormal finding. Multiple x-rays of the chest, skull and cervical spine were also taken although here again no abnormality was ever revealed. This type of overservicing was similarly provided to many other patients in this same hospital.

The federal government, which had set off the gold rush, stood by indifferently. Early on it had occurred to Washington that Medicare (which is federally administered) would generate millions of hospital and doctor bills to be audited. The Federals looked around for agencies to whom they could delegate the task of checking these claims, and came up with—Blue Cross! Blue Shield! At the intersection of the health and government monopolies, it was solemnly decided that the hospitals' claims should be audited by the hospitals' friend, and the doctors' claims by the doctors' friend. When the Medicaid scandals could no longer be ignored, Washington appointed the inevitable commission—headed by Walter McNerney, president of the Blue Cross Association. The states, which administer Medicaid, also usually chose the Blues as auditors. The results were as might be expected: in California, for example, much of what little effective regulation had previously existed was disbanded when the auditing of Medicaid (known in that state as Medi-Cal) was placed in those friendly Blue hands. The Blues found that, besides approving their friends' claims, they could pad out their own bills for conducting the audits. Godfrey Hodgson, in the October 1973 *Atlantic*, tells how the Virginia Blues passed on to Medicare the cost of all manner of administrative luxuries; the most notable of these capers was charging Medicare for part of the $2,138.50 cost of thirteen dozen golf balls imprinted with the Blue Cross/Blue Shield monogram.

Towering over such petty hustlers is the imposing figure of H. Ross Perot. Hardly anyone had heard of Perot when, in 1969, he was made a director of the Nixon Foundation. Only a few years before, he was just a

$20,000 employee of Texas Blue Cross. But Perot had seen his future, and he knew it would work. By the following year, 1970, H. Ross Perot was worth around $1.5 billion, and *Fortune* magazine offered the observation that no American had ever made so much money in so short a time. Perot, unlike his nineteenth-century precursors, made his fortune out of government funds for the old and the poor. He founded an electronic data processing firm which picked off Medicare and Medicaid contracts all over the country. His bid was often higher than anyone else's, but somehow he landed the contracts, and his profit rate ran as high as 41 per cent. Perot was evidently hard to resist; when New York State bureaucrats chose another bidder, Perot appeared in the office of then Governor Nelson A. Rockefeller, and on the governor's orders Perot got back on the inside track. For the statistical-minded, it might be pointed out that the fortune Perot made out of public money works out to an average contribution of almost $19 from each taxpayer in the land. Perot himself is reluctant to give any of it back. Recently turned statesman, Perot has been advocating more tax loopholes for people like himself.

The disaster that Medicare and Medicaid represented for most people—the underwriting of inflation and gigantic waste—led inevitably to the next idea: third-party the entire health bill. By the early 1970s everyone involved in the politics of health was peddling some version of a national health insurance program. Even the AMA, by now appreciating the benefits of socialism for the rich, was offering its own plan. None of the plans, with the possible exception of Senator Edward Kennedy's, seemed to take into account the experience of the 1960s. Even when, as in Kennedy's case, there was some suggestion that health costs should be controlled, nothing in the record of government regulation held out hope that the health industry would not easily be able to avoid whatever controls were instituted. In late 1973, Senator Russell Long offered a plan that promised working people a double screwing: it would have the usual inflationary effect, and would be paid for out of the Social Security payroll tax. Thus the cost of Long's plan would be paid entirely out of income earned by work, with the heaviest burden falling on those who earned the least, and unearned income would pay nothing at all. Whatever their sponsorship, all the plans currently offered seemed designed to repeat the Medicare-Medicaid fiasco on a much larger scale. Much more money would be pumped into the same old health industry, prices would go up even faster—but, with the bill now entirely third-partied, the American public would not see the connection between its "free" health care and a soaring tax bill.

The ills of the health industry are not easy to diagnose, still less to treat. Much of the endless debate among health reformers concerns organization of health care delivery. The medical school-hospital empires are loud in their contempt for the old-fashioned fee-for-service generalist in solo practice; much better, they say, to group doctors together, preferably under the wing of the empire, with some third party paying the bills. Yet that solo practice gives the consumer a wide range of choice and brings the doctors into the neighborhood, instead of forcing the patient to travel to the medical center. The solo doctor may be out of touch with the latest achievements of medical research, but those wonders have nothing to do with the great bulk of the doctor's business. Doctors are over-, not under-trained; most common ailments could be diagnosed and treated by someone who learned his trade in far less time than it took the doctor. Fee-for-service, for all its glaring faults, at least permits the patient to make some connection between what he is paying and what he is getting.

The currently fashionable HMO (health maintenance organization) is an example of a well-meant idea that is going astray. Doctors overtreat because they make their money in sickness not in health; therefore—so the HMO fans argue—if they are paid a flat fee per patient per year it will be in the doctors' financial interest to keep people healthy and out of the hospital. The proponents always point to their favorite HMO, the Kaiser-Permanente plan in California, which seems to work as an HMO should; they rarely mention New York City's Health Insurance Plan, which recently was on the verge of financial and administrative collapse. Of course, the easiest way for an HMO to make money is not to keep people healthy, but to avoid treating them whether they are well or not. Or, as economist Gelvin Stevenson suggested, "start a prepaid cafeteria and watch the sandwiches get smaller." Complaint handlers in businesses as diverse as car dealers and government have been proving for years that with determination you can keep the public away; an HMO ought to be able to do as well as, say, an automobile dealer faced with a warranty claim. Some inkling that HMO spells money has gotten through to the industry and some of the smartest hustlers are positioning themselves to grab this new opportunity. *Fortune* magazine called one doctor who got into the HMO business a "fast-moving entrepreneur," and went on to suggest that the profit rate in HMOs might be as high as it is in oil companies.

The average man is not likely to gain much, if anything, from the kind of organizational shadowboxing represented by the HMO debate. More than most of the swindles described in other chapters, the screwing we take from the health industry mirrors the society in which it takes place; it is unlikely that a society that produces an H. Ross Perot can also enjoy a healthy medical system. This conclusion is reinforced by the familiar comparison between American and foreign health systems. We are frequently told that we pay more and get less than other nations; our bills are richer, but our health statistics are poorer, than theirs. The countries cited are, most often, Sweden and Britain, sometimes Israel, and, most recently, China. Those countries, though very different in many ways, share a greater sense of unity, of common purpose, than can still be found in our fragmented and suspicious nation. Their health systems work, not because of the way in which they are organized, which differ greatly, but because their societies work at least relatively well. Health care is delivered because caring is possible and because a certain measure of trust exists. Trust is necessary because the relationship between scared patient and omniscient doctor is bound to remain profoundly unequal; we can arm ourselves against the others who hustle us, the landlord and the lawyer and the rest, but never against the person who holds life and death in his hands. Our health industry, then, cannot do much better by the American public until we have healed our body politic.

7

Education: Catch-85 and the
Arithmetic of the Diploma

IT IS THE MOST UNUSUAL OF SCREWINGS.

The pirates we have been meeting in other chapters rob us of money, but school takes us in another currency: time. Money also, but mainly time. Most extraordinary, the education industry doesn't even intend to screw its victims, and those who administer the treatment in most cases derive no personal benefit from it. It is a crime without a criminal, a used car without a dealer. The infernal machine proceeds with no one in the driver's seat. If the average man looks inside the education machine to identify who's putting it to him, he'll find out no one is there.

In other ways, the education industry resembles the more familiar kinds of hustle. It is financed mainly by third-party payments, and so the average man has little or no say over who gets his money. It is run by experts, and so the average man is not allowed to criticize their performance. It is a monopoly, and so the product is standardized, shoddy and overpriced (though the monopoly cost is expressed in years instead of dollars). The wordnoise that protects education is especially deafen-

ing—louder even than the noise that surrounds its two
main rivals, government and automobiles.

Education is, most of all, the place that the average
man cannot avoid. He may be able to avoid having a
checking account, and even owning a car—but hardly
anyone escapes school (the rare exceptions occur mainly
among the very rich and the very poor). The average
man cannot even escape *more* school: measured by time,
school is growing faster than any other occupation, including watching pro football. At any given time about
one third of the American population is in school in one
form or another, and it seems probable that the average
man's years in school are growing faster than his life ex-
pectancy.

The imperative reason for going to school is to find a
place on the upper end of the net screwing scale. If you
want to enjoy a favorable balance of screwings—that is,
to do onto others more than they do onto you—it seems
you pretty well have to stay in school at least through
college. School is the passport to the favorable terrain
occupied by the 15 per cent for whom Catch-85 was written. The professions with their lucrative hustles are
barred to those who have not hung in there long enough
to get an advanced degree; you may be able to outlawyer
a Clarence Darrow, but you'll never get a chance to show
your stuff without the law school diploma. Even in business it is hard nowadays to get very far up the scale without at least college, preferably an advanced degree.

Certainly increasing one's future income is not the only
value one can get out of schooling. We are all aware of
the other kinds of advantages that education, at its best,
can offer both to students and to society. People who
have learned more are likely to be more useful to

the rest of us, materially because they will probably be more productive, and less tangibly because they may be more knowledgeable citizens. They are likely also to be more useful to themselves. People who know and think more about a variety of things are likely to find more variety and pleasure in their lives, and there is some hard evidence that people with more years of schooling as a group are less susceptible to snake oil salesmen, whether commercial or political. And certainly teachers as a rule view their vocation along those lines rather than as agents for their students' future earnings. But these are reasons why it is a good idea for people who are so inclined to be able to stay in school until they have acquired what they want to learn. This is quite different from the cold imperative of learn-and-earn: if you don't stay in school, you're going to get screwed in the job market.

Years-in-school therefore provide a rough measure of where we all stand (again, with the exception of the born rich). Anyone with a professional degree figures to be ahead on net screwing; if not, he's either saintly or stupid (not always easy to tell which). This does not mean that the professional is immune to screwing, only that he dishes out more than he takes. The doctor, for example, patronizes the auto mechanic and lawyer and he has a title search on his house, but these tolls do not seriously affect the doctor's relative standing: they are leeches on the belly of a shark. If, at the other extreme, you didn't finish high school, you are just about certain to be in the great army of losers. You may have your own hustle, but, satisfying to the soul as that may be, it does not put you ahead of the game. The auto mechanic charges flat-rate labor on the doctor's car—and still comes out far behind. In between is the rapidly growing population of college graduates. This is where the dividing line is found, for holders of a college diploma can go either way. Increasingly, however, they are ending up as net losers. The dilemma of the average man is that the more of him go to college, the less the chance that any one of them will be able to get what he expected out of his diploma.

That calculation is vastly different from the way it was figured two generations ago. Only yesterday, the college diploma was a guarantee of entry into the favored class, and even some high school graduates were able to go all the way. But in those days, of course, the average man didn't go to college. The college was the boot camp of the elite, reserved largely for those who held the right passport by inheritance. It was birth, not years-in-school, that gave them their place. Then, in the great expansion of college after World War II, the average man appeared in droves on campus—and his very presence in itself destroyed the promise held out to him by college.

The promise was that, since college graduates all get good jobs, more college graduates would mean more people getting good jobs: democracy through education. The fallacy in the promise is one of arithmetic, similar to the principle of Catch-85, which dictates that all but 15 per cent of us must lose out on tax loopholes. If, in an unequal society like ours, there are 15 per cent who end up in the black on net screwing, there can never be room at the top for more than 15 per cent of the population—no matter how many go to college. If only 15 per cent go to college, including those with inherited places, then the system works, and everyone with the diploma finds himself on the sunny side of the street. But if 30 per cent get the diploma, only half of them can cash in on its promise. The rest will be headed off at the pass. And if, as soon will be the case, half of the population gets a college degree, fewer than one in three graduates will get what he paid for. This simple arithmetic is what is screwing the average man out of the supposed value of his diploma. But few people seem to be aware of the odds they are facing. For example, a 1973 survey of 38,200 high school students found that half of them thought they could become millionaires if they tried. Now, that is clearly impossible: no matter how hard they try, that group of students is not going to turn out 19,100 millionaires. But, because the mechanical rabbit of opportunity is theoretically in everyone's reach, each thinks he could catch it if only he ran fast enough.

When the average man started going to college in great numbers, he set off a kind of arms race in degrees. The diploma had been a good method of rationing privilege. It saved trouble for the personnel department. Instead of having to judge applicants on their merits—trying to pick the ten winners out of 200 pieces of paper—personnel simply classified them by diploma and took the ten with bachelor's degrees. This worked well as long as diplomas were scarce, but the system broke down when the graduates started marching in by the thousands. This had two consequences distressing to the average man who had paid his four years on the premise that his sheepskin was also a meal ticket, just as the learn-and-earn propagandists had told him.

First came a glut of diplomas. In one privileged job after another, a growth-maddened education industry turned out more graduates than the market could absorb. Obscured somewhat during the boom years of the 1960s, the change became painfully evident in the early 1970s. In 1973, according to the "Occupational Outlook Hand-

book" of the Department of Labor, the outlook was bleak
for many graduates. School would turn out 2,000 forest-
ers, but there were only 1,000 jobs. The education industry itself produced 108,000 jobs while it turned out
191,000 degrees in education. And so on. Graduates
who expected to go on to professional schools faced
equally poor odds; law schools, for example, could take
only one in four applicants. In May of 1973, the Carnegie
Commission estimated that during the 1970s the education industry would produce three million more graduates than the market would produce jobs. With the
children of the rich jogging along easily on the inside
track, the great majority of those three million losers will
be the sons and daughters of working-class parents who
grasped at the illusion of opportunity.

Too many diplomas chasing too few jobs also produced
an inflation in degree requirements as the personnel department, desperately trying to sort out the crowd, began
asking for more schooling for the same jobs. The inflation
began with the postwar flood of graduates. In *Education
of the American Population,* a study of the 1960 census,
John K. Folger and Charles B. Nam found that in the
decade of the 1950s, only 15 per cent of employers' increased demands for diplomas could be accounted for
by changes in the nature of work. The other 85 per cent
was due to added diploma requirements for the same
jobs. The education industry is one of the major contributors to the inflation. Schoolteachers in the 1930s needed
two years past high school; then it became four and now
it is creeping up to five years. Even the ultimate in academic trophies, the Ph.D., may not be immune to inflation. Doctorates are in surplus in many fields. President
James M. Hester of New York University saw the solution.

There will be a need, he prophesied not long ago, for "advanced degrees beyond the Ph.D."—a kind of Super-doctor. For the average man, the diploma inflation means that he has to invest more years for the same result. He can even start college on the promise of a job four years later, then on graduation find either that there are too many of him or that someone has tacked on an extra two years, and he has to go back to school.

Still, most of us have been convinced of the basic learn-and-earn equation: income rises with years in school. We are bombarded with studies showing those hundreds of thousands of extra dollars earned by college graduates. Those years must be a good investment—at least if you're a white male, which is what those studies typically high-light. If you're female, or black, or otherwise genetically afflicted, the payoff on the college years will be a lot smaller. Now comes Christopher Jencks in his book *Inequality* to challenge the validity of learn-and-earn. This careful study by Jencks and seven others produced results upsetting to the education industry. They found, not surprisingly, that if you started higher up on the lad-der you'll earn more from your learning: an extra year of schooling does twice as much for the middle-class as for the working-class student. Almost half the difference in earnings among people with different amounts of school can be accounted for, not by the schooling, but by the class they come from—you travel further if you're run-ning on the inside track. Jencks also found that the return on education comes not because the educated are more productive, but because their diplomas give them access to higher-paid occupations; within any given occupation, there is no evidence that those with more school or better grades earn more. So, of course, if there is no more room in the well-paid occupations, your payoff on school might well be down around zero. Jencks is skeptical about the notion that the average man can make it to the promised land via school:

> Rate-of-return estimates do tell us that efforts to keep everyone in school longer make little economic sense. The average rate of return for postsecondary education is quite low. For the kinds of students who are not now in college, it is even lower. For working-class whites, blacks and women, dropping out seems in many cases to be the most economically rational decision.

Despite this discouraging assessment, the education industry's product is still selling well. Although as time goes by each year of school buys less in future earnings, although it is possible to put in all those years and still emerge screwed, people are still patronizing school in increasing numbers. And with good reason: the average man goes to school because it is the only game in town. Like the compulsive gambler, he may know the wheel is fixed, but he plays anyway because he has no alternative. If he goes to school, the odds on the payoff are getting worse, but if he doesn't go, as Jencks seems to be suggesting, he is *sure* to lose. So he goes.

The average man has no choice because school has acquired a monopoly over access to well-paid jobs. There are, nowadays, few potentially lucrative occupations he can enter without school credentials. Among the rare holdouts are the arts, some sports (not pro football), and those remaining areas of crime that have not been legitimized and credentialized. For all other opportunities, the route passes through the educational industry. This monopoly, unlike any other, seems to have been acquired without conscious design. Where the Morgans and Rockefellers expended ulcer-making efforts in destroying the capitalist free market, the schoolmen seem to have drifted into their empire. There is no evidence that the education industry's leaders—indeed, it does not appear to have any central leadership—stayed up nights scheming ways to stomp their competitors. Nor, for that matter, do the members of the industry profit greatly from their monopoly: most of them, in fact, come out in the red on net screwing, and no great American family fortunes have been won out of school.

The school monopoly was brought about mainly by the efforts of people outside the industry. Do-gooders, observing that some school was good for everybody and a lot was good for a few people, decided that a lot must be good for everybody. Unions saw compulsory education as a way to keep low-priced teen-agers off the labor market, and guilds of course saw more school as a means of restricting membership and keeping prices up. Industry had its own reasons for favoring more school. In the nineteenth century, much of the pressure for compulsory public schooling came from industrialists. Industry figured school would give its future employees their first taste of discipline. Let school break them in, discarding those that refuse to fit, and industry would get—free—a docile labor force.* Nowadays, with the general growth of hypocrisy, the employers' line is less blunt. More school is needed, we are told, because a modern economy requires more people with more advanced skills. Of course that target has already been overshot—the average man stays in school far longer than needed to acquire the

---

* This basic notion, that school should beat us into shape for the assembly line, is today being marketed under the brand name of "career education."

skills involved in the job for which his diploma will qualify him. Besides, the process is extremely wasteful. Each industry could train people in the particular skills it needs in a fraction of the time it takes schools, including trade schools, to do the job. But this doesn't matter to industry: it has successfully shifted to others the cost of preparing, sorting and grading its labor force. The cost is paid twice over by the average man in two kinds of currency. He sits in school, bored, to learn in two years what he could have learned on the job in six months, and he pays the cost of school either in tuition or taxes. But industry profited: he paid for the twenty-four months, while his future employer got the six months worth of training free.

The average man might as well go to school, since to a large degree he's paying for it anyhow. The cost of education has been so successfully third-partied that everyone, consumer or not, is helping foot the bill. Grade school education has of course been overwhelmingly public for a long time, and now higher education is heading in the same direction. Public colleges are growing much faster than their private counterparts, and tax exemption (see chapter 12) assures that everyone contributes his mite to private schooling of all varieties. The laudable aim of public higher education is that everyone should be able to afford college; the unfortunate side effect is that the average man can less and less afford *not* to go to college.

The rich as usual have been quicker than the average man in seizing the opportunity to get their career credentials at someone else's expense. According to a study by W. Lee Hansen and Barton Weisbrod, free public higher education in California benefits the well-to-do at the expense of those of lower income. The wealthy collect more in free schooling than they pay in taxes; the rest pay more than they collect. Ironically, it was Governor Ronald Reagan, the defender of the rich, who pushed through tuition for the state universities against liberal opposition, although the effect of tuition was to make the wealthy pay more of their share. The fact that Reagan was doing the average man a favor seems to have been kept from everyone, including, presumably, the governor himself.

The third-party system evidently enjoys general approval. At least Governor John J. Gilligan of Ohio must feel it does. A few years ago, Gilligan proposed that Ohio's public colleges raise their tuition to cover the entire cost of schooling, and that the state provide enough loan money so anyone could go to college and later pay back the cost out of those extra earnings his diploma would bring him. The purpose was to make the beneficiary, rather than the public, bear the cost of college. The idea was too good: the Ohio school establishment shouted that it would set public education back a hundred years, and Gilligan's proposal went down the drain.

Despite that setback, support for the basic idea of the Gilligan proposal—unthird-partying the bill—seems to be growing as more and more parents, even in the upper middle class, find themselves unable to pay tuition for their children and think that someone, even the kids themselves, should help pick up the tab. Take, for example, the Long Island judge who recently announced that he was relinquishing his coveted post and returning to the private practice of law. It wasn't that he had grown tired of the black robes, rather it was that he felt that he couldn't afford to live on his $37,000-a-year judicial salary. It wasn't that the jurist raced yachts or was paying alimony to four former wives, it was that he had two children who were about to enter college.

That sounds ludicrous until you remember that it now costs more than $5,000 a year to support a daughter at Radcliffe—and that's without counting clothes, doctor bills, or long-distance telephone calls. Unless the student lives at home and studies at the dining room table, a year at a state university can now run as much as $3,000. For a family that is living on $25,000 a year with two children in college, this means that as much as half their income after taxes may be going toward college costs.

And scholarship aid is unlikely to provide much consolation. Until recently, the federal government (which has been setting the pattern in this department since 1965 through its guaranteed loans) would not subsidize loans to a student whose family has an income of $15,000 or more. Because college costs have risen 80 per cent in the last decade and place an intolerable burden on families with more than one child to support at school, the government dropped this $15,000 ceiling in 1972. But the federal bureaucrats who were suddenly forced to review each application on its merits, instead of applying a flat numerical formula pegged to family income, responded by cutting back by 40 per cent the number of guaranteed loans that they approve. This cut came right out of the average man's hide. As the financial aid officer at Georgetown University explained it, the rich could of course continue to paddle their own canoes, some of the poor could pick up scholarships, but families earning between $9,000 and $25,000, the bracket where the average man lives, could no longer afford to send their children to Georgetown.

The costs of such a financial burden accompanying

higher education are obvious. At a time when the job prospects of a college graduate with no special skills, save a well-rounded liberal education, are at an all-time low, the pressures on the student's parents are unrelenting. It might be all right to scrimp and save so that junior could be a doctor or a stockbroker, but what do you think when you sacrificed so that your child could have the best education possible and he ends up driving a cab?

Not only do financial pressures like these exacerbate the inevitable generational conflicts, but they place strong pressures on parents not to deviate from orthodoxy. A man may be locked into a well-paying, but spiritually deadening sinecure, and want to endure the challenges of going into business for himself, but if he has college-age children, he can't afford to take the chance.

Despite its peculiarities, the education industry's product is similar to that of other monopolies: overpriced in time, frequently shoddy and undifferentiated. This has little to do with the people who operate the industry— many of whom are, as we all know, capable and well-intentioned—but is part of the nature of any monopoly. In the absence of competition, there is no compelling reason to improve the product; the customers are lining up anyway. And since the diploma arms race requires the average man to stay in school for more years without necessarily learning any more, school is induced to thin out the content of education so it will spread out over the extra time—much as the automobile industry must make sure its cars wear out fast enough to keep up annual sales. It is a form of Parkinson's law: the busywork of school must expand to fill the time available for it.

Critics of education tend to miss that basic point. In the past decade, there has been a flood of criticism of the education industry; school has been under greater siege than any other of our institutions. Much of the criticism centers on the boredom of those years in which we are incarcerated in a series of classrooms. The vast exciting world outside is transformed in that classroom into the trivial tedium of a textbook, and learning about that world, a process that should be as exciting and varied as the subject itself, becomes the regurgitation on command of disconnected information that is meaningless to teacher and student alike. Our natural curiosity is gradually snuffed out, ending, to pick the worst example, in the patient compiling of trivia for a doctoral dissertation. These are familiar observations, but too often the critics think the solution lies in a specific change—fire the superintendent, make schools of education train better teachers, adopt the latest fad in teaching methods—rather than in coping with the fact that school is a monopoly. Expecting school to perform better under monopoly conditions is like expecting General Motors to make a better car before someone else does.

All this should not lead to the conclusion that education is entirely free of the mundane kind of screwings we have come to expect from, say, the auto industry and the banks. Such practices are particularly common in higher education, the area where learning is generally immune to the political pressures of school board elections. Yet because higher education is wrapped in such a mantle of respectability and reverence (we blandly accept an advertising pitch which says, "Send Your Money to College"—how would we react to an ad campaign around the theme "Send Your Money to an Orthodontist"?) we rarely even acknowledge that we have been screwed.

Because we have been indoctrinated to accept the

premise that higher education is perpetually facing a severe financial crisis, few parents do anything more than mutter into their checkbooks about the tuition-grubbing practices of academic institutions. Because education is such a third-party transaction and no one is directly lining his pockets with our tuition money (although a dean of Washington's Federal City College was recently convicted of pocketing student scholarship money) few people get exercised about such questions as the refund policies of our major colleges and universities.

If we buy a television and return it three days later undamaged, any reputable department store or appliance chain will give us our money back. But if our child registers as a freshman at Siwash Tech on Tuesday and returns home ten days later because he is homesick and has decided to make pumping gas his life's work, we are usually out half of his tuition, as well as a hefty chunk for room and board. At the University of Michigan, for example, an out-of-state student is only refunded half his $1,235 tuition if he withdraws after two weeks, while at George Washington University in the nation's capital, a hasty retreat home will cost a recalcitrant freshman's parents $540 if he stayed more than a week.

It's hard to say what the money goes for. It's certainly not in exchange for the portion of the semester's education the student has absorbed, since these penalty fees are generally assessed even if the student has not attended any classes or communed with any great professors, but merely passed through the registration line. These practices can't even be justified by the argument that a reluctant student at a competitive institution is depriving someone else of an opportunity to attend that school. All schools overadmit incoming students based on carefully nurtured projections about how many students will decide to go to college elsewhere and how many will drop out early in the semester. In a sense, a student's disenrollment has already been anticipated by the collegiate computer. Nor is it any more convincing to argue that this money compensates the university for the paperwork involved in enrollment and disenrollment. Most university registration work is done by gaunt graduate students, grateful to be paid the minimum wage for alphabetizing student enrollment cards. The rest of the academic bureaucracy reflects an inefficiency that would have been the envy of the nineteenth-century Russian civil service. Although processing academic forms often takes weeks, there is rarely an educational transaction that could not be carried out within fifteen minutes of intensive work.

The meagerness of tuition refunds is just another way that academic institutions meet their deficits or avoid dipping into their endowments to pay for current operations. What makes the matter galling to the parents who are footing the bill is that they can't even claim this lost tuition money as a charitable contribution on their income taxes. This tax shelter is also denied aspiring professionals, who often spend hundreds of dollars in application fees trying to find an accredited school which will accept them. Since the paperwork in assessing a student's application often consists of combining the college board scores with the grade-point average and dividing by two, it is difficult to justify these twenty-five-dollar fees (which no longer seem petty if you have to apply to, say, eight schools). But in the non-competitive world of education, if you want to go to Yale Law School, you really must do business with the Yale Admissions Office.

Although the diversity of American higher education is more geographic than intellectual, when they are applying to college, most students have, at least, some choice. But when it comes to what he must do to get in to all but the least selective schools, the student has no alternatives. In addition to the inevitable essays on "What I Want To Be When I Grow Up" (they phrase them a bit more subtly these days), a student must take a standardized test. Not just any test, but in all likelihood one prepared for the College Entrance Examination Board by Educational Testing Service in Princeton, New Jersey.

The College Boards of ETS are a monopoly within the larger school monopoly. Freed from almost all competition in the marketplace (potential students have no choice but to use their services, and college admissions offices can only turn to one other standardized test that is administered nationwide), the people who run ETS are also immune from outside scrutiny because they are professionals. Although ETS is a non-profit institution (which, of course, does not preclude high salaries or extensive fringe benefits), it suffers the same expansionist urges that afflict conglomerates like ITT. Helped along by public subsidy in the form of tax exemption, ETS has been doubling its gross every five years; much of the added business consists of tests the need for which had not been recognized until pointed out by ETS. Starting with multiple choice tests, ETS quickly cornered the market on scholarship information (all notions of privacy of one's financial affairs are discarded when one fills out the "Parents Confidential" financial statement), and has now moved into other facets of the higher education business, as well. A few years ago ETS decided to expand its law school operations by going into the transcript and academic recommendation business with something they called Law School Data Assembly Service (LSDAS). Perhaps reflecting the insensitivity to the marketplace that monopoly fosters, ETS did not begin to anticipate the rapid boom in law school applications at the start of the decade. What happened is that a number of students were rejected by law schools around the country because their recommendations and transcripts got lost in the bowels of the ETS's computerized operations. For many it meant a year's delay in their legal educations, for a few it meant a permanent change in their career plans. One student applied to eight law schools through LSDAS and to another on her own. The ninth school accepted her, which was fortunate, since none of the other eight ever received her records from LSDAS. Rather than accepting any moral or financial responsibility for the debacle, ETS shrugged it off the same way ITT might minimize the loss of a truckload of Hostess Twinkies. The only difference is that one monopoly shapes people's careers, while the other merely manufactures gooey synthetic food.

As yet no serious dent has been made in school's monopoly of access to jobs. The Supreme Court recently outlawed the use of "irrelevant" educational credentials to deny people jobs, but there is no evidence that the decision has had any great impact—or even been widely noticed. Economist Milton Friedman's idea of school vouchers enjoys a certain vogue, at least for discussion. Friedman proposed that parents be issued vouchers paid by tax money which they could then use to send their children to any school, public or private, that would admit them. Friedman's purpose is to make all schools compete for the voucher dollars. As this is written, the voucher plan is being tested in Alum Rock, California. However, as Friedman himself must know, what he is proposing is not true competition. His vouchers could only be used in a school, not to finance other ways of learning like independent study or apprenticeship. Friedman's voucher plan might well produce only the kind of false competition that exists in the auto industry. We can buy any of a million varieties of car, but they are all the same, because public policy protects the automobile against competition from other forms of transportation. Within the education industry itself, a number of brave reformers have started "alternate" or "free" schools as a way of differentiating the product. But these efforts usually peter out pretty quickly: it is hard to innovate in an industry that is under no competitive pressure, though some of that pressure may be felt now that many colleges have excess capacity.

The industry adopts a benevolent attitude toward the average man. It does not hard-sell its product. Though there is undoubtedly more propaganda for school than for Chevrolets or deodorants, the tone is more genteel than commercial. School is there, after all, for the average man's good—to give him an opportunity his parents never had. As we have seen, there is just enough truth in that statement to make it convincing to the great majority of Americans. The corollary is that if the average man does not stay in school and ends up screwed, it's his fault, not that of the system. He dropped out and became a factory worker when he could have stayed in and become a doctor. This process is known in another kind of con game as "cooling out the mark." When two con men finish skinning their victim, or mark, the one who posed as his ally will often stay with the victim to convince him that it's useless to call the cops: that is cooling out the mark. Similarly, the education industry cools out its mark by convincing him he is to blame if he did not grab the brass ring promised him by school. This is another sign of progress in a democratic society. It used to be that the average man was doomed to be a loser simply because he was born in the wrong class: it was the system that did it to him. Now he is screwed by the shell game of the diploma—and persuaded that it's nobody's fault but his own.

8

The Automobile
and Accessory Swindles

WE HAVE ALL been told often enough that the car sym-
bolizes the American Dream, that the love affair between
America and the car is a distinctive part of our culture.
Only yesterday the popular historian Frederick Lewis
Allen was writing of the year 1950, when the number of
drivers first surpassed the number of jobs in the nation:

> Never before in human history, perhaps, had any such
> proportion of the nationals of any land known the lifting
> of the spirit that the free exercise of power can bring.

Today that sounds painfully old-fashioned—a glimpse,
almost, into an Easter egg past—and yet there is still a
good deal of truth in what Allen wrote. The car has indeed given us what the theorists tell us—a sense of free-
dom, of mobility, of privacy and adulthood. Those
benefits may be illusions, or they may be about to vanish
in smog and fuel shortages, but they are real for most
people most of the time, and they feel just fine. The benefits of the car are the kind of youtooism that is typically
associated with major screwings of the public. What he
gets may not be worth anywhere near what he paid, may

be much less than what he's told he's getting, may be a fraction of what those who are putting it to him are getting—still, the average man is getting something from the car, and he knows it. Most important, he is getting enough so that he can't live without the car: this dependence is what makes him such an easy victim.

The automobile hustle by now has assumed gigantic proportions. It is a fair estimate that the American as car owner is swindled each year out of more money than the average man earns in the poorer parts of the world—a remarkable tribute to the skills of the auto makers and their related industries, as well as the occasion for a kind of stoic pride on the part of those paying the bill. The average owner was spending $1,190 per year on his car even before the price increases of 1973–74. Senator Philip Hart estimates that the figure includes $235 of swindle; the calculations in this chapter indicate a much higher total. Iván Illich, the radical priest-philosopher, adds the bill in time rather than money. Illich figures the average American car owner works 1,500 hours a year—more than four and a half hours a day—to support his car and its related costs, drive it, and park it. If the car travels 7,500 miles a year, it is moving, in terms of the owner's time spent on it, at five miles an hour. That's walking speed, which is where we humans came in.

The massive hustle that lies behind these figures falls into the patterns described in chapter 1: the victim is softened up by youtooism, and then he is screwed by monopoly power, by unnecessary complexity, by experts, or by a combination of some or all three components, while the nature of the transaction is obscured by wordnoise. To see how it works, let us follow the average man as car owner through his experience, recording the major screwings at each step, beginning with the buying of the car.

But first—let's ask it before he signs the papers—why does he want to buy a car anyhow? Perhaps, as students of the American psyche tell us, he is in love with the car. He needs it to be socially and sexually adequate. If he is male, he may have heard that women cruising by car on the Los Angeles freeways decide whether to let themselves be picked up by the brand of the male's car —no Volkswagens. But maybe he is utterly indifferent to the car's status attributes. That won't keep him out of the showroom. He's still about to buy a car, and for the soundest of reasons: it's the only way he can get from here to there.

Alternatives to the auto existed in the old days: trains, trolleys, buses. Trains are occasionally sighted, though if they aren't extinct those still in existence provide wretched service and barely tolerable discomfort. The buses still run, now and then, but it has been made clear to everyone that riding the bus, even in front, is a symbol of failure—an impression the bus companies do nothing to dispel.

These other means of travel have been pretty well disposed of by the Highwaymen. The Highwaymen, known also as the Road Gang, are all those who make their money from the auto and activities related to the auto. The major figures in the gang are the auto manufacturers, the oil producers, lawyers, and insurance companies, and a host of government officials. When they get together on an issue of common interest—like protecting the "highway trust fund"—the Highwaymen go into battle with more economic and political firepower than any other outfit in the nation. Traditionally first place among lobbies has been accorded to the military-industrial combine. Doubtless this is because the defense people cut a larger slice of the federal budget, and because their coups are more spectacular. When Lockheed gets itself on the welfare rolls at $250 million, or when Litton Industries places its president, Roy Ash, as head of the Office of Management and Budget, or when another cost overrun record is set, these achievements make the front pages. The activities of the auto industry are less newsworthy. Every car made is as much a consumer fraud as the F-111 plane, but no one writes about it. Indeed, as we shall see in this chapter, the auto business is an institutionalized, year-after-year cost overrun.

The auto business' clout is clearly greater. Of the ten largest corporations in the nation, six are auto makers or oil producers, and the auto business takes a larger share of the national income (twenty-five cents on every retail dollar) than any other industry. Officeholders at all levels of government live off political money generated by the auto. The $21 billion spent annually on highway construction is matched by a large, though necessarily unknown, sum made on land speculation in connection with the location of new highways. Of that $21 billion, about $4 billion comes from the federal government in the so-called "highway trust fund", financed by the federal gas tax of four cents a gallon. The fund, one of the great coups in lobbying history, was sold on the grounds of national defense: presumably the troops would use the highways to get to the beach where the Russians had landed. Interstate highways built under this program get 90 per cent of their financing from the fund, 10 per cent from the local authorities. The cost-benefit potential for local officeholders is remarkable. For ten cents of local money, he can get ninety cents of federal action; if he has any ingenuity at all, he will also share in the speculative money made on the highway's location. That's more miles per gallon than you can get from any other kind of government money. (One seldom-mentioned by-product of highway building affects the average homeowner. Any land taken for a highway goes off the tax rolls, meaning that all other property owners in the affected community must pay higher taxes to make up the difference.) Because of the special attractiveness of highway money, officials at all levels are, with rare exceptions, firm in their support of policies that favor the car and the truck over other ways of transporting people and goods. These officials join the Highwaymen in rejecting any support of competing means of travel comparable to the subsidy of the auto.

Given the policies pushed through by the Highwaymen, it's not surprising that the average workingman spends 13 per cent of his working day getting to and from work in a car. He has no choice, and so he is now entering the dealer's showroom.

As he contemplates the new cars available to him, the average buyer has a virtually infinite number of choices. Or, to put it another way, he has no choice at all. In recent years the industry has offered the customer so many options—in body styles, gadgets, decor, etc., etc.—that the buyer can feel he is designing his own car, as indeed Ford once said of its Mustang. Marshall McLuhan estimated the possible variations on one model at 25 million, and a Yale physicist is said to have calculated that the "number of different cars that a Chevrolet customer conceivably could order was greater than the number of atoms in the universe." This was truly the American Dream—every man not a king but a car designer, which is probably better anyhow.

But dreams are not reality, and in the real world—so artful is the technique—the average buyer is offered no choice at all. In all their important characteristics, those cars—those choices ranging up from 25 million—are all the same. Though constantly redesigned, their parts are identical across many models, mere reshufflings of the same deck. In what matters—basic design, performance, workmanship, gas consumption, durability—there is not, as George Wallace said in another context, a dime's worth of difference among all the varieties of car. Not only similar, they are all inferior to what the auto industry could do if it so chose—inferior, indeed, to what it had already done, when it made the Model T Ford more than half a century ago.

This dreary sameness under the cover of apparent diversity is possible because competition was killed off long ago. In the early years of the industry, there were up to 100 firms making automobiles and offering the buyer choices ranging from the standard transportation of the Model T to all sorts of individualistic variants like Stutz, Cord, and so on. The little firms were gobbled up or driven out one by one. Now the industry is a monopoly dominated by one company, General Motors, and including three hangers-on. Either to preserve the appearance of competition, or because it just can't digest any more, GM permits the others to stay in business, though it admittedly could easily drive them to the wall. One result is that technology stagnates. In the absence of true competition, there is no reason to improve the product. The point was made many years ago by Alfred P. Sloan, president of GM, when he turned down the idea of using safety glass because the other companies would use it also: "Our gain would be a purely temporary one and the net result would be that the competition and ourselves would have reduced the return on our capital and the public would have obtained still more value per dollar expended." The latter danger—more value for money for the public—has been successfully avoided ever since. The companies compete loudly, of course, in everything except what matters: price and quality. The cost of advertising competition in non-essentials is, in a monopoly market, simply passed on to the consumer in higher prices. Beneath the frantic wordnoise of advertising, the reality is that GM sets standards and prices for everyone.

Thus the car offered to the buyer is a product of GM policy. It was a General Motors executive who coined the term "dynamic obsolescence," the industry's final solution to the peril of overproduction. Dynamic obsolescence means that the exterior of the car will be frequently changed so that the car appears old a year after it was made, that the insides will be so flimsy that the car will indeed grow old before its time, and that each year a pretense of dramatic improvement will be made—although, with real improvements ruled out by technological stagnation, this has come to consist of rearranging a few gimmicks. The cost of dynamic obsolescence is passed on to the buyer twice: first, by tacking the cost of style changes onto the price of the car (about 25 per cent of the price), and, second, in the car's unnecessarily rapid loss of value.

The essential nature of the car is hidden from the average owner by the policy of complexity. As in so many other transactions, deliberate complexity makes it impossible for the average car owner to figure out what is going on in his machine. His grandfather understood his Model T far better than he understands his Chevrolet Impala. His grandfather could easily observe the simple machinery that made the Model T go; he could, when driving it, feel how its various parts were performing; if it wasn't working properly, he could in many cases fix it himself, or at least analyze what was wrong—and therefore he could determine later on if the mechanic had done what he was supposed to do.

No more. Complexity has made strangers of the owner and his car. The effect of the many changes in car design is to reduce communications between car and driver. Automatic transmission prevents the driver from understanding or feeling how the gears work; power steering and squishy suspension reduce the driver's feel for the car and for the road. Pointless complication makes the car hard to understand and harder still to fix. In this hazy atmosphere, the screwing of the customer proceeds at a lively pace. He is at the mercy of the experts—the publicists and mechanics who tell him what his auto is all about.

We are, it should be noted, going through the process of buying a new rather than a used car. Hustling used cars is an old-fashioned game, like peddling a broken-down horse, while selling new cars illustrates the swindles most characteristic of our times. It is typical of our failed perception that we ask, "Would you buy a *used* car from this man?" In fact, it is probable that the buyer is hustled out of more of his money in a new car rather than a used car transaction. But the old-time hustle is obvious in that seedy barker down at the used car lot, while the new car showroom is shiny, the salesman smoothly suburban, the deal is complex, and the buyer leaves hardly aware that his shirt is no longer on his back.

The odds on the buyer are poor. As one dealer observed: "I sell two or three hundred cars a year and the customer buys one every two or three years. You're going to tell me he's going to come in here and beat me in a deal?" Our smoothly suburban dealer has to work around the clock for his money, furthermore, which he makes on a strictly commission basis. He belongs to no union, he earns no salary, and there are no retirement benefits to ease his way. This master hustler has an array of tricks to pad his pocket and to relieve you effortlessly of your money. Perhaps he's already torn the price tag off the car window before you've entered the showroom, so that he can quote a higher price to you—and then lower it if need be during the bargaining process. Or possibly he's set up a demonstration model for your inspection (if you've given him advance notice by phone) that's seen thousands of miles, and switched odometers to your eternal ignorance.

More likely, however, you've just been to the dealer up the street, who quoted you what seems an exorbitant price and you've decided to try for a better price elsewhere. "Oh, I can give you a better deal than that by far," our dealer tells you, and he quotes a figure far below the price at which he can afford to sell the car. It's a technique called "low balling." If you bring a car in for a trade in he'll offer you a price higher than he can afford to go, and that's a "high ball." All quoted phone prices are balled prices, and they're known as "verbal balls." For him, the essential point is to get you, the customer, to sign a contract, any contract, because as soon as you've done that, you've signed a pact that you'll work with him right down the line. This is the stage when he'll begin to go to work on you in earnest. Once a contract is signed (it isn't valid anyway until the dealership manager has signed the purchase order, but you aren't expected to know that) the dealer has any number of ways to work the price up. He'll probably just start laying the extras on you so fast that you won't know if you're coming or going, and in a daze of surfeit you'll just pay along. If you happen to be an obstinate consumer, he'll take you out and apologetically show you the ugliest paint job you ever saw and explain it's the only car he has for that price. "Elimination ball" is what the salesman "forgets" to include in the contract— the price of the automatic transmission, for example. After elimination ball, the salesman "bumps" you, that is, he jolts the extra money out of you, usually when you've come with the wife and kids to pick up the new car. To avoid embarrassment you reach into the checkbook and pull out an extra hundred and maybe more, for there's always that extra mistake in subtraction in the contract which is revealed in a last-minute check—an error the customer may have seen, or certainly can be made to feel he's seen, on the original signing. Now, shamefaced, he has to shell out even more. You have of course already paid extra for items already included in the price of the car, but this larceny is so obscured by now you're happy just to hang onto the car.

Despite the poor odds on the customer, let us for the moment join John Jerome, in his *The Death of the Automobile*, in the fantasy of Superconsumer: the car buyer who beat the house. As Jerome describes him, this buyer knows every aspect of the system. He knows all the ways of balling and he knows the other games: the pack in all its forms (top pack, plain pack, finance pack), the blitz, the balloon, unhorsing, paper-trading. He knows the dealer can sell him the car at the dealer's price and still make money, because the company will pay him a rebate on the sale. He knows the dealer's profit on the optional extras, so he bargains him down from a 50 per cent profit to only 25 per cent. He pays cash and he sells his old car himself, clearing one quarter or so more (the dealer might have offered him more, but he would have gotten it back somewhere else in the deal.)

He buys a $3,000 car for $3,000. He beats the dealer at every turn. He is indeed Superconsumer.

Victorious, he drives his new car off the lot—and immediately loses $1,000, the amount by which the car depreciated the moment it was sold. (Depreciation, to the businessman, means a way to avoid paying taxes. To the average man, it is a dead loss.) This screwing is probably a record in its class: one is hard put to think of another "durable" good that loses so much of its value so fast. Unless he is rich, in which case he will buy a Rolls-Royce that will increase in value.

This is how the average buyer stands at this point: He is out, let us say, some $500 on monopoly pricing and quality. This is admittedly a guess, but the figure is a modest one. It is made up of three elements: monopoly pricing on the car as it is, monopoly prices passed on by others, like the steel industry, that sell materials that go into the car, and the poor quality of a product not subject to competition—the difference, that is, between the car he got and the car the industry could have built. He also is out $1,000 in depreciation. So he has laid out $3,000 and gotten $1,500 worth of car. (That's only if he didn't finance and if he beat the dealer in their negotiations. Otherwise, he would be out still more.)

He is out half his money, then, in the best of circumstances. And there is more to come—much more.

Before he can drive off in his new car, the buyer must get it insured. He will now get caught in the cross fire between experts. The mechanism used in this screwing is what has come to be known as the fault insurance system.

Under the theory of fault insurance, a person injured in an auto accident can only be compensated if, first, the fault for the accident can be laid on someone else, second, the victim was not even partially to blame, and, third, the person at fault is either rich or insured. Only the minds of experts or puritans could have conceived a system that so flatly contradicts what common sense tells us. We know that we are just as injured if our car hits a tree rather than another car, but the fault system tells us we cannot collect because there is no one else to take the blame. We know that in many accidents both drivers are in part at fault, but the system tells us no one can collect because the blame cannot be placed entirely on one of them. (In some jurisdictions there is an occasional exception: the so-called "doctrine of last clear chance," which allows you to collect, even if you were negligent, if the other fellow had the last clear chance to avoid the accident.) Nor, of course, does it make any sense for our right to compensation to depend on the other driver's ability to pay. The system does, however, make sense if it is viewed as a form of welfare for professionals. A large proportion of American lawyers' income is generated by fault insurance: auto cases provide 57 per cent of court time in this nation.

The end result of fault insurance, as described by the Department of Transportation, is this: three out of five victims will get nothing at all, and half of the rest will get less than the accident cost them in medical bills and lost time at work. A more detailed analysis of the system in one state, New York, was made by Richard E. Stewart when he was that state's Superintendent of Insurance. According to Stewart, this is how the premium dollar paid by the customer is spent:

33¢ to insurance companies and agents;

23¢ to lawyers and claims investigators;

8¢ to losses compensated by some other source, usually health insurance;

21.5¢ for "pain and suffering": this is an intangible which depends on how well your lawyer bargains, which in turn depends on how long you can afford to wait for the money; the less you need the money, the more you collect for your pain and suffering;

Leaving just 14.5¢ on the dollar for payments for actual economic loss—medical bills and lost work time.

So, as the average man gets up his insurance premium, he may reflect on his prospects if he has an accident: the odds are less than fifty–fifty that he will collect anything at all if he is hurt, and only one in five that he will break even; if he has to go to court, it is likely to take him years to collect; so many people make their living off his premium dollar that only 14.5¢ will come back to pay the actual costs of his injury.

(Unless he lives in one of the few states, led by Massachusetts, that have adopted some form of no-fault insurance. No-fault cuts insurance costs by abandoning the effort to determine who is to blame and simply paying victims what the accident cost them. According to Stewart's calculation, a complete no-fault system, which none of those in effect is, would cut costs by more than half. No-fault is progressing slowly, and the versions adopted so far range from partial to token. Resistance is strong in state legislatures, which are heavily infested with both lawyers and insurance men. The only reason no-fault has been adopted even in part is that the insurance industry is divided on the issue. One faction sticks with the present system. The other faction would ditch their allies, the lawyers, on the grounds that the lawyers are cutting themselves too big a slice of what is, after all, the insurance men's business. Cutting out the lawyers would raise profits for the insurance men. It would also, coincidentally, help out the average man. It is in such conflicts between two predators that the public interest sometimes sneaks through.)

The odds are good that our new owner will soon learn these insurance realities for himself. The average driver has a fifty–fifty chance of getting into an accident within three years, and very little chance of avoiding accident through a lifetime of driving. Of course this is mainly his own fault, as the industry-financed National Safety Council never tires of telling him: if he has an accident, it was either because he was drunk or because he lacked sufficient driver education. This version of blaming the victim has just enough truth in it to keep it afloat. Clearly, alcohol doesn't sharpen the driver's wits, and it is well to learn how to drive before taking the wheel. Still, the presence of alcohol and the absence of a driving school diploma are neither the only nor the likeliest explanations of an accident. Omitted are those possible explanations that the industry doesn't want to hear: that the car is, in Ralph Nader's phrase, unsafe at any speed; that it was defective either at birth or because of faulty repair; or that driving the modern auto is so soporific that the act of driving, rather than the booze, put him to sleep. These possibilities are ruled out because they would leave the victim blameless.

The deal the car owner makes on his insurance is pretty bad, but in fact it is worse than it appears by our calculation. The flimsy, unsafe construction of his car will produce unnecessary accidents and injuries and repairs. This will drive up the cost of insurance; for each 14.5¢ more of injury, the premium will have to go up one dollar to take care of the industry's many dependents. We will come back to the issue of repairs, after a stop at the gas station.

Now our new owner has to fuel his machine. As he turns into the station, he is about to confront monopoly power in its purest form. The fact that he has to patronize the gas pump so often—because the manufacturers design cars to travel an ever shorter distance on the same gallon—is only the beginning of the treatment.

At the pump, the driver sees that sign indicating, along with the price, the state and federal taxes to be paid on each gallon. A revised version of this sign, a form of truth-in-gas-selling, would include a line for monopoly profit: ten cents per gallon.

Notes appended to the sign would offer explanations. Under the federal tax, the customer would be reminded that almost all the money will be used for highway construction, not for any other form of transportation, thus guaranteeing that he will be back early and often. Under monopoly profit, the customer would be advised not to expect the oil companies to pay back any substantial part of that profit in the form of taxes. In fact, the average man pays taxes at a higher rate than most oil companies; over six recent years, five major oil firms paid income tax at the rate of 4.7 per cent. Thus the average car owner pays for those excess profits once at the station, and then he pays again in his taxes to make up for the taxes not paid by the oil companies. (See chapter 13 for more on taxes.)

There is only one gas pump, just as there is only one car: the buyer has no choice here either. Even less, indeed, since the oil companies hardly go through the motions of pretending their products differ. As an official of Phillips Petroleum said: "We have an additive that allows us to advertise. I don't know whether it does anything for gasoline." Even the credulous American consumer does not seem to pay much attention; he seems instinctively aware that the major oil companies often swap their oil, so that the tiger in the consumer's tank may in fact be a different breed of cat. What competition has occurred centered on goodies like green stamps or free drinking glasses, until the shortages engineered by the companies permitted them to drop even that small sop to the consumer.

The price, like the gas itself, is the same everywhere. Until 1973, the big companies allowed independent dealers to sell their product under a different label at a discount of, usually, no more than a penny a gallon. If the customer could find an independent station, he could reduce the screwing by that penny a gallon. By 1973, however, the majors evidently had decided they could do without the independents, and they used the first "shortage" of that year to drive some 2,000 of the cut-rate dealers out of business, and the second one to run up the price.

The 1973–74 "shortages" are a good example of a basic principle in wordnoise: dealing with reality by claiming the exact opposite. It was not the first time the oil industry had tried to convince the public there was not, or soon wouldn't be, enough oil to go around. Back in the forties, for example, the press was reporting the industry's claim that the United States had oil reserves sufficient for only around twelve years. In each case, the industry ran its arguments up the flagpole: if the United States ran short of oil, no matter how much was available from abroad, the national security would be at the mercy of (then) Germans and Japanese, or (now) Arabs who have Russian friends.

These recurrent threats of shortage are the industry's way of coping with what has been since the earliest days its basic problem: there is in this world an abundance of oil that could be delivered to the consumer at a price far lower than the one he can be made to pay. (This is because oil is much cheaper to produce than competing fuels. As protection against the day when this might change, the oil companies recently have been buying control of such other fuels as coal and uranium.) The danger from the oil producers' point of view is that, if competition prevailed, the oil would reach the consumer at a much lower price. The difference between the competitive price and the price the consumer can be made to pay would stay in the consumer's pocket, and immense profits would be lost. The eternal problem, then, is how to prevent competitive pricing.

The first Rockefeller, John D., solved the problem in the late nineteenth century by stomping rival producers and distributors out of business and creating his Standard Oil monopoly. This worked until Standard Oil was in part broken up in the turn-of-the-century anti-trust days. The simple monopoly was succeeded by more sophisticated ways of avoiding price competition. If there had to be several oil companies, they could at least agree to hold production down and prices up. The federal government pointed out the path in 1929 with a recommendation for legislation permitting "agreements among oil producers for the curtailment of production." Texas got the point, and in 1929 passed the Market Demand Act, empowering the oddly named Texas Railroad Commission to regulate production in order to restrict "economic" waste ("economic" as opposed to the physical waste that occurs from unrestrained drilling in a single oil field; the latter was already regulated at that time). "Economic waste," of course, is money left unnecessarily in the consumer's pocket. Other oil-producing states passed similar laws. To make sure no cheap oil leaked through to the public, Congress passed the Connolly "Hot Oil" Act, which prohibits interstate shipment of any oil produced in excess of state regulations.

The industry had achieved its purpose: monopoly pricing without monopoly ownership. The refinement of tax loopholes—permitting oil companies not to pay taxes—ensured that the profits would not find their way back to the consumer via the internal revenue. All was well, until the 1950s. Then foreign oil appeared in quantity: all over the world, wells were opening up that could sell oil at far below the artificial U.S. price. If that oil were allowed on the American market, the game of monopoly would be broken up.

How to keep that cheap oil under control and prevent economic waste? The device chosen by the oil companies was the quota system. The quotas, adopted during the Eisenhower administration, worked like this: the government figured how much foreign oil was needed after all domestic oil was sold, and then gave to the companies the right to import that amount (usually about 20 per cent of total consumption). As a raid on the public, the quotas were on a scale similar to the "highway trust fund." The companies were able to sell cheap foreign oil at the high domestic price, without paying for their quota rights. Like the trust fund, the oil quotas sailed under the flag of national security. The quotas were supposedly needed to prevent the United States from running out of oil, though how importing less would preserve the domestic supply was never entirely clear.

The effect of the quotas, during their fourteen-year existence, was to take the consumer for $5–$7 billion a year. That works out to 5¢–6¢ per gallon at the pump, and about $100 a year for a home heated by fuel oil. The quotas were removed in early 1973 by the federal government. This was no pro-consumer act. By then the quotas no longer served the purposes of the industry, so they permitted the government to remove the quotas while they pursued their goal—keeping cheap oil off the market —by other means.

By 1973, the oil companies had gotten that cheap foreign oil under control at its source in the Middle East. In the early 1970s, with the help of the U. S. State Department, the companies had worked out cartel agreements with the oil sheikhs of the Persian Gulf. They had a common interest in restricting production and raising prices. Although the companies had no more reason to quarrel with the sheikhs than with the governor of Texas, for public consumption there were stories about "struggles" over the amount of royalties the companies were to pay to the landowning sheikhs. In fact, the amount was meaningless to the companies. Since the price of oil is twenty to thirty times the cost of production, an increase in royalty need not affect the price, which is determined by the power of the monopoly. In any case, the companies had devised a way to pass the royalty cost along to the American public. They had gotten the Treasury to class their royalty payments not as business expenses but as income taxes, so that the royalties were deducted, dollar for dollar, from the companies' U.S. tax bill. Every time the sheikhs raised the royalty, the companies simply forwarded the bill to the United States for payment by the American taxpayer. Once the cartel agreement was in force, the companies no longer needed the quotas. What they now wanted was to raise the price and also to squelch opposition to such oil projects as the Alaska pipeline. Hence the "shortage." Here again the State Department chimed in to help the companies scare the consumer into the proper attitude. Officials promoted the idea of a worldwide shortage, and James Akins, director of the Department of State's Office of Fuels and Energy, professed that "by 1976 our position could be nothing short of desperate." Officials put forward the fear that the United States and other industrial nations would face disaster if "the Arabs" imposed an oil boycott. But the Persian Gulf has more oil than ever and, as the events of the winter of 1973–74 demonstrated, the Arab nations could not successfully organize a boycott on their own. What they were able to do, in co-operation with the oil companies, was to restrict production enough to force a huge increase in prices. In what was undoubtedly history's greatest single screwing of the consumer all over the world, the oil companies and the sheikhs each tripled their profits within a few months, with the supposed boycott providing a political cover for their mutual greed.

Thus the entry for monopoly profit on our hypothetical sign at the gas pump will continue to rise in years to come. As the average man drives off, he may reflect that he has bought twice as much gas as a more economic engine would require, and that he has been taken for at least ten cents on each gallon. (This is not the only time he pays tribute to the oil monopoly. His home may be heated by fuel oil, and any industrial user—an oil-burning power plant, for example—passes the extra cost of monopoly-priced oil on to the consumer.)

At last the car owner is on the open road. By now, he has dropped half what he paid for the car, more than half his insurance bill, and more than half also on his fuel. He'll be back soon for his next screwing. This one is called "repairs."

He need not break or wear out anything on his new car in order to encounter the repair system—his car is likely to have reached him already in need of attention. *Consumer Reports* found an average of thirty-six birth defects per car when they tested new 1973 models. This, it should be noted, applies only to the average man's car. If he is an auto company executive, a celebrity, or a major public official, the buyer may qualify for a "Dealer's Special Order." Employees are required actually to check such a car, even to the extent of pulling it off the assembly line, to make sure there's nothing wrong with it. The policy seems to be to make sure that those who could make trouble get trouble-free cars without going to the expense of also checking all those average-man cars coming down the line.

When he becomes aware of one of his car's thirty-six birth flaws, our new owner will doubtless take it back and try to get it fixed under the warranty—if he notices it in time, for the companies, in response to an increasing number of claims, have reduced the length of their warranties. From 1967 to 1973, the standard warranty shrank from two years and 24,000 miles to one year and 12,000 miles. The owner will now be involved in a test of patience with the dealer. The dealer is not anxious to do the work, since he earns less on it than on straight repairs, and, of course, the company is reluctant to pay. So the owner will find it difficult to make an appointment, if indeed he can make his case that the warranty covers what's wrong with the car. (He will not, in any event, get coverage for anything that happened because of a defective part. If his new brakes fail and he drives his monster into a brick wall, totaling it and perhaps himself as well, the warranty will pay for fixing—the brakes.) If, however, the owner persists and gets the appointment, the shop may well discover other non-warranty work that needs to be done, and if the owner refuses to pay this tribute, his nice new car is likely to get vengeful treatment.

Once past the warranty—when he is paying for the work himself—the owner will find that his repair bills include two distinct swindles: flat-rate labor costs, and the parts monopoly.

The flat-rate system is a set of rules devised to prove to the consumer that what is happening to him is legitimate because that's the way it's always done: if everyone else is getting taken at the same rate, what's he got to kick about?* Under flat rates, labor for repairs is charged according to the theoretical amount of time a given job is supposed to take, according to the experts (the authors

* Yes, there are honest repair shops and honest dealers. The point is that the system penalizes them, and so they are an endangered species.

of the two manuals available to the trade). The repair is not charged according to the time it actually took. If, for example, the manual says the job takes two hours, when in fact it was done in forty-five minutes, the customer will be charged for two hours of labor. In theory, he would only pay for two hours if the work took three hours—but in practice that won't happen. Both the shop and the mechanic, who typically splits the labor fee with the shop, stand to lose if the time goes over the flat rate, so he will see to it that the job is finished, for better or for worse, inside the allotted two hours; if he fails too often, he'll be looking for another job. Here complexity protects the shop and the flat-rate system from the customer, for in the complicated, mushy modern auto, it is virtually impossible to figure out what if anything was done, never mind how well, or how long it should take.

The other entry on the repair bill is for parts. Now the customer is back on monopoly territory. The manufacturers' grip on the spare parts market is even more complete than on the car itself, for while the buyer has the illusion of choice among manufacturers, when he wants parts he has to go to the one firm that made the car. Frequent style changes serve, along with other purposes, to make it prohibitively expensive for outsiders to make spare parts; as a result, 90 per cent of parts are available only from the original manufacturer. This makes it possible for the firms to set prices at satisfyingly high levels. The effect of monopoly can be seen by comparing parts prices with the prices of other products made by the same companies. A hood for a 1969 Chrysler Newport cost $101.90 ($171.40 installed) at the same time that Chrysler was selling an Airtemp air conditioner for $148. An air conditioner has a motor, compressor, and condenser, while the hood is just a piece of steel. Similarly, GM was selling a 1969 Buick bumper face bar at $154.35 ($235.83 installed) while it was selling a Frigidaire dishwasher for $228.88. As for Ford, they were charging $181.65 ($235.85 installed) for a 1969 Mercury station wagon door, and $166 for a Philco freezer.

The price is high but still rising, as the companies use their monopoly power to sop up an ever-larger share of the car owner's available cash. One auto insurer, State Farm, said the prices it had to pay for replacement parts rose by almost two thirds from 1963 to 1972, when new car prices were rising by less than 8 per cent. From 1967 to 1973, the cost of four frequently replaced parts on a standard Chevrolet (bumper, grille, hood, front fender) rose from $231.65 to $496.11—more than double in six years. One result of the parts monopoly is that the sum of the parts equals a lot more than the whole—*Money* magazine figured out that if you bought a whole car as separate parts, it would cost two and one half times as much as buying the same parts as a new car. Another result of the inflated price of parts is to stimulate the sale of new cars by hastening the day when, looking over the estimate for repairs, the owner decides to junk his car and buy a new one.

Demand for parts is stimulated by the needless complexity and flimsiness of the car. The poorer the construction, the more the customer will have to come back to buy those overpriced parts. About $1 billion a year is added to the repair bill by designing that causes extensive damage in low-speed accidents. Flimsy construction guarantees that the front end will collapse when it is bumped, and monopoly guarantees that the manufacturer can raise the cost of replacement pretty much at will. When, for example, the Chevrolet Impala was "restyled" from 1970 to 1971, one effect was to raise the cost of repairing the results of a front-end collision at five miles per hour (that's slower than the walking speed of two people) from $196 to $376. Those bumper cars at the amusement park are not made by auto manufacturers.

The totals are impressive. Americans spend around $25 billion a year on auto repairs, an average of more than $200 per car. Senator Hart estimates the rate of swindle at 40 per cent, or $10 billion, or $80 per car. Hart's estimate includes overcharging at the shop, work poorly done, and unnecessary repairs. It does not, however, include monopoly pricing of parts. Add that in, and the cut of the consumer dollar rises over 50 per cent, passing the magic figure that distinguishes big league screwings from the lesser efforts.

The repair industry also provides an excellent illustration of the principle that nowadays crime doesn't pay. You are in the shop complaining about how the motor sounds, and the mechanic tells you your 8-cylinder engine needs new sparkplugs. By John Jerome's 1972 calculation, those plugs cost the manufacturer five cents each; the shop, sixty cents; and will cost you $1.25. An old-fashioned mechanic, mired in nineteenth-century methods of theft, would clean your old plugs and charge you for new ones. That, in Talleyrand's phrase, would be worse than a crime; it would be a blunder. It will take the mechanic about twenty minutes to clean the plugs in order to clean you out of ten dollars. But he could have taken you for $5.20 (ten dollars minus the cost of the plugs to the shop) in only five minutes by putting in new plugs. By practicing the legal method, he can screw four customers for a total of $20.80 in the time it would take to take one person for ten dollars by the old method—a major increase in his productivity. The old-time mechanic seems rather pathetically behind the times, like the mafioso who shakes down local bars when, if he'd gone into real estate, he could be making more money without the risk of being shot by the competition.

By now we have covered the major screwings practiced on the American car owner. Aside from the sheer magnitude of the hustle—somewhere around half of every dollar spent on the automobile—an important factor to notice is the existence of carom screwings. In the auto industry, the carom effect of shoddy construction produces benefits all the way down the line. The repair shop will get more business; the manufacturer will sell more monopoly-priced parts; the lawyers will do more lawyering; and the insurance men will write higher premiums. Similarly, the design of cars to go fewer miles per gallon increases the take of the oil monopoly. If the driver stops to consider that his car could have been built to go twice as far on a gallon, he will figure that half the gas he just bought was sheer waste, so that he had to pay double tribute to the oil industry.

Monopolies feed on each other and on their control of politics. Americans have to buy the one brand of car and the overpriced gas and repairs and insurance because there is no other way to travel; there is no other way because the Highwaymen have used their control of politics to eliminate alternatives; they control politics because they have enough money to buy control; they have the money because they have the monopolies that earn them excess profits. Once the monopoly exists, therefore, it has the power to defend itself from political attack. General Motors is immune from attack, either by anti-trust or by the competition of other forms of transportation, simply because it is General Motors. By now so much of American politics lives on money generated by the auto that a major change in transportation policy would impoverish thousands of officeholders. That means Al Riordan, among others, shouldn't worry. Riordan is a columnist for the Seaside Heights, N.J., *Review*. When the Environmental Protection Agency in mid-1973 said New Jersey would have to reduce car use to meet clean air standards, Riordan perceived that this would "create the greatest crisis America has ever known. The indifference to the pending crisis by the American Public, up till now, has helped the managers of this pending crisis in American life advance toward the goal. Destruction of the American way of life, and perhaps America itself." Riordan did not identify the crisis managers, but he did see that "if this tyranny continues unabated, the riots in this country will make the race riots of five years ago look like a barroom brawl." The idea of automobiles rioting is intriguing, but it doesn't seem likely to happen soon, although their big brothers, the trucks, did riot for a while early in 1974. The same government that warned New Jersey to cut down on its habit was helping out the auto manufacturers by restricting imports of foreign cars and removing the excise tax on domestic cars, and helping the oil companies make their case that the shortages were due to the Arabs rather than to the companies themselves. With that aid, both the auto and the oil industries scored record profits in 1973, with the oil companies doing it in proper monopoly fashion: the big companies raised their profits by 50 per cent or more, even though they actually sold less oil than they had the year before. As for the average car owner, he was experiencing a record screwing.

9

Pensions: The Broken Promise

PENSION PLANS are an intricate and reasonably boring
topic, at least until that day when, to our surprise, we
turn sixty-five and when, to our even greater surprise,
we find that the promised pension isn't waiting for us. No
gold for the golden years; nothing but Social Security.
No little home in the country or condominium in the sun
—only the trailer park. The pension disappeared somewhere along the years, and it's too late now to go back. It
happens to up to nine out of ten of the 23 million people
who think they are enrolled in private pension plans—
why? The easy answer is that you didn't read the fine
print: another case of screwing by complexity. The hard
answer is that even if you read the fine print, you'd still
lose the pension. Either way, the odds against you are
ten to one.

To understand how this screwing works, it is best to
begin with the motives of the person who administers it
—the employer who set up the pension plan. When private pension plans first appeared in large numbers, during
the Second World War, employers conceived of them as
a tactic to hang on to their workers at a time when wages

were controlled and labor was scarce. By now, pensions have blossomed into a major industry that supplies great benefits to employers and banks, some pickings to a few unions, and a living to the parasitic pension administration industry that has attached itself like a $4-billion leech to the nation's total of $150 billion in pension funds. To the employer, the primary value of the pension fund is that it offers him an opportunity to con his employees out of wage increases in return for a promise he need not keep. The employer says: if you will give up all or part of a wage increase, I'll put some money aside in a fund, and I'll pay you a pension, in addition to your Social Security, when you retire. The employer gets the hard cash, and the employees get the promise that will be broken: all of them give up the raise, but only a very few will ever collect the pension.

From the employer's point of view, the question is not so much the amount of the pension he is promising as it is how many people he will eventually have to pay off. If he promises $100 a month to 100 employees, and all of them collect, his promise someday will cost him $10,000 a month. If he can cut the number who collect down to ten, his bill will be only $1,000 a month—even though he is making the same promise of $100 a month. If he is particularly skillful, he can get down closer to the magic number of zero employees collecting—and then it doesn't matter how much he promised. Meanwhile the employees have given up a much larger amount in foregone wage increases in return for a promise that is worth about as much as most other lifetime guarantees. All the employer has to do is convince enough of his employees to go along with the scheme, and in this task he can usually count on the help of the union leadership—if there is a union; if not, he can screw his employees without going to the trouble of corrupting their representatives. He can also be confident that neither government nor anyone else will interfere to make him keep the promise.

The employer does put some money aside in a pension fund, though typically not enough to finance pensions for any great number of employees. He doesn't mind doing this, because government has declared his contribution tax-exempt, making the pension fund a better kind of money than profits, which are taxed. Since in most cases the employer has a free hand in administering the pension fund, he can use it for any worthy purpose of his choice—like investing it in the stock of his own company; if the stock collapses, it's the employees' loss, not his. Or he can turn it over to his favorite bank to invest, an act which will make him a preferred customer at the bank. The bank in turn will use the money to further its own projects. Thus that $150 billion in pension reserves has become a giant slush fund flowing through the economy at the whim of employers and bank trust departments, and, in a few cases, union officials. The employees for whom the money is supposedly in trust—and whose lost wages it represents—have no say in its use.

In these circumstances, it is not surprising that so few employees ever collect on the pension promise. Just how few is not exactly known. Not long ago Peter Flanigan, the business representative in the White House, was able to say that "the problem cannot be considered overwhelming, despite the very real pathos of the few hardship cases." Since then the evidence has been accumulating. Two studies of plans covering ten million workers found that in one case 4 per cent, and in the second, 8 per cent, of the retired employees were col-

lecting their anticipated benefits. At AT&T, 3 per cent of
the women who left over a period of twenty years collected a pension. Other surveys show one in six and one
in ten collecting. In this context, Ralph Nader's view that
"at least half the people covered by pensions will never
collect a penny" is relatively optimistic. The figure used
here, that the odds against the employee are nine to one,
is a compromise among these varying estimates.

Some of the victims have achieved a minor fame in the
pension literature, where their names appear and reap-
pear like those of martyred saints on the church calendar.
Here are, mainly from Ralph Nader and Kate Blackwell's
You and Your Pension, some of the best-known martyrs
and the ways in which they were screwed out of their
pensions:

JAMES TYLER: a construction worker from Lakewood,
California. He belonged to the same union for thirty-one
years. After he had worked as a member of one local for
several years, he was told he would have to change locals
to take a job six miles from his home. When, on retirement, he applied for his pension, he was told he wasn't
eligible because—after thirty-one years—he didn't have
enough time in with either union local. Under the rules
of that plan, an employee lost all his accumulated credit
when he switched from one union local to another.

JOSEPH MINTZ: he has been in aerospace work for more
than thirty years. He has no pension rights because he
has always been laid off before reaching the ten-year
minimum for becoming eligible for pension. One company laid him off after nine years and ten months. (Another man in a similar situation wrote Senator Jacob
Javits that after nineteen and a half years with one
company he was let go "for cause. I guess the cause was

because at 20 years I would have been entitled to the pension plan.")

HARRY OAKES: he worked in a department store in St. Paul, Minnesota, for fifty-two years. He retired at sixty-six. He received his pension for thirteen months. Then the company went bankrupt, the pension fund disappeared, and neither Oakes nor anyone else got any more pension payments.

IRIS KWEK: she was laid off, after working for the Anaconda American Brass Co. in Detroit for thirty consecutive years, when she was forty-eight. She was not entitled to a pension—in that plan, you had to be sixty-five, or sixty with fifteen years employment, to be eligible. Anaconda's personnel director explained that "the plan is not designed to provide benefits for those who leave the service of the company while still employable." (In an unusual variant of the carom effect, Iris Kwek also got screwed out of her chance to complain. She passed up a chance to testify before a congressional committee because the company told her it would find her another job. She learned that there was to be no other job—when it was too late to testify.)

STEVE DUANE: he went to work for A&P at a Jersey City, New Jersey, warehouse at the age of nineteen, and worked there for thirty-two years, with time out only for the Second World War. When he was fifty-two, A&P decided to close the warehouse, putting Duane out of work. Duane didn't get a pension—you have to be fifty-five to qualify in that plan.

CHARLES REED: he went to work as a coal miner for Jones & Laughlin Steel Corp. at twenty-one. After twenty-three years, he was laid off and never called back. Reed finally found work outside the mines. When he reached retirement age thirteen years later, he applied for his pension, for which miners become eligible after twenty years. He found he was entitled to no pension because of a provision (which did not appear in the booklet describing the plan) that those twenty years had to have been worked within the thirty years preceding his application for benefits. Reed began looking around southeastern Pennsylvania and soon found 1,200 other miners who had worked the required twenty years and gotten no pension.

JOSEPH ORIGLIO: he worked for twenty-three years in shoe factories and belonged to a pension plan administered by his union, the United Shoe Workers of America. He lost his job, because of automation, at the age of fifty-five. He was unemployed for three years and ten months, and was unable to pay his union dues during that time. Then he got a job again in the shoe industry. He offered to pay his back dues, but was told only to pay a fifteen-dollar reinstatement fee. He worked for another seven years, then retired and asked for his pension. No pension: the plan required twenty-five continuous years. It permitted a break because of unemployment of up to three years—and Origlio had been out ten months too long.

Most of these screwings result from the employer's effort to hold down the number of people who qualify for pensions—without the employees becoming aware of what is going on. Making the ground rules as complex as possible is the obvious strategy; lawyers are called upon to practice the expert's art of putting the plan into language that no one can understand. One pension expert testified that "I don't think there's a plan I've looked at that two men could get the same answer out of, especially men who are not college men or lawyers."

Sometimes, indeed, the victims include those who are supposed to know what is going on. Nader tells the story of the man who left his firm confident of his pension rights because he was over forty-five and had put in fifteen years, as the plan required. But the employer pointed to some very fine print and canceled his pension on the grounds that the man had gone to work for a firm that he, the employer, considered to be a competitor. Ironically, the man had been the firm's personnel manager, the person in charge of explaining the pension plan to other employees.

Because of the high cost of lawyers, the employer can count on winning the great majority of the close ones. If the plan is ambiguous, the employer can simply deny the person's application, knowing that the great majority of his ex-employees will lack the resources to take him to court.

Rules designed to hold down the number of winners also have adverse side effects on the employees. The existence of the pension plan makes it more difficult to change jobs, because, after a certain age, many people can no longer qualify for a pension with a new employer. If, for example, the person is fifty and the pension plan at the new job requires twenty years to be eligible, he would have to work till the age of seventy to qualify. So he turns down the better job and stays where he is. He also becomes a more docile employee. Far from using another job offer as a threat to brandish against his boss, he has to walk softly to avoid being fired. As for the employer, he begins to look with a calculating eye at the worker who is approaching eligibility: if he can fire him, or lay him off, or harass him into quitting before that fatal day, he will save a bundle on the man's pension.

Similarly, the employer will be reluctant to hire some-one at an age that makes him just able to qualify for the pension. If the plan requires fifteen years of work, the employer will look with disfavor on a fifty-year-old applicant: he'll be around just long enough to start collecting his pension. The employer will prefer to hire a twenty-five-year-old, who will do one of two things: leave without becoming eligible, or put in forty years before he collects. In these several ways, then, the fool's gold of the pension becomes a chain binding the employee more tightly to his present boss.

The average man has little chance of protecting himself against an arcane sentence in the plan which, in the employer's interpretation, does him out of his pension. He has no chance at all against another way in which many people enter the loser's circle: underfunding. Nothing in the law requires the employer to put enough in the fund to cover his potential pension bill. He puts in as much as he wants to, and in most cases, human nature being what it is, that's not enough. Even some of the larger corporations skimp on their pension funds. Nader cites the examples of Western Union, which at one point had assets in its fifty-year-old fund covering only 12 per cent of its liabilities, and Uniroyal, where the fund's assets covered 35 per cent. A Senate committee turned up a mining company whose fund had assets of $33.3 million and liabilities of $107 million, and a utility whose fund, after twenty-six years, had $66 million in assets and pension liabilities of $133.5 million. One cause of underfunding is acquisitive conglomerates: some of them are fond of skimming the cream off the pension funds of companies they acquire.

When fate catches up with an underfunded fund, it is

the beneficiaries, not the employer, who pay the check. Take, for example, the case of Joseph Gallagher. He was told, at age sixty-four, that he would get no pension after his forty-two years with the Haws Refractories of Johnstown, Pennsylvania. The reason Gallagher would get no pension was that there was no money in the fund. The company was not broke, just the pension fund. The law requires the company to pay out any money in the fund to qualified pensioners, but that requirement has little significance when the fund itself is empty. Gallagher's was far from the only fund to go dry; by the estimate of the Internal Revenue Service, about one in fourteen plans goes under; in 1971, no less than 3,335 plans went under, stranding their beneficiaries. When the United Auto Workers studied the history of pension plans covering its members, it found that ninety-nine plans had folded in ten years, and that almost three quarters of the people theoretically covered were receiving reduced benefits or nothing at all. The remarkable fact is that the eligible person has no legal claim against a prosperous employer who has allowed his pension fund to run dry.

The auto workers had good reason to study their pension plans, since their industry was the scene of one of the best-known pension disasters. In 1963, the Studebaker Corporation closed down its plant in South Bend, Indiana, putting more than 4,000 out of work. The pension fund didn't have enough money to meet the promises made in union contracts. Some of the older employees got pensions, while the younger ones lost their rights in return for a lump-sum settlement: a man of forty with twenty years at the plant, for example, got $350. This was not the first such event in that part of the automobile world. Five years earlier Packard had merged with Studebaker, and the company had announced a 65 per cent cut in the pensions of retired Packard employees, for the usual reason that there wasn't enough money in the fund. (The union was able to negotiate the restoration of part of that cut.)

The average man is alone when he confronts the employer and that band of actuaries, lawyers, and administrators who stand between him and his pension. Only rarely can he count on any solidarity from the leaders of his union. In most cases—the best-known exceptions being the United Auto Workers and the United Steelworkers—unions are willing to go along with the pension charade. For one thing, negotiating a pension plan allows the union officials to cut a fine figure in front of their constituents. The more the membership believes that they in fact will get the pension that has just been negotiated, the more impressed they will be with their leaders' performance. For the workers to know the truth—that few of them will get the pension for which all of them have just given up a raise—is as unpalatable to the union as to the employer. Nor does the union's angle of vision include the largest category of workers who lose their pension rights: those who change jobs. When a worker leaves his job, he is no longer a member of the union leaders' constituency, and the leaders no longer have any interest in him and his rights. Unions vary in their degree of parochialism. Some have negotiated industry-wide plans that allow an employee to carry his pension rights to another job as long as he is still represented by the union. Others, like the Teamsters and some construction unions, have acquiesced in plans under which their members lose their accumulated rights when a change of job forces them to change union locals. In the teaching field, an outside agency, the Carnegie Corporation, set up a pension plan called the Teachers Insurance and Annuity Association. Under that plan, teachers can change jobs as much as they want and keep their rights; they can even leave teaching and go on making payments into the plan on their own. By contrast, the plan designed by the New Jersey Education Association does not permit teachers to take their rights off the New Jersey turf; if they leave, their own contributions (not the employers') are returned to them —with interest of just 2 per cent.

Some alert union leaders have managed to cut themselves in on the booty available through the pension plan. If union officials can get a share in administering the fund, they can do, though admittedly only in a modest way, the same sort of thing management does. (They can't get all of the action, because the Taft-Hartley Act limits union representatives to half of the fund's trustees.) The Teamsters, not surprisingly, have pioneered in this field. Officials of the Central States Teamsters fund, one of the country's largest, were caught not long ago wheeling and dealing with their members' pension money. The fund had loaned $35 million to a California resort operation with only a second mortgage as security, had dipped into the smelly waters of Las Vegas, and had been doing business through Mafia intermediaries. As for the Journeymen Barbers, Hairdressers, Cosmetologists and Proprietors International Union, its fund was clipped by a hustler named Thomas A. Shaheen. Shaheen showed up in 1966 and convinced the union that its $21-million fund was being mismanaged by the Indiana National Bank. He could do better, he said, and besides his services were free. With Shaheen as its consultant, the fund made a loan to the Winthrop Lawrence Corp., of which

Shaheen was chief executive. The fund also made a second-mortgage loan to Bobby Baker, the U. S. Senate operator convicted of tax evasion. By the time Shaheen and the union president were indicted in 1971, the fund's assets had shrunk from $21 million to less than $14 million.

The United Mine Workers have easily outpaced their rivals—except, perhaps, the Teamsters—on the union side of the pension hustle. The UMW, which in the years it was headed by Tony Boyle was increasingly difficult to distinguish from management, would loan pension funds to companies it favored. One was the Eaton Company. The union liked Eaton so much that it neglected to collect money owed the pension fund by West Kentucky Coal Company, which was controlled by Eaton—and the union. The UMW pension fund is financed by a royalty of eighty cents on each ton of mined coal; the union leadership was willing to overlook the fact that West Kentucky was at one time $700,000 in arrears in its royalties. The most spectacular of the union's dealings with the pension fund had to do with the National Bank of Washington, which the union owned. The UMW had evidently learned a lesson from government: they kept up to $75 million of pension money in non-interest-bearing accounts in their bank, just as the Treasury Department deposits all that free money in Rockefeller banks. The bank loaned out that free money at its usual rates; the income it produced meant higher profits for the bank; the profits went in the form of dividends to the union; the union used the money to pay the outlandish salaries and expense accounts of then President Tony Boyle and his fellow pirates. The U. S. District Court for the District of Columbia, ruling on a suit brought by the dissident miners who eventually gained control of the union, found that the pension fund had lost $12 million in interest on the money held in the union's bank—an amount paid ultimately by the union membership in the form of lost pensions, for, as the court observed, "the beneficiaries were not in any way assisted by these cash accumulations, while the union and bank profited."

These union swindles, while perhaps distasteful to those who believe that unions should protect their members, are not an important factor in the screwing of pension plan members. As Charles Leinenweber observed in his article on "The Great American Pension Machine" (*Ramparts*, June 1972), "Corruption can be a diversionary issue, especially where workers are led to believe that the only reason they receive no pension is because their union officials and pension trustees drive Cadillacs." What the corrupt union leaders do suffers from the stigma of being both illegal—all the cases reported here ended up in court—and small in scale. The games played by management with the members' pension money are, in the modern manner, big enough to be legal.

Management can do pretty much what it wants with pension funds it controls. One favorite practice is to invest the fund in the company's stock—in effect, using the employees' pension money to prop up the firm. Sears, Roebuck puts 80 per cent of its fund, now around $3 billion, into its own stock, and Genesco Co. has $15 million of its $80 million fund in Genesco stocks. A Chicago firm's pension fund put $250,000, or 69 per cent of the fund, into its stock, and a year later the stock was worth $13,500.

Company officials who administer a pension fund can further their personal interests as well as those of the company by using the money to perform the sucker role played by the small investor in the stock market. Officers of the McGrory Corporation put pension fund money into McGrory stock, thus holding up the price while they were selling off their own shares; when the fund stopped buying, McGrory stock dropped by two thirds. The pension fund lost $4.5 million on its stock investments. At the Kropp Forge Co. of Chicago, the fund bought 206,318 shares of Kropp stock from two officers who were leaving the company at three dollars a share—at a time when, according to a fund report, the stock was worth $1.875 a share. Taking a somewhat different approach, the trustees of the Winn-Dixie Corp. fund made loans to other companies owned by the officers of Winn-Dixie.

Company executives can benefit most directly by paying themselves handsomely for their work in administering the pension fund. In one instance, the five trustees of a fund—three of them past or present executives of the company—paid themselves $300,000 a year in trustees' fees. On top of that, the fund paid $130,000 to another corporation, controlled by the same trustees, which had been set up to administer the fund. Payments like these are what finance the growing pension administration industry, which now skims $4 billion a year out of the pension funds. Besides paying company executives as trustees, pension funds hire outsiders to manage the employees' money. Some of these outsiders are the insurance companies and banks that manage the majority of pension funds. Others are newcomers rising to the opportunity; as Leinenweber put it, "small companies with distinctively sinister names, like Certified Portfolios, Inc., Incentive Industries, and Incentive Plans of America." What with so much else on their minds, like manipulating stock prices and making loans to their friends or themselves, the experts of pension fund administration have a poor record of earning money for the employees: in 1971, funds earned an average of 4 per cent, which is no more than they could have gotten from a savings account, and in 1973 the average fund lost almost three years' worth of contributions. All told, with its high costs and poor performance, the pension administration industry provides still another reason why nine out of ten employees find when they reach retirement that there's nothing left in the till. Everyone else got there first.

The banks are, in their quiet gray way, the biggest beneficiaries of pension funds. About two thirds of the $150 billion in pension funds is managed by banks, and most of that by the biggest banks: one third of the banks' share is held by three Wall Street giants, Morgan Guaranty Trust, Bankers Trust, and Chase Manhattan. These holdings represent an increasing share of the instruments of control over American industry; by 1970, bank-managed pension funds held 7.9 per cent of the common stock of *all* U.S. corporations. The power inherent in that stock is wielded by the banks, not by the companies to which the pension funds are attached, or, needless to say, by the employees for whose pensions the money is supposedly intended. Most agreements between pension funds and banks give the bank complete control over the investment of the money and the voting of the stock held for the fund. Chase Manhattan's sample contract, for instance, gives the bank "uncontrolled discretion" in its investing; it also includes a provision relieving the bank of any responsibility toward the members of the pension fund. Thus money which originated from wage increases foregone by employees in the hopes of a pension has now slipped not only out of their hands but out of those of their employers as well and has become a power tool for bankers.

The banks are using the growing bulk of the pension funds—they are expected to reach $250 billion by 1980—to extend their control of the American economy. Morgan Guaranty has used its pension funds to build an empire far greater than the conquests of old J. P. himself. It has, for example, gained effective control of the copper industry; through the use of pension funds, Morgan has bought itself a commanding position in four of the five largest copper companies. Usually these conquests are carried out with the stodgy respectability that we have come to expect of bankers. But on at least one occasion Chase Manhattan got into a deal that momentarily gave David Rockefeller the buccaneer aura of his illustrious grandfather. The deal involved a company called Resorts International. Earlier, under the name of Mary Carter Paint Co., it had acquired a shady reputation. Now it was a Caribbean resort operator that wanted control of an airline and, thinking big, it had selected Pan American as its target. Enter Chase Manhattan, which through its pension fund holdings controlled 7 per cent of Pan Am's stock. Chase agreed to swap its shares in Pan Am for shares in Resorts International, which would have given Resorts a grip on Pan Am and Chase a grip on Resorts and, through it, on Pan Am; rather than losing an airline, the bank would have gained a string of resorts. Ultimately the deal fell through when the press published the backgrounds of some of those involved in Resorts International—unfit company for the present generation of Rockefellers. Chase withdrew in embarrassment. In defense of the bank, one Chase executive observed—this was in 1969—that the head of Resorts "is an acquaintance of

President Nixon and we assume that Mr. Nixon would not associate with people of questionable character." Leinenweber, in telling the story, observes that those who unwittingly put up the money for Chase's aborted deal included pension plan members at General Motors, Ford, Western Electric, Standard Oil, and Westinghouse.

Government looks on with benign indifference as the average man's money is lifted out of his pocket by the various hustlers who make up the pension industry. Right after the Second World War, government gave the industry a big boost by declaring employer contributions to pension funds exempt from the corporate income tax. That act now costs the general public $3 billion in taxes that must be made up from other taxpayers. That is just the first installment of the bill paid by the public for pension swindles. A good number of retired people who have been screwed out of their pensions are forced to go on welfare, and some of them—the "healthy patients" mentioned in the next chapter—will end up in nursing homes with the public paying through Medicaid.

The pension industry is subject to only the most token regulation. No control is exercised over how the pension industry swings that $150 billion around. In order to achieve tax exemption, the operators of a pension plan must file a form with the Internal Revenue Service, but of 115,000 such forms on file, no more than 1,000 are examined, much less acted on, in any given year. Under IRS rules, pension plans are not supposed to discriminate against one class of employees in favor of another. Standard Oil, for example, cannot get exemption for a fund only intended to pay the pension of chairman of the board J. K. Jamieson (his pension is expected to be

between $96,000 and $208,000). However, the finding in
the landmark court case on discrimination suggests that
employers are on a very loose rein. The Ryan Aviation
pension fund in 1944 covered four officers, one super-
visory employee, and 115 other employees. In 1951, the
plan had just ten participants: five officers, three of the
original employees, and two more recent employees. Of
the $71,000 in the fund, $52,000 was earmarked for the
officers. The court decided that the plan was not dis-
criminatory, which seems fairly close to saying that anything goes. Another, less obvious form of discrimination
takes place in the majority of plans, those that figure your
pension in conjunction with Social Security. In these
plans, employees are promised an amount as pension that
includes Social Security. Take, using Ralph Nader's example, a plan that promises retirement pay (Social Security plus pension) equal to 50 per cent of your salary
at retirement. A person making $50,000 a year would get
$25,000—very little of that coming from Social Security,
almost all from the pension plan. A person making $5,000
on retirement would get a pension of $2,500—almost all
from Social Security, very little from the pension plan.
The higher your pay, the more of your pension comes
from the pension plan. So, although employees pay in
equally (in foregone wage increases), the benefits go un-
equally to those who earn more. This sort of plan is legal,
which is perhaps not surprising, since as noted earlier it
would be equally legal if the fund had no money in it for
anyone.

Rumblings from pension plan victims in the trailer
parks, amplified by Ralph Nader and other critics, have
given rise to mild expressions of interest in harnessing the
pension industry. In recent years reform proposals have

been put forward by the Nixon administration and Senators Javits of New York and Williams of New Jersey, among others. As William V. Shannon of the New York *Times* has pointed out repeatedly, none of the major proposals would do much reforming. They would buttress the present system by snipping off its most notorious excesses. Even these mild reforms have been vigorously resisted by the pension industry. Describing the issues involved here forces us to use pension jargon: "vesting," which means what you must do to become eligible for a pension—you are vested, say, after you have worked so many years and reached such an age; "portability," your right to take your pension credits with you to another job; "funding," how much is put in the pension fund; "fiduciary responsibility," what they do with the money in the fund; and "insurance," any provision that guarantees pensions to members of a plan that goes broke.

Employers are understandably opposed to any law that would force them to put enough money in the pension fund, because most plans are underfunded, and equally opposed to any regulation of what they do with the money once it's there, because that would wreck the pension administration industry. Compulsory insurance is opposed on the grounds that well-run plans would have to pay for the irresponsible ones that go under (an argument that could equally well be made against compulsory automobile insurance). The central issues, however, are vesting and portability. The only way to increase significantly the number of people collecting from the present one in ten—to make it a pension rather than a lottery ticket—is through quicker vesting or greater portability. This is because many more lose their pension to the fine print than to the fund going broke. The number of winners would be increased if either the right to a pension with the present employer were more quickly earned, or if it were easier to transfer pension credits into the fund of another employer. This is the point of greatest employer resistance, joined in many cases by unions. Easier vesting or portability, they say, would be too expensive. Recall that the employer's motive is to make a promise he will only rarely have to keep; such promises are cheap. The union goes along because it was an accomplice in negotiating the promise. Both are happy with that "$100-a-month pension" they just negotiated, the employer because in nine times out of ten he won't have to pay it, the union leaders because the amount makes them look good. Only the membership doesn't know what's going on.

Now, if the law were to set minimum standards for eligibility—so that, say, five out of ten employees would collect—the employer's promise would cost him five times as much. At the same cost he could only offer a pension of twenty dollars a month, but that would hardly motivate his workers to give up as much in raises as they would for the $100 promise. He would not be able to con them as much. Reforms that make it more likely people will collect are resisted, therefore, because they would raise the percentage of truth in the pension promise, to no one's advantage except that of the average man.

At this writing, both houses of Congress had passed pension bills, and it seemed certain that something calling itself pension reform would become law in 1974. The press, bored perhaps by the intricacy of the issues involved, hailed Congress' proposals as true pension reform. A closer look showed that both bills contained more holes than they did cheese, at least for the average man. Indeed, in the loud promises they made, and the paltry changes they would actually achieve, both bills resembled nothing so much as the illusory pension plans they purported to reform. Merton C. Bernstein of Ohio State University, author of *The Future of Private Pensions*, pointed out that relatively few workers would be protected against the standard pension screwings, that their added benefits would be small, and that some provisions of the bills would not come into effect until the 1980s. That would seem to leave a lot of people still headed for the trailer park. If the average man was due once more to be paid with a promise rather than a pension, such was not the case with his superiors. Taking advantage of the situation, a group of lobbyists headed by the American Medical Association and the American Bankers Association darted in to enrich a tax loophole for self-employed professionals: the annual amount they are allowed to put into tax-free retirement funds was to be raised from $2,500 to $7,500. This should enable the well-to-do to improve on their already excellent record: at present, half the tax advantages from private pension plans go to the upper 8 per cent of the population.

The private pension system makes Social Security look good. Social Security is a swindle on working people for reasons detailed in chapter 13. Still, the print is easy to read, everyone covered collects, it costs less to run than private plans, and no one has ever parlayed the Social Security fund away on the stock market. The average man, beset by experts and deserted by his union, might well conclude that he would be better off with more Social Security, for all its faults, than with a one-to-ten shot in the pension lottery.

10

Nursing Home: The Last Stop

THE AVERAGE MAN'S CHOICES NARROW as the years wear on. He has lost most of his encounters with the world around him. He had some opportunities, but he was never able to get ahead of the game. He earned the diploma, and somehow it never brought him what he expected in the job market. He took a flier on some stocks, and came up with one lemon instead of three cherries. He got taken on everything from his car to his mortgage. Only yesterday, he found out, on his retirement, that he wasn't eligible for the pension plan. You may see him now, lingering in a cheap cafeteria, trying to stretch the price of two cups of coffee across an empty evening. You will see him, that is, if he is fortunate enough still to be able to manage on his own. If he isn't, you won't see him at all: he is in a nursing home.

It is the final screwing, and it is happening to more and more people. The nursing home is a sad way to go, and a grim reflection on how we treat the old among us. For that reason, the nursing home remains a dark place that few want to peer into. Most people with relatives in nursing homes would rather think about practically anything else.

The average person in a nursing home is the victim of private greed and government indifference. His presence there is yet another sign of the death of the family. Indeed, that death was officially noted when the federal government decided that the resources of the children should not be included in determining whether a person is eligible for Medicaid: parent and child alike, we're all on our own. Once the extended family would have taken care of the older person in trouble; now his closest relative is government. Once his children would have decided whether he needed to be in an institution and, if so, which one; now the place where he will end his life is chosen by a caseworker whom often he will never see. He has been reduced to a piece of paper on a bureaucrat's desk. Control over his life has been third-partied out of the hands of his family into those of—nobody.

The average man will not necessarily go to the nursing home because he is sick enough to require its "skilled nursing care." According to various investigators, from 30 to 90 per cent of people in nursing homes are healthy enough to be somewhere else: sometimes they could be at home, with a certain amount of personal assistance. The wealthy can pay for their own care, and stay out of the institution. But the average man, once he can no longer function completely on his own, has no place else to go and no one to turn to: of the million people in nursing homes half have no immediate family, and, of the rest, half have no relatives that take an interest in their plight. The nursing home takes a person's unwanted relatives and, later on, it will take that person too.

The patient is alone in the hands of the people who

run nursing homes. This is bad news for him, for the sudden flood of government money into nursing homes has attracted a greedy horde of traders in human lives. Drugs are the weapon typically used to keep the patient in line. Medicaid alone spends some $200 million a year for drugs for nursing homes, and of that, 40 per cent goes to tranquilizers and sedatives. Many of the drugs do not actually reach the patients, having been siphoned off in various swindles, but that 40 per cent usually hits its target. There is, for example, one California operator who practices the pre-emptive strike; she zaps each incoming patient with a tranquilizer to "make him feel at home." A retired nursing home administrator once described how tranquillity is maintained:

> A layman doesn't know what to look for in a nursing home. He walks in and sees a patient is nice and quiet and he thinks this guy is happy. And the nurse tells him: "This is John. John is one of our best patients. He sits here and watches television."
>
> But you just take a look at John's pupils and you'll see what condition John is in. John is so full of thorazine that it's coming out his ears. Thorazine—that's a tranquilizer they use. It's a brown pill. It looks like an M&M candy.
>
> The nursing home where I worked kept at least 90 percent of the patients on thorazine all the time. They do it for the money. If they can keep John a vegetable, then they don't have to bother with him. They never have to spend anything to rehabilitate him.

Once doped, the patient is less likely to complain about what is done to him, or not done for him. If he's fortunate, neglect is the worst that will happen to him. The government is paying a doctor to treat him, but the patient only catches a glimpse of the doctor as he flashes past in that

Medicaid phenomenon known as the "gang visit." The doctor gallops through the nursing home, glancing for a moment at the most urgent cases, then bills Medicaid for a personal call on each patient. One doctor billed Medicaid for seventy-one patient visits on one day and fifty-six on another; he charged for 960 visits in a three-month period. Another doctor racked up ninety on one day and eighty-six on another; 487 calls in sixteen days. Both doctors were also carrying their usual non-Medicaid practice. If the patient calls for a nurse, he may find there is none on duty, because the operator is saving money; he may, however, spot an aide wearing a nurse's cap when the inspectors are in the home. He may be fed slop; nursing homes are good customers for merchants selling spoiled meat and stale bread. According to the Senate Nutrition Subcommittee, a lot of nursing home patients die before their time from diets that are too sweet and too starchy, as well as too cheap.

Neglect can sometimes be costly: each year a certain number of nursing home patients are burned to death when a home that was in violation of fire regulations goes up in flames. One day it may be the home whose owner told Mary Adelaide Mendelson, author of *Tender Loving Greed*, about his new set of sprinklers, then jovially added that he had saved the money it would cost to hook them into the water supply: the sprinklers, he said, were only there to fool the inspectors.

If our patient is unlucky, he may land in a home where patients are actively abused as well as neglected. Such homes, though not standard, are far too common. Here, shut off from the world outside, he may be beaten at the whim of an aide for any reason or none; especially if he is in that home where a few years ago, among other cruelties, a nineteen-year-old aide was seen slapping a ninety-year-old patient because he had dropped something on her shoe. Patient abuse develops naturally in the environment of some kinds of nursing homes. The cruelty of aides and nurses simply mirrors the indifference of the owner. The aide is likely to be tired and irritable. Nursing homes pay rock-bottom wages, so many employees are holding down two full-time jobs. Some couldn't get a job anywhere else, like the employees of one nursing home whose operator regularly recruits his staff from the city's skid row. Such people are likely to take their revenge on the world at the expense of helpless patients.

The patient's luck has run out entirely if he finds himself in the home of a Benjamin Cohen or a Daniel Slader. Cohen owned and operated the Kenmore Nursing Home in Chicago where, according to an undercover investigator, the stench from neglected patients pervaded even the dining room; he fed his patients in 1970 on $.78 a day. Slader, who was Treasurer of the Metropolitan Chicago Nursing Home Association, was even more frugal: he fed patients on $.58 a day. His home was still in business despite fifty recent violations and an inspector's report that found the "overall picture of the third floor to be in deplorable condition. The stench permeated the area . . . broken plumbing, peeling plaster, inadequate food." Both operators were getting rich on their underfed patients. Cohen was making two for one on his investment. He had bought the home for $40,000 cash, and in one year he had a net profit of $50,292, plus another $31,-000 in depreciation (in effect, tax-free income), plus another $14,000 in salaries for his wife and himself. As for Slader, he and his associates were said to have made

$185,000 the previous year on their investment of $40,-000. There was, it seemed, plenty of money in nursing homes if you ran them right.

The patient has little chance of escaping. No locked door prevents him from leaving (in most cases; some homes do actually lock their clients in). Assuming he can still move around on that fifty-eight-cent-a-day diet, he nonetheless has little prospect of getting away. He has no money for a fresh start. His Social Security check is cashed by the operator and he has no idea how long it would take to pry the check loose if he left the home. Even his small monthly allowance for personal expenses is likely to have been intercepted by the operator. He has only the clothes he's wearing—frequently not his own, for some operators take the clothes and put the patients in Salvation Army rags. He can no longer cope with the world—that in fact is why he's there—and whatever ability he had is now eroded by the quality of nursing home life. He is free to leave, but he has no place to go.

He could, if he is on Medicaid, call his caseworker and ask to be transferred. The caseworker put him there in the first place. She knows all about that home: the stench, the lousy food, the early deaths . . . She keeps on sending patients there for any of several reasons. The other homes in the area are just as bad or the better ones are all full. Or she has an understanding with the operator. The caseworker is essential to that steady flow of patients on which the operator's prosperity is based. The operator may reward a co-operative caseworker with, say, a fur coat at Christmas, or, as happened in one city, a bounty of $100 a head. The patient, on the other hand, will not give her a fur coat for moving him to a better home. Or, even without the fur coat, the caseworker may feel it better to do nothing. If she takes the patient out, it means trouble with the operator . . . arguments . . . other patients asking to be moved . . . the patient doesn't have that long to live anyway. The caseworker hangs up the phone.

The patient could complain to the nursing home inspector, if he can find him. Like the caseworker, the inspector knows all about that home: he inspects it every year. Even if he's not on the take, he knows that he has written up the home's violations year after year and nothing has happened. The violations remain uncorrected, his office fails to prosecute the operator. So he too hangs up on the patient.

Neither caseworker nor inspector, nor anyone else, is likely to respond if the patient complains to them about how he is being treated. The regulators shield themselves by demanding impossible evidence before acting. Mrs. Mendelson, for example, presented Ohio authorities with complaints of cruelty in one nursing home, including the account of an eighty-one-year-old woman who said that two nurses "dragged her to the bathroom and threw her in the bathtub . . . when they were giving her a bath after throwing her in, they broke her tail bone, which hurts her very much, when, sitting her in a hard chair, they tie her in that chair . . . she does not want to be spit on and beaten any more." The authorities said they would not listen to the case unless a witness other than the patient was willing to sign a complaint. Of course those two nurses were hardly likely to sign complaints against themselves, and in general the only witness other than the patient is the person who is inflicting the abuse on him.

By now the patient may be showing symptoms of paranoia. He sees a gigantic conspiracy against him that includes the people who run the nursing home, the government in the persons of the caseworker and the inspector, and the relatives who abandoned him. That's not paranoia—the patient is right.

The relatives, if any, are almost as helpless as the patients. Many of us have had the experience of looking in to the closed world of the nursing home, often with considerable guilt, because someone in the family can no longer make it on the outside. Other than word of mouth, there is little to guide us in trying to pick the rare good home out of a herd that includes numerous mediocre homes and an occasional Auschwitz. Once having chosen a home, the relatives can expect, if the patient is on Medicaid, to have the operator ask them to pay something extra under the table. If the relatives object, or if they complain about conditions in the home, they are typically told, "If you don't like it here, take your mother someplace else."

Government, which licenses and inspects the homes, could enlighten us, for the inspectors' reports are the best, in fact virtually the only, outside information about the quality of a nursing home. But government, and especially the Department of Health, Education, and Welfare, seems determined to keep us in the dark. At this writing, HEW is engaged in a stubborn rear action to keep those inspectors' reports from the public eye. HEW seemed to have lost in early 1972, when a newsman, Mal Schechter of the magazine *Hospital Practice*, won a suit granting him access to inspection reports on homes licensed for Medicare (which is federally administered). In the case of Medicaid, which is administered by the states, similar cases were being fought in state courts.

HEW gave ground inch by inch. It interpreted the court decision to mean only that Schechter himself could have access to the eight reports on which he based his suit, not that the general public could see all Medicare reports. Later that year Congress adopted legislation requiring HEW to make public both Medicare and Medicaid inspections. Still HEW hung on grimly. It interpreted the law to mean that the public could see, not the report, but an "extract" from it. It further ruled that the reports could not be obtained at the nursing home or by telephone or mail; if you want to see that "extract," you have to go to the regional Social Security office (Medicare homes) or the local welfare office (Medicaid homes). HEW had succeeded, within the limits of the new law, in making it as hard as possible for a person considering a nursing home to find out what the last inspector had written about the place. Certainly it had avoided the obvious action: posting the report at the entrance to the nursing home. In fact, Washington vetoed a New York State proposal to post the reports. Such an action might have had considerable effect in, say, New York City, where state inspectors in 1973 found that two thirds of 104 profit-making homes were deficient.

The nursing home industry was also the scene of an effort by HEW to implement a new approach to government regulation: if the people you regulate don't obey your rules, change the rules to fit their behavior. In the early 1970s, HEW was beset by complaints that the nursing homes were not following the regulations that came with their Medicaid and Medicare money. The General Accounting Office found that the majority of homes it studied in three states were failing to comply with the regulations; one frequently disregarded rule was that each patient must be seen by a doctor every thirty days. The HEW response in 1973 was to rewrite its regulations eliminating the thirty-day rule and many other specific requirements. Thus at one bold stroke the nursing homes were brought into compliance with the regulations. The industry would be able to increase its profits at the expense of the patients without unduly disturbing the authorities in Washington.

Government's role as the industry's third-party friend dates mainly from 1966, that seminal year in the health industry, when Medicaid and Medicare came into effect. In the previous decade enough new money, both public and private, had come into the industry to attract some smart pioneers who today are among the industry's most eminent hustlers. But that was only a trickle compared to what happened after 1966. By now, government provides some three quarters of the industry's annual revenue of $3.5 billion, and Medicaid alone supports more than half the one million people in nursing homes.

The average man as taxpayer had been added to the patient as a victim of the nursing home industry. How the flood of third-party government money after 1966 aroused the innovative greed of the health industry was described in chapter 6; most of the major swindles listed there are to be found in the nursing homes, plus a few peculiar to the local habitat. As the money poured in, a carom effect was soon observed. The industry raised its prices in response to the new money; as the prices went up, fewer and fewer patients could afford to pay their own way, and yesterday's private patient today is on Medicaid. The outcome of the carom effect is that the average man has to pay out more dollars in taxes than the industry receives in extra revenue. If a private patient at twelve dollars a day goes on Medicaid when the rate goes to fifteen, the operator has gained three dollars while the taxpayer has lost fifteen.

The many ways in which nursing homes swindle the average man can be divided into two general categories: one group is small, old-fashioned, and illegal; the second is bigger, newer, and, usually, within the law. The difference between nursing home operators who practice one or the other kind of swindle is the difference between a Mafia don and his counterpart at ITT.

The old-fashioned swindler usually is someone who grew up in the industry and is working with little capital. He is found chasing nickels and dimes. This is the kind of operator who pilfers the small amount—usually five to ten dollars a month—that patients are supposed to get out of the Medicaid check for their personal use. Typically he is working against a flat-rate Medicaid payment system. He gets, say, fifteen dollars a day for each patient; the way to increase his net is to cut his expenses. He can't do anything with such fixed costs as rent and taxes. What he can cut is what comes out of the patient's hide: food and service. Hence the rotten meat and spoiled produce to keep the food budget under a dollar a day, and hence, at the extreme, the operator who hired his help from skid row.

There is, for example, Herbert Cook in California buying substandard eggs known as "checks and dirties" for his patients; Cook got in trouble not because the eggs are banned for human consumption, which they are, but because they were stolen. The old-fashioned type on a somewhat larger scale is Eugene Woods, a Cleveland operator who fled town when his operations caved in. Woods intercepted Social Security checks addressed to his patients, endorsed and cashed them himself. The reason was that the amount paid the nursing home by Medicaid is determined by subtracting the patient's Social Security payment from the nursing home's monthly rate; the lower the Social Security amount, the more Medicaid will pay. If the operator intercepts the checks—the patients have no reason to care, since they don't get the money in any case—he can understate how much Social Security is paying and collect correspondingly more from Medicaid. Woods also practiced some more exotic swindles. Once he got an old man from a rooming house, put him in his nursing home and later bilked him for close to $30,000. When Woods left town, among his papers was found a list of coins in a collection owned by one of his patients, with the most valuable items marked by asterisks.

The drugstore kickback is the classic old-fashioned fraud. The nursing home is the best customer a drugstore could hope to have. If, as is frequently the case, the home gives all its business to one pharmacist, he is guaranteed a large volume of business at the top price (often, in fact, at over the top price). Anyone bringing in that kind of business would be entitled to demand a discount. But the nursing home operator doesn't ask for a discount, which would have to be passed on to the taxpayers, who ultimately pay the bill. Instead, the operator extracts a kickback, the taxpayer pays the full bill, and operator and pharmacist split the difference. Typically, also, the pharmacy charges the nursing home for its bulk purchases more than it charges the person who comes in off the street and buys a single prescription. Refinements on the scheme are based on the generic-brand-name hustle described in chapter 6. Most obviously, the nursing home will always choose the more expensive brand name over the generic drug, leaving more margin for the kickback. This can be improved by billing the government for the brand name and delivering the generic equivalent. Best of all is to order the brand name—and not deliver anything at all to the patient.

At times these hustles reach a volume that can no longer be called small. Yet they retain enough of the two-bit flavor, and are clear enough in their illegality, to be disreputable. The great contribution of the new breed of nursing home operators, those who came in during the 1960s, was to make swindling respectable. They come from respectable backgrounds—many are lawyers or business school graduates—and they understand the modern world far better than the small-timers ever did. They saw that the nursing home plus government money offered a setting for large-scale financial hustles that had the virtue of being legal—most of the time, anyway; a few of the new breed in their eagerness crossed the line and a couple have even been caught. But in general their swindles are both far bigger and far safer than the nickel-and-diming of their predecessors (who are still in business). The newcomers excelled in the cost-plus situation. Medicare, and in some states Medicaid as well, pays nursing homes their costs plus a "reasonable" profit. The new operators quickly devised ways to pad their costs and make their profits unreasonable. They build or buy a nursing home and then lease it to themselves at an outlandish rental that then becomes a cost to be reimbursed by government. Or they set up separate corporations to sell goods and services at unreasonable prices to their nursing homes; the government pays at a higher rate and the profit is drained off to the other companies. Two officers of a nursing home chain bearing the strange name of Convalariums of America were among those who pushed this game a bit too far. They set up six dummy corporations which rendered phony invoices to Convalariums at inflated prices. These invoices were paid by Convalariums, while payment to the actual suppliers, at lower prices, was made by the dummy corporations, with the two executives pocketing the difference.

Some business leaders also saw that a nursing home with guaranteed government revenue provided an excellent base for usury. The idea is to load the home down with mortgages—the interest to be paid by government —and then perhaps use the resulting capital for other enterprises. One Joseph Kosow of Boston, for example, has grown rich by placing second and third mortgages on nursing homes at rates of interest that, according to one investigator, have run as high as 40 per cent a year. In some homes doing business with Kosow, mortgage payments alone have eaten up one quarter of their revenue. Government is not alone in bearing the cost —when costs have to be cut to meet the interest payments, the patients pay too. In one such home, where rent, including mortgage payments, took almost one third of the budget, everything else was cut: payroll, which in most homes takes close to two thirds, got only one third—less help to take care of the patients—and all other costs, including food and linen and utilities, had to come out of the remaining third. The patients were paying off the moneylender.

The most farsighted among the new breed saw that the list of victims—the patient and the taxpayer—was incomplete. So they formed public companies and sold stock in nursing home chains—thus offering the average man as investor a chance to take a seat alongside the taxpayer and the patient. The public, as greedy as it was innocent, gladly took up the invitation, and the boom in nursing home stocks was on, one aspect of the great stock market hustle described in chapter 3. In 1969 the hottest of these stocks were known as the "fevered fifty" of Wall Street, and J. Richard Elliott, Jr., of *Barron's* wrote that a ". . . kind of frenzy seems to grip the stock market at the merest mention of those magic words 'convalescent care,' 'extended care,' 'continued care.' All euphemisms for the services provided by nursing homes, they stand for the hottest investment around today." The chains bore the kinds of names that, in retrospect, might have caused the buyer to beware: Medic-Home Enterprises, Geri-Care (later rebaptized Lifestyle Companies), Metrocare Enterprises, United Convalescent Hospitals, etc. Among the chain operators were promoters who performed all the latter-day magic described in chapter 3—selling the stock to the public at one price, to themselves for much less; bleeding the nursing homes white before getting out—and some of them did it with unequaled skill.

There was, said one analyst, "no way" to lose money in this business. What the average man as investor failed to see was that, while there was no way for the promoters to lose, there was ample opportunity for the investor to lose his shirt; he thought he was being invited to get in on the take, but the fine print said it was an invitation to a screwing—his own. The boom burned itself out by 1971, and the average investor found that the stock he bought when it was headed for the moon was now permanently attached to the ground.

None did worse than those caught with shares in Four

Seasons Nursing Centers of America. First offered at eleven dollars a share, it shot up to a peak of $181.50, then shot down just as fast, and was worth fifty cents when trading was suspended. The chain went into bankruptcy. In 1972 officers of Four Seasons, including its president, and employees of its accountants (Arthur Andersen & Co.) and its brokerage firm (Walson & Co.) were indicted on charges of defrauding the investors. According to the charges, the officers phonied Four Seasons figures in order to run up the price of the stock, and the accountants certified the figures; then, when the stock began to fade, the officers bailed out by selling their own shares through secret accounts at the brokerage house. That left the average investor holding an empty bag. The loss to the stockholders of $200 million was said to be a record for a stock-fraud indictment—a remarkable tribute to the ability of the new breed of nursing home operators, for they were in an industry that had not even been on Wall Street a few years earlier. Old Daniel Drew, the inventor of watered stock, must have smiled down appreciatively from hustlers' heaven. Of course, the Four Seasons operators got caught, which is poor form, but the size of their fraud guaranteed them against any substantial retribution. This became evident when the former president of Four Seasons, Jack L. Clark of Oklahoma, came up for sentencing. Clark was said to have made $10 million as his share of the swindle. Judge Thomas P. Griesa sentenced him to one year, meaning parole in four months, and imposed no fine at all. If Clark can be considered to be earning his swindle with his jail time, he was getting paid at the rate of $2.5 million a month; the average man doubtless would gladly put in a little jail time at that salary. As for the investor, he could reflect that Clark was putting in one month for each $50 million that the stockholders lost on Four Seasons.

The record of the nursing home industry is the best argument in sight for the revival of that sense of community that would make it intolerable for us to allow the old to live out their last years in the cold hands of an indifferent bureaucracy. Until that day comes, the average man seems doomed to paying out extra taxes to support the industry's hustles and excess profits, while heeding, if he can, this advice: don't get caught alive in a nursing home.

11

Government and Other Monopolies

For CITIZENS, government is the greatest of third-party transactions. Government takes our money in taxes and then decides to whom, and for what purpose, that money should go. Government as regulator sets the ground rules on how business can treat us as consumers. All our daily transactions are colored by what government does or does not choose to do. The subject is encyclopedic. We could go on and on, and on some more, exploring the many ways in which what government does and fails to do affects the average man. Instead, we shall limit ourselves to three aspects of government most important to the screwing of the public: monopoly, the subject of this chapter, and subsidies and the tax system, the subjects of the next two chapters.

Government and monopoly are natural allies. Both share the ideology of socialism for the rich and capitalism for the poor. In this view, the bracing chill of capitalist competition is good for the poor; it toughens their fiber so they can better work their way up out of poverty. The rich, on the other hand, have already made that climb and are tired; they deserve to be excused from further effort. They are to be supported under our form of socialism.

The average man can get the point simply by comparing how his government treats him if he is flattened by a catastrophic illness—as a sturdy fellow who can stand on his own two feet with both legs broken—with the tender loving care that same government applies to the slightest sign of corporate ill health, even if brought on by the corporations' own indulgence in riotous living. If the average man is mugged on his way to the store, the government will denounce crime in the streets, while if an industry is menaced by foreign competition, the government will apply tariffs or quotas to protect it from the realities of free enterprise. If the average man goes broke, that's his problem, but when in 1974 the Franklin National Bank got in financial trouble—at a time when it was almost impossible for a bank to avoid making money—the Federal Reserve Bank rushed to the rescue with a loan of $1 billion at below market interest.

On a strictly dollar basis, the alliance of government and monopoly can be explained by the fact that only the monopolists can afford to purchase officeholders in large enough lots to determine national policy. Putting it somewhat differently, the rich get socialism because they have the money to buy it. True enough, but this focus is too narrow. Government has other, less obviously tangible affinities to monopoly. They share a horror of competition. Government is itself a natural monopoly, like AT&T. Whatever a government agency does, be it the Post Office or the Department of Agriculture, no one else is allowed to be in the same line of business and thereby offer the threat of better service at a lower price. When on rare occasions the threat of competition arises, it is greeted with shocked indignation. For example, John DeLury, head of the New York City sanitation men's union, was never so furious as when it was pointed out that private collectors can pick up the garbage for one third what it costs the city to employ DeLury's men. In a perfect monopoly, such odious comparisons are avoided.

All government monopolies claim to be natural, suggesting perhaps that DeLury's uniformed sanitation men were picking up apple cores in the Garden of Eden, but the logic behind this judgment seems to be more political than economic. Take what happened when Congress decided that a study should be made to determine whether there was a role for private enterprise in the postal business. Whom did they select to make this study? None other than the U. S. Postal Service, thereby raising the possibility that studying the Post Office, as well as delivering the mail, may be a natural monopoly best left to the Post Office itself.

The 1973 postal survey was actually an evaluation of the utility of maintaining the private express statutes dating from the mid-nineteenth century that make it a crime for anyone but the government to deliver letter mail. (The statutes have since been changed to permit courier services to make deliveries that have to be at their destination within twelve hours.) Technically, the express statutes require private courier services to put U.S. stamps on all letters they deliver, thereby paying the postal service full rates for not delivering your letter.

According to the Postal Service, a governmental monopoly is needed to prevent "skimming." This doesn't relate to milk, but refers to the belief that profit-mad private industry would handle only the easy deliveries, leaving it to the federal government to bear the unprofitable burden of delivering your Christmas card to Aunt Sadie, who lives in a farmhouse forty-seven miles north of Hays, Kansas. All this sounds very reasonable and equitable until you realize that you don't know anyone who lives on a remote Kansas farm. What the Post Office is really saying is that you should cheerfully endure an increasingly expensive and inefficient federal monopoly to uphold the right of someone else's Aunt Sadie to get holiday mail. It is strange that although the federal government's agricultural policies have done everything they can to drive the small farmer off his land, the Post Office is still vigilant in upholding the right of Aunt Sadie, like every other American, to receive her mail three and four days late.

Admittedly, the Post Office advanced some other reasons to justify its continuing shelter from competition. Perhaps the most innovative was the contention that "under competition, funds for Inspection Service enforcement of postal laws might be severely limited and made available strictly in accordance with a business justification . . ." Part of the job of the Inspection Service is scouring the mails for explosive or potentially dangerous materials—an activity that clearly would have a business justification. Interestingly enough, the main task of the Inspection Service that would probably have to be abandoned under competitive conditions would be the enforcement of the laws designed to protect bluenoses from the psychic burden of receiving pornography—or what they perceive to be obscene materials—in the mail.

If anything, the postal unions have been even more zealous than their superiors in trying to thwart private operations like the Independent Postal System. Not only have they filed suit against the IPS, but several union locals have tried to curb the activities of the private carriers by means of "anti-littering laws." These statutes would virtually ban the use of plastic bags which private carriers must utilize because your little wicker mailbox is considered to be government property and its use by anyone else from the paper boy to a political candidate is strictly forbidden. Perhaps the most scorching attack on these little plastic bags was mounted by a Springfield, Missouri, postman who published an open letter charging that not only were the bags unsightly, but they also were a menace to small children and an indication to burglars that no one was at home.

The glittering success of the MGIC Investment Corp., which directly competes with the government's FHA mortgage insurance, may explain why the Post Office so bitterly fears competition. Starting from scratch in 1966, its founder, Max Karl, has turned MGIC into a company that currently insures more home mortgages than FHA. Karl has made $30 million in the process, though MGIC premiums are often 50 per cent less than those charged by FHA. MGIC's selling point is speed. While it takes FHA six to eight weeks to process an application, MGIC, which Karl started to bypass governmental red tape, can do the job in a day or two. There is little doubt that the FHA is constantly reminded of the performance of MGIC when it comes to Congress at appropriations time. It is this kind of external performance evaluation that is the anathema of any bureaucrat. The "softer" the bureaucracy, the fuzzier its rationale for existence, the more desperately its denizens will resist any attempt by the outside world to determine what they are doing, how well it is being accomplished, and whether it was worth carrying out in the first place.

What the bureaucrat is constantly striving for is what the industrial and professional monopolies have already achieved. In industry, the goal of the monopolist is to keep out other firms and jack up the price of the product; in the professional world of doctors and lawyers, the game is to keep your numbers small and maintain a minimum fee schedule for members of the guild. Another, less familiar purpose is to avoid effort. Protected from the rigors of competition, you can let the business slide a bit, save on research, don't worry too much if productivity is dropping at the plant and, generally speaking, spend the afternoon at the golf course. Professionals can bury their mistakes (so to speak), secure in the knowledge that class solidarity will keep their colleagues from spreading the word. Government bureaucrats seek the same goal of relaxation. What all these three groups have in common—bureaucrats, monopolists, and professionals—is the goal of self-regulation, which means: we set the price for our services and we decide how well we're doing our job. Much of the secrecy that enshrouds monopolies of all sorts—bureaucratic, business, and professional—is intended to prevent outsiders from evaluating them, for fear that the general public will discover the secret:

BUREAUCRAT: This agency hasn't done anything worthwhile since 1937.

BUSINESSMAN: Any fool willing to work an eight-hour day could turn out a better product at half the price.

PROFESSIONAL: My secretary fills out the forms and I charge the client fifty dollars an hour for my expertise.

Monopolists, then, share a common aversion to evaluation of what they make or do. When private and public monopolists join in common enterprise, their resistance to evaluation reaches a fever pitch. A couple of years ago, when the Administration proposed that taxpayers put up $250 million to bail the Lockheed Aircraft Corp. out of the consequences of its own ineptitude, someone in Congress asked how Lockheed's performance would be guaranteed. John B. Connally, then Secretary of the Treasury, made the classic response: "What do we care whether they perform? We are guaranteeing them basically a $250 million loan. Why for? Basically, so they can hopefully minimize their losses, so they can provide employment for 31,000 people throughout the country at a time when we desperately need that kind of employment. That is basically the rationale and justification." Connally's ideology was presumably acquired in his years in government as well as in his association with the monopoly-bound oil industry. In any event, his viewpoint seems entirely consistent with the socialist principle of "from each according to his ability, to each according to his needs." Lockheed's need was for $250 million; its ability, on past performance, was nil, and that was all the corporation could legitimately be expected to deliver.

Under the benevolent gaze of government, monopolies flourish in America at painful cost to the average man. Of the two basic types of monopoly, guilds are both the less familiar and the more rapidly expanding. The professional monopolies are scarcely recognized for what they are in conventional economic theory, possibly because the theory is written by professional economists, who, as academicians, are themselves members of a professional monopoly. The cost to the public of guild monopolies is difficult to estimate in the absence of competing services. (But see chapters 5 and 6 for examples of the cost in medicine and law.) It is fair to say, however, that when anyone buys a service from a member of a self-regulating professional monopoly he will pay more than that service would cost under competitive conditions—often he will pay a lot more.

Government's role is to protect the monopoly by authorizing the guild to regulate itself. Professional monopolies do not achieve their control of the market in head-on battle with the consumer; they get the government, the states in most cases, to do it for them. The first step is to convince the government that, in order to protect the public, the service must be restricted to *licensed* practitioners. This prevents the evil of comparative shopping—buying the same service from a non-guild member—and the public accepts the monopoly price because it is the only one available. Secondly, the guild gets control of the regulatory machinery. Consumers are fended off by the din of expertism: the public must be protected by experts who can judge how well the guild members are doing their jobs, and all the experts are members of the guild. Thus most of the people who sit on those hundreds of state boards that regulate guild activities are themselves members of the guilds they are regulating. The guild's purposes are helped along by the fact that, since serving on a board to regulate, say, cosmetology, is not one of the juicier plums of state government, it is often difficult to get someone without an ax to grind to serve on those regulatory commissions.

Government, itself an aspiring professional monopoly, is usually willing to help out the guilds. The guilds often are far from politically powerful—cosmeticians and well diggers cannot be anything but small potatoes as lobbies —but no countervailing force is exercised on behalf of the public and, as is well known, you can't beat somebody, even an egg grader, with nobody. Resistance to the guilds pays no political dividends, as Richard J. Hughes found out when he was governor of New Jersey. Hughes vetoed several bills that would have created new licensing boards, but got no credit for it from the voters; his actions, indeed, were hardly known to anyone except the small groups he offended. Accordingly, every month or so, another state government surrenders to another guild, and events proceed along the lines foreseen by Adam Smith two centuries ago: "People of the same trade seldom meet together, even for merriment and diversion, but the conversation ends in a conspiracy against the public or in some contrivance to raise prices."

The surest protection of the guild is occupational birth control: hold down the membership, and they can all raise their rates until supply and demand come into equilibrium at a satisfyingly high level. In the early days of guilds, this was accomplished by apprenticeship. Those seven-year apprenticeships in the London crafts did not reflect the difficulty of the tasks to be mastered but rather the eagerness of those on the inside to make entry as difficult as possible. (Parliament by then had outlawed such blunt methods as simply limiting the number of members.) School is the modern apprenticeship. The guilds control their numbers by imposing a diploma requirement and making that diploma difficult to get. Lengthening the years in school helps discourage entry into the guild: the opinion is widespread, for example, that you could learn to be a doctor or a lawyer in no more than half the time schooling for those two professions now takes. The American Medical Association, queen of guilds, does it most straightforwardly by rationing the number of seats in medical schools (which means, of course, that no matter how much the population of premedical students increases, the number who can go on to become doctors remains the same). Guilds are typically vigilant in blocking any side entrances leading into their occupations. Lawyers used to learn their trade by apprenticeship, and in New York State it was possible until recently to apprentice yourself for four years to a practicing lawyer and then take the bar examination. Then the state bar association stepped in with a requirement that an apprentice spend at least one year in law school, thus giving the schools absolute control over the number (and type) of people who will be permitted to take the bar examination. The lawyers were being particularly cautious, as is their habit, since the guild already controls its numbers by deciding each year how many candidates will be allowed to pass the bar examination.

Other, less powerful guilds have to use less direct tactics. Take, for example, the beauticians of Louisiana, as reported by Jethro K. Lieberman in *The Tyranny of the Experts.* They started out by lobbying through a rather mild law providing that their business be regulated by a Board of Control of Cosmetic Therapy, with only one beautician among its three members. A few years later muscle was added to the law. The board was expanded to six members, and now five were beauticians. The board was given the power to fix prices and prevent "unfair" competition. Finally, the board was given extensive powers over the schools through which aspirants had to pass on the way to the beauty shoppe—the board promptly fixed a minimum tuition fee "lest competition among the schools drive down their income." Similarly with barbers: in Rhode Island, it takes 1,500 hours of education to learn how to cut male hair. And with "ophthalmic dispensers" (they put the glasses in your frames):

there are only three schools in the nation, and the state boards have so rigged the licensing examination that it is very difficult to pass unless you attended one of those schools; someone who learned the trade on the job has virtually no chance of passing. This one is particularly silly, since most lenses come ready-made from a manufacturer and need only be fitted to the frames, but it serves the essential purpose of keeping the numbers down. Sometimes even fellow guild members are fair game if they try to cross state lines. The State Optometry Board of Michigan denied a license to an optometrist who had attended an Illinois school which "did not provide a long enough course of instruction." Nurses have been campaigning for years to restrict the R.N. title to those who went through a four-year college course, excluding graduates of two- and three-year training programs, although no one else believes you can tell the difference among the three kinds of nurses after they are on the job. Lengthening the years in school is always defended by the guild as a means of protecting the public against undertrained practitioners, but this claim is undermined by the typical inclusion of a grandfather clause exempting those already in the guild from the new requirements—evidently the public does not need to be protected from *them*.

Once in control, the guilds raise prices and make sure that their members do not lapse into old-fashioned free enterprise. Regulating "unfair" competition is usually done by setting minimum prices that all guild members must observe. That is the method practiced by the American Bar Association, though it is now under siege (see chapter 5). Barbers and dry cleaners have also imposed minimum prices, and, with a hand from the legal guild, gotten the approval of the courts. If, despite occupational birth control, there still isn't enough trade for all the members, the guild may take up what Jethro Lieberman calls "inconspicuous production": charging the public for a service that doesn't need doing. One example comes from the undertakers. There just aren't enough bodies to go around any more: in 1880, there were 993,000 deaths for 5,100 undertakers; in 1960, 1,700,000 corpses but 25,000 undertakers (funeral directors by then). The inconspicuous production answer is the requirement that all corpses be embalmed; there is no health reason for this, especially in the case of those that are cremated. Other examples mentioned in other chapters include the surgeon's unnecessary operations, the lawyer's unneeded litigation, and of course the best of them all: title insurance.

Each time the average man does business with a guild, he pays the costs of monopoly: poorer service and higher prices, including that extra the guild member tacks on to his bill to make up for the earnings he lost while he was in school.* Our meetings with the guilds grow more frequent, for guilds are spreading in American life. Each year a host of groups are lobbying the legislatures in an effort to make themselves into monopolies; sometimes they lose, but they'll be back next year, and once they gain their monopoly they never lose it. Lieberman dragged together this list of people outside the usual professions who are guilded in one state or another:

---

* The doctors' guild, by a clever application of the third-party principle, has managed to bill the average man twice for doctors' education. The federal government now pays about half the cost of training physicians in medical school. So the average man with his taxes helps put through school the very person who later will overcharge him as a member of the guild.

abstracters, boiler inspectors, private detectives, egg graders, electricians, electrologists, elevator operators, guide-dog trainers, hoisting engineers, homeopaths, horseshoers, librarians, manicurists, masseurs, mechano-therapists, milk certifiers, mine inspectors, motor vehicle dealers and salesmen(!), motion picture operators, naturopaths, occultists, pest controllers, physical thera-pists, drugless physicians, plumbers, psychologists, certi-fied shorthand reporters, sanitarians, social workers, watchmakers, well drillers, and yacht brokers and sales-men.

The logical end result is for everyone to belong to a guild. Then everyone can be simultaneously exploiter and victim, winner and loser, until the whole system is paralyzed. That apparently is what happened in the me-dieval city of Liége, where government collapsed after a long period of guild rule.

The average man who finds his way into a guild after his stretched-out years in school is in the ambiguous po-sition known as transfer screwing. He is taking every-body outside his guild; but the other guilds, and the other screwers, are all taking him. If he belongs to one of the more modest guilds, his balance of payments may not be favorable enough to justify the years he spent in school. He belongs to a monopoly, but it just isn't good enough, like the player who ends up with only Baltic and Mediter-ranean.

Industrial monopoly is more familiar than the guild variety. It flourishes in the modern sectors of the econ-omy, those whose leaders have grasped the fact that cold capitalist competition is an affliction they need not en-dure. This is, in Galbraith's term, the "planning sector": those firms that take no noise from the consumer, but rather dictate what he wants and how much he'll have to pay for it. The "market sector," where competition survives, is for the old-fashioned and the retarded. How much of America is under monopoly control depends on your choice of definition. One widely accepted measure is the four-firm 50 per cent rule: if an oligopoly of no more than four firms controls 50 per cent or more of the market in that field, the prices will rise to monopoly-like levels. By this measure, more than half of all manufacturing, and at least 35–45 per cent of all marketing, take place under monopoly conditions. If anything, this measure understates the extent of monopoly. The industry where the most notorious monopolistic pricing prevails, oil, does not fit the four-firm 50 per cent definition; neither do those industries in which several ostensible independent producers are controlled by a single outsider, as the leading copper producers are controlled by a single bank. The total annual cost of this lack of competition to the consumer, according to who is doing the figuring, may be anywhere from $16 billion, the most conservative estimate, to $100 billion (Ralph Nader), or even $230 billion (Senator Philip Hart). Although calculating the exact surcharge that a lack of price competition adds to each item you buy is understandably difficult, it is possible to identify some of the components that comprise monopoly pricing. Economist William Shepherd of the University of Michigan has estimated that the inefficiency caused by a monopoly market structure adds a 5 per cent surcharge to the cost of each product; and another 3 per cent is due to a misallocation of corporate resources because of the lack of feedback from a competitive market. Putting this in another perspective, this means that these two results of monopoly alone add a penny to the cost of each Trac II razor blade we buy.

It is important to realize that monopoly is by no means limited to technologically complex industries like aircraft engines. If we were willing to invest in a printing press and had a flair for composing saccharine lyrics to "Dad on Father's Day," it would be relatively easy to set up a greeting card business in our basement. But rather than serving as a bastion of the free enterprise system, the structure of the greeting card business looks suspiciously like that of the automobile industry. Playing the role of GM is Hallmark, the company that has made the fifty-cent birthday card a drugstore staple. In the same way, expensive technology cannot be used to justify why the razor blade industry is totally subject to the whims of Gillette or that chewing gum is virtually synonymous with Wrigley. Names like these are almost as much a part of the language as Kleenex and Xerox, and each time we put a piece of Doublemint under a movie seat we have just paid another monopoly surcharge.

Admittedly, most people do not buy such products as locomotives, primary aluminum, blown glass, or blast furnaces—though their monopoly prices ultimately come out of the consumer's pocket. Still, in everyday life we get plenty of opportunities to reflect on the effects of monopoly. Here are a few selections from a list of common products that come from monopolistic industries:

Razors and razor blades
Sewing machines
Electric lamps
Soaps and other detergents
Pharmaceutical preparations
Chewing gum

Chocolate and cocoa products
Photographic equipment
Householder laundry equipment
Typewriters
Householder vacuum cleaners and refrigerators

Finally, if the consumer decides in exasperation to blow up the store, he will have to pay extra for his materials, explosives being an industry in which four firms hold 72 per cent of the market.

In recent years even the once-competitive food and food-related industries have begun to taste the pleasures of monopoly. Profits in the monopolized parts of the industry are twice as high as in the remaining areas of food competition and, according to a Federal Trade Commission study, the overall result is to raise the public's eating bill by $2.6 billion a year. Monopoly goes particularly well with soft drinks, where four firms (Coca-Cola, Pepsi-Cola, Royal Crown Cola and Seven-Up) control 70 per cent of the market. These firms sell their syrup to bottlers, who in turn sell to the stores. But each bottler has his exclusive territory, so a store cannot get more than one bid on any brand of bottled synthetic. With competition, the store (and eventually the public) could get, if not twice as much for a nickel, at least a lower price than it now has to pay.

The monopoly surcharge the average man pays for all those goods goes to support socialism for the rich. It must not be supposed, however, that the surcharge all goes to extra profit, for, as noted earlier, relaxation is an equally important goal of monopolists. Accordingly, a large part of the extra amount paid by the consumer is devoted to waste. It does not show up in the books as profit; it just leaks out around the edges. One example from an anti-trust case concerns a conspiracy to fix the prices of folding chairs sold to schools. The conspirators raised the price of the chairs by 32 per cent, but of that amount, only 9 per cent appeared as extra profit, the rest having dribbled away in waste. When the price fix was broken up, competition evidently forced more efficiency on the companies involved, for prices fell by the full 32 per cent that they had been jacked up, not just the 9 per cent of excess profit.

The waste in the American system of monopoly tends to bear out those gloomy critics who have been telling us for decades that socialism is bound to be inefficient. This is particularly true when a private monopoly collaborates with its government counterpart—pooling, as it were, their reserves of incompetence. The wreck of the Penn Central Railroad is the classic case of waste over profit—a transport monopoly steered into bankruptcy by a management inept even by the easygoing standards of the railroads, aided lackadaisically by its government regulators. Karl Marx would doubtless have rent his beard at this example of socialism gone insane, but Joseph Stalin, product of a less idealistic age, would have understood. Had he lived to see the Penn Central driven off the rails, Stalin might have given a chuckle for the comrades who had staged a disaster reminiscent of his own stupendous blunders in Russian agriculture.

The purest form of American monopoly socialism is, of course, the defense industry. Here the fuel of national security rockets the natural inefficiencies of both monopolies to heights never scaled before by mankind—no one, not the Emperor Caligula, nor the highway lobby, nor the Chinese contractors who sold the Great Wall to the Ming emperors, nor yet Joseph Stalin himself, no one in history has wasted so much on so little in so few years. The case of Lockheed is again illuminating. Favored with the opportunity to make profits beyond the dreams of most men's greed, Lockheed chose instead to loaf its way to the edge of bankruptcy. Most of Lockheed's troubles have grown out of its contract for the C-5A transport plane. Now, 1969 was the last year in which Congress authorized the military to buy planes under that contract. Yet each year since then Congress has voted hundreds of millions for cost overruns on that project, which produces no planes—*no planes at all,* just cost overruns. Congress and the Administration had perceived the fundamental truth that no one needed the C-5A anyhow, while all involved needed the cost overruns to avoid the alternatives of work or welfare. John Connally was right after all: there was indeed no reason to hound Lockheed to perform.

The principle involved here was stated succinctly by Major General "Zeke" Zoeckler, program chief at the Pentagon on the famous F-111, the fighter-bomber on which General Dynamics rang up a cost overrun of 500 per cent. Responding to critics, the general explained that attaining "social goals" necessarily involved waste. In the course of his explanation, he made the observation that "inefficiency is national policy." Until then it had been widely assumed that inefficiency was a by-product of government policy, not the policy itself. Incidentally, the average man has here a rare opportunity to cut himself in on a tiny bit of the action. If he works for a monopoly firm, chances are much better that he can loaf on the job than if his employer is under the lash of competition.

He should, however, avoid the smaller defense contractors. These firms are likely to be forced by the Pentagon to live up to their contracts, evidently on the grounds that they do not yet qualify for socialism for the rich, whereas the big contractors with the worst records of meeting their commitments are, following the Zoeckler principle, the ones that show the highest profits.

The respective sagas of Litton Industries and A. Ernest Fitzgerald round out this aspect of monopoly and government. Litton, a relative newcomer in the field, has been coming on fast. In recent years, it has scored excellent cost overruns on two big shipbuilding contracts for the military; on one comic occasion, a ship Litton was building had to be cut in half and then put right back together to satisfy some obscure front-office principle. Such fidelity to General Zoeckler's law did not go unrewarded. Litton, fourteenth on the list of defense contractors in 1968, moved up to ninth after the election of Richard Nixon, and in 1972, after Nixon's re-election, Roy Ash, Litton's president, became director of the Office of Management and Budget, a vantage point from which he could extend the principles of monopoly socialism from its military pioneers to the rest of the U. S. Government. Fitzgerald, on the other hand, is a believer in free enterprise capitalism. He was fired from his job in the Pentagon (he was later reinstated over the protests of his Pentagon superiors) when he tried to blow the whistle on Lockheed's C-5A. With Ash's accession to power, and the suspension of the capitalist sympathizer Fitzgerald, the triumph of American socialism was complete.

Government does not boast of its liaison with monopoly. American policy is clothed, in the modern manner, in verbal apparel designed to make the unwary see the opposite of reality. Government spokesmen are loud in their devotion to free enterprise and capitalist competition. Whenever the economy is sickly, we are told that controls would be bad because they would interfere with the workings of the free market—which tends to distract us from observing that government is helping the free market out of business without controls. The illusion is fostered also by two forms of governmental pretense: the anti-trust laws and the regulatory agencies.

Anti-trust laws have decorated the law books since the Sherman Act was passed in 1890. There is little in the record to suggest that anti-trust law has had any deterrent effect on American monopolies; rather it seems like a fig leaf modestly concealing the harsh fact of consumer exploitation. Take, for example, the case of General Motors, possibly the most glaring and most expensive to the public of all American monopoly enterprises. In the last forty years, seventeen anti-trust actions have been brought against GM, and the company has lost all but three of them. But none of those cases has lessened General Motors' grip on the car market, and the largest fine it ever had to pay, $56,000, amounted to less than 10 per cent of GM Chairman Richard Gerstenberg's 1973 pay of $923,000. In fairness to the members of the anti-trust division of the Justice Department, it should probably be said that there is something incongruous in the idea that they could take on a firm with the power of General Motors—it sounds like Finland attacking the Soviet Union.

On the rare occasions when an anti-trust move is successful in affecting what happens in the market—always against a relatively small opponent—the reward to the consumer is so high as to suggest the vast benefits that the average man would gain if the monopolized half of our economy were returned to competition. When in 1964 a price-fixing conspiracy among bakers in the state of Washington was broken up, the price of bread dropped 20 per cent, and when a conspiracy in pricing the antibiotic drug tetracycline was ended, its price went down by no less than 75 per cent. These examples, however, are exceptions to the rule that government plays with monopoly, not against it.

The other form of government pretense, regulation, functions to buttress monopoly and its by-product, waste. The government regulatory agencies, as is well known, typically end up as captives of the monopolists they are supposed to be combatting. The agency is created in a burst of indignation and functions well with its first enthusiastic leaders: then the job becomes routine, and the public loses interest; the next generation of regulators is subject only to the pressures of the industry they watch over, and soon they slide comfortably into the arms of the monopolist. (In earlier chapters we have noted the failures of regulation in banking, the stock market, and nursing homes.) It is significant that the new Federal Product Safety Commission has been in the news frequently since its formation in 1973. If it follows the life history of other regulatory agencies, the initial zeal should wear off within the next year or two and bureaucratic torpor will begin to set in. Regulatory commissions become a resting place for semi-retired hacks—Nicholas Johnson, late of the Federal Communications Commission, is just about the only federal regulator in recent years who has visibly rocked his industry's boat. Once the agency has decayed to its normal state, it can bring its bureaucratic viewpoint to bear on the problem and thereby enhance the monopolists' natural tendency to reduce competition, raise prices, and multiply waste.

The value to monopoly of pretended government regulation was seen as long ago as 1894 by one Richard Olney, the U. S. Attorney General of the time. Here is Olney telling a railroad president why he shouldn't support abolishing the Interstate Commerce Commission:

> The Commission . . . is, or can be made, of great use to the railroads. It satisfies the popular clamor for a government supervision of railroads, at the same time that the supervision is almost entirely nominal. Furthermore, the older such a commission gets to be, the more inclined it will be to take the business and railroad view of things. It becomes a sort of barrier between the business corporations and the people . . .

The Interstate Commerce Commission, which presided languidly over the wreck of the Penn Central, is generally conceded to be the worst of the sorry lot of regulators. It is thought to be so incompetent that it not only runs counter to the public interest, but it also isn't even a very effective handmaiden to industry. The ICC manages to raise the cost of transportation in the purported interest of competition: railroads, for example, are required to charge artificially high freight rates so that truckers can compete with them over the same routes. The ICC is notable also for the mindless detail in which it regulates transportation. Freight is required to move over specified routes, often going far out of its way, for some long-forgotten reason. Not long ago, in a triumph of the regulatory mind, the ICC received—and denied—a petition for a reduction in the transport rate on yak fat. Yak fat consumers, whoever they are, will continue to pay more, as will the rest of us, because of ICC. One estimate is that the hand of the ICC in transportation costs the consumer from $4 to $8.7 billion a year—a cost that reaches the average man in higher prices on anything he buys that ever took a trip on a train or a truck. The Federal Maritime Commission and the Civil Aeronautics Board weigh in, in their cost to the consumer, at $2.5 billion and $3 billion respectively. To get the full flavor of CAB's performance in regulating the airlines, the consumer should take a flight on Pacific Southwest Airlines (PSA), which is unregulated because it operates only within the state of California. On Pacific, he will pay about 30 per cent less per mile than he would on a CAB-regulated flight; Pacific's price for the Los Angeles-San Francisco run is about half the regulated price elsewhere for flights of similar distance. Admittedly, PSA avoids some of the wasteful practices we associate with commercial airlines. Like the Eastern shuttle, PSA operates a one-class service. Since first class does not pay its own way, this means that our coach fare helps cover the airline's deficit on its luxury service: in effect, the rich travelers in first class are subsidized by the peasantry in coach—the screwing of the average traveler proceeds as usual even at 30,000 feet.† Once again, the extra amount the regulators charge the consumer seems to go to waste rather than profit, since airlines are not in most years a particularly profitable business.

The liaison between government and monopoly is expressed in hard dollar language during election cam-

† In March 1974, the CAB ordered a revision of fares and in the process admitted that under its rules "The coach passenger is now and for many years has been in effect subsidizing the luxury travel of the first-class passenger." At the same time, the board firmly rejected a proposal that the airlines be allowed to engage in price competition.

paigns. What is remarkable is the rate of return that can be earned on a skillful investment in a politician. On Wall Street, a short-term investment that enables you to double or triple your money is the stuff that legends are made of. In politics, such a meager profit would be considered a bad investment. Senator Russell Long of Louisiana, who certainly should know, once observed of campaign contributions that "investments in this area can be viewed as monetary bread cast upon the waters to be returned one thousand-fold." The repayment comes in the form of higher prices for regulated industries or government contracts fat enough to pay off the contribution and leave a lot more for the giver. Investment in Senator Long may pay unusually high dividends, but his basic point is sound: each dollar an industry invests in an officeholder must be paid for by many more dollars out of the consumer's pocket. The 1972 campaign produced some fine examples. Dairymen contributed $422,000 to the Nixon campaign, and two days later the Department of Agriculture raised milk support prices, which had the effect of costing milk drinkers an extra $500 to $700 million a year. The diarymen also had to put out about $2 million for senators' campaigns, so that the rate of return on investment—though still better than one hundred to one—was less than would appear from the Nixon transaction alone. Another case, that of financier Robert L. Vesco, actually exceeded Senator Long's guidelines. Vesco wanted to get off the hook on charges brought by the Securities and Exchange Commission that he looted $224 million in stockholder money from the International Overseas Services mutual fund complex. Maurice Stans, Nixon's finance chairman, suggested a contribution of $250,000, all but

$50,000 of it in $100 bills. Had the deal not fallen through as a by-product of Watergate, Vesco's return on his investment would have been almost exactly one thousand to one. The same game goes on routinely in state legislatures with the public utilities, whose prices are state-regulated. Utilities invest heavily in state officeholders and are rewarded with higher prices, plus a decent cloak in the form of creative accounting that conceals their excess profits. An example is the Colonial Pipeline, whose regulated profits, by friendly accounting, are figured to be under 10 per cent. That's on its "total assets." But of those assets, only 10 per cent were put up by the stockholders, the rest being borrowed from banks and insurance companies. If the return is calculated on the stockholders' investment, it comes out to a profit of 95 per cent. But the regulators don't figure that way.

Critics since time out of mind have been advocating the public financing of campaigns because, among other reasons, it would save the average man a lot of money. The reasoning is simple, if not entirely convincing. Why give the dairymen $500 million so they can pay $422,000 to Nixon? Why not give the $442,000 directly to Nixon through public campaign finances, eliminate the middle man, in this case the dairy lobby, and save $500 million on the milk bill? Monopolists naturally don't like the idea of public financing, and neither does a considerable section of public opinion. Some people have a natural revulsion against paying tax money to candidates so they can get elected to positions of power and privilege. There is, in any event, no assurance that public financing of campaigns would produce the desired result. Why, after all, should officeholders stop selling their services to private interests just because the public is paying for their campaigns? If public financing were put into effect, we might find that investment in a senator still paid a return of a thousand to one.

The themes of this chapter all come together in perfect symmetry with the case of International Telephone and Telegraph. ITT is of course the worldwide multiglomerate that received its greatest advance in consumer recognition with the publication in 1972 of the memo by its lobbyist, Dita Beard, discussing an offer of $400,000 for the 1972 Republican convention in return for the dropping of Justice Department objections to ITT's acquisition by merger of the $2 billion Hartford Fire Insurance Co. (That one is far over the thousand-to-one ratio, by the way.) The publicity about the deal did not prevent ITT from continuing to pick up more companies after Hartford. By now chances are fairly good that the average person is now working, has worked, or will in the future work for an ITT subsidiary. ITT makes most of its money through its government connections, and the skills it has acquired over the years have enabled the company to survive adversity with profits unruffled. During World War II, the company worked for both sides, much like Milo Minderbinder in Joseph Heller's *Catch-22*. One ITT firm made the Focke-Wulf fighter plane for Nazi Germany, another made electronic equipment for the U. S. Air Force. After the war, in a remarkably bold stroke of lobbying, ITT actually got the U. S. Foreign Claims Settlement Commission to give it $27 million for the damage American bombers had done to its German war plants.

The difference between the monopolist—the American

Medical Association or ITT—and government becomes fuzzy. Ultimately, we cannot tell their faces apart and we begin to suspect that, in Taylor Branch's phrase, we're all working for the Penn Central.

12

Government: Subsidies to Those That Have

SUBSIDIES ARE THE LEAST FAMILIAR of the methods by which government screws the average man. As recently as 1972, economist Carl Shoup was able to say: "Federal subsidies are the great fiscal unknown. The federal budget presents no comprehensive summary of subsidies. Most public finance textbooks in the United States either do not list the word 'subsidy' in their indexes or give only a page or two of reference."

Cloaked by the general indifference, subsidies have been coming on fast, and can now take their rightful place alongside the income tax code as instruments to implement socialism for the rich. Former Senator Fred R. Harris made the point when he testified before the Joint Economic Committee, which had just made the first study ever of federal subsidies. Harris said: "Subsidies are to modern politics what patronage was to the politics of the 19th century. Subsidies, in other words, are the lifeblood, tainted to be sure, of our electoral system; and this is precisely the reason why it is so hard to eliminate a subsidy once established. . . . Many of our historians and journalists, suffering from a sort of historical hangover, continue to focus on politics primarily from the standpoint of who gets what job in the wake of victory and how he uses or misuses his position for financial gain. But the real raid on the public treasury, which makes mere graft pale by comparison, is taking place elsewhere"—in subsidies. Note that Harris shows here his understanding of the modern world: all the good swindles are legal; breaking the law is the mark of an amateur crook.

Here we will be describing two kinds of subsidies. One is the federal variety, which comes sometimes in the form of cash and sometimes as a tax break. The other is subsidy in the form of exemptions from local property taxes. The latter all operate, like income tax loopholes, on the fail-to-collect principle: rather than issuing cash to your friends, you help them by not collecting taxes from them. The consumption of public funds is thus less conspicuous.

Subsidies are in theory justified, to the extent that any-one still bothers to try to justify them, on the grounds that government is paying to accomplish something that would not otherwise happen. Each subsidy, in some for-gotten day when it originated, was supposed to help someone, not just by paying them cash, but by paying them to do something useful.*

Whatever their origins, subsidies now conform to two general rules: most of the money goes to people who are already well off; most of it goes to pay people to do what

* We are omitting here the so-called transfer payments, payments like Social Security, disability, unemployment, welfare, and so on, which are intended to transfer income to those in need without asking any per-formance in return. But the general point about subsidies—those that have, get—applies even here. Those programs supply $296 per person to peo-ple making less than $5,000—and $1,146, or nearly four times as much, to people making $25–50,000.

they would do anyhow, without the subsidy. As President Franklin D. Roosevelt said in one case, subsidies go "not for the needy but for the greedy." That was in 1943, and Roosevelt was vetoing a bill to support timber growers. Congress overrode his veto, and now timber growers get $140 million a year in tax breaks—$100 million of which goes to the five biggest companies in the industry.

Subsidizing industry to control pollution is, it would seem, a fine thing to do. Here is how it works, under a provision in the 1969 Tax Reform Act allowing rapid depreciation on investment to clean up water pollution. If a corporation buys a $150,000 pollution control device, it will receive a subsidy of:

+$11,952, if the company's profits are above $25,000;

+$5,479, if its profits are less than $25,000;

+$0, if the company has no profits, or a loss;

And $0, if the company spends its pollution control money on measures that require no capital expense, like using low-sulfur fuel.

The effects of such subsidies reach the average man only by a roundabout route, when he pays a bit more tax to support those who have established themselves on subsidy. One subsidy, however, until recently reached each American each time he sat himself at table—the farm subsidies. Until the 1973 changes, whose effects are still unclear, the farm subsidies were costing the consumer about $10 billion a year, half in direct payments to farmers and half in crop limitations that had the effect of raising food prices an average of 15 per cent.

Farm subsidies historically were sold on the grounds that they protect our sturdy yeoman farmer—a good man to have around in a crisis, as was proved on Concord Bridge so many years ago. That's not how it worked out, according to a detailed study by economist Charles Schultze, the one-time federal Budget Director. Schultze found that the wealthiest 7 per cent of farm families got federal benefits averaging $14,000 per family, bringing their net farm income up to $27,500. Meanwhile, the poorest 40 per cent of farmers got $300 apiece, for an average income of $1,100. Of the total subsidy to the farms, 63 per cent went to the wealthiest 19 per cent, while the poorest half of the farm population shared 9 per cent of the pie.

The consumer may have trouble digesting all this. The government was picking out the richest farmers, who already made more than the average eater, and was writing them checks that doubled their pay, while the poor yeoman remained just that. Still, the eating public, unhappy about food prices, has aimed little of its fury at the farm subsidies. This was true even in 1972, when the farm swindle went international, and the beneficiaries were not just rich American socialists, but real foreign socialists, over there in that Russia. That was the year of the great Russian grain deal, which, besides enriching a few insiders in the grain business (who were alert enough to ask for a tax break on their profits), had as its main effect the driving up of food prices in the United States, so that Russians were paying less than Americans for bread made from American wheat. Even that did not arouse much visible anger, perhaps because the whole transaction was so complicated. Its meaning was not hard to comprehend, however, as Lester G. Maddox of Georgia proved when he distilled its essence into one sentence: "The Russians got our grain, the Administration got credit for the deal, the speculators got the profit, and the rest of us got the bill."

The abandonment in 1973 of the farm subsidies will not in any case help the average man, something he could figure out for himself by looking at last week's food bill. In keeping with its general policy of encouraging monopoly, the federal government in recent years has helped a few huge food companies gain control over agricultural markets that were once highly competitive. The resulting monopoly pricing of domestic food plus government subsidized export sales were the root causes of the abrupt rise in food prices in 1973–74. The subsidies were no longer needed—it was possible to screw the consumer without them.

When Washington is disturbed by public complaint about subsidies, the official in charge will frequently invoke the small-change defense: O.K., the program doesn't make much sense, but the amount it costs you is trivial, so why don't you think about something else? A good recent example is the federal subsidy to the maritime industry, which totals about three quarters of a billion dollars.

About one third of that is paid to fourteen shipping companies to subsidize the difference in earnings between American and foreign seamen. The companies pay Filipino wages out of their own money, and the taxpayers make up the difference between that and an acceptable American wage—which in this industry runs between $16,000 and $30,000 a year. Since the government picks up the difference, the companies have no reason to hold down wages. Each seaman's job is subsidized by about $12,000, considerably above the average wage in the United States. Another third of the total subsidy goes to support the construction of ships in American yards; the 13,000 workers in this part of the industry are subsidized an average of $8,000 apiece. The rest of the subsidy goes in payments to shippers who, under Buy-American rules, are required to send their goods in American vessels. One result of all this, of course, is to guarantee that the American industry will never be able to compete in the international marketplace.

Careful study has been unable to uncover any valid reason for the maritime subsidies—they are useless to the national defense, the balance of payments, the general welfare, and, in fact, everyone except the cozy handful who receive them. This being so, Maritime Administrator Emory S. Land had to tack back to the small-change argument in his defense: "The operating differential subsidy [on wages], per capita, amounts to the cost of one Scotch highball. The construction differential subsidy may amount to the cost of one bottle of beer. It seems to me we might relinquish two libations per annum and support a proper shipbuilding industry and a prosperous U.S. Merchant Marine."

That's a fine sentiment, but unfortunately it's impossible to put it into practice because of the third-party principle. Third-partying, normally the government's first line of defense, here prevents us from hoisting two empty glasses to the U.S. Merchant Marine. With all the money third-partied into a lump sum, we have no way of knowing who will get the proceeds of those two drinks we just failed to have. It might be J. Paul Getty, asking us to go dry so he doesn't have to pay his income tax, or Senator Eastland soliciting for his farm subsidies, or anyone else on the subsidy take—yet we may not choose, if we've just been listening to Mr. Land, to do our non-drinking for someone other than the merchant marine. About this time, it may occur to the average man that it would be a great idea if everyone *else* gave up a scotch and a beer so that he could live like a shipping magnate. This dream is dashed by the harsh reality of Catch-85. As described earlier, Catch-85 holds that in our system the benefits of governmental favors like subsidies or tax loopholes must be effectively restricted to no more than 15 per cent of the population, so that the other 85 per cent can pay the freight. The trouble with the average man is that there are too many of him. The end result, if everyone passed those two drinks to the person on his left, is that we'd all end up with the same amount in our glasses.

Small change is far from the only defense invoked for subsidy. In his book *Public Policy Toward Aviation,* economist Jeremy J. Warford detailed the four predictable arguments put forth by anyone enjoying a federal subsidy. Private aircraft make up 98 per cent of the 130,000 planes in the country. They get subsidies of various kinds, the great majority of the money originating in Washington, that work out to $3,500 per year per plane. That kind of success requires that we pay attention to the plane owners' tactics. These are the four main arguments put forward for the aircraft subsidy, and, in one form or another, most other kinds of governmental largesse:

Highest Common Denominator: if someone else is getting it, we should too. The Aircraft Owners and Pilots Association will point out that other forms of transport are subsidized—autos through free highway construction, and, as noted, the maritime industry—so equity demands that the planes get their share as well. The trick here, then, is to find some similarity between yourself and someone else who is already on the take. The principle was affirmed in another context by John B. Connally, the theoretician of socialism for the rich, whom we met earlier in the Lockheed case. At issue was the so-called

DISC loophole, under which U.S. firms with subsidiaries abroad are able to escape some of their taxes. This, it was said, was unfair to firms that don't have foreign interests. True enough, said Connally, and the solution is to create another loophole to take care of those industrialists left out of the first one. It should be noted that Highest Common Denominator is limited by Catch-85: you have to be a member of the 15 per cent in order for your argument to be taken seriously.

Don't Hurt the Little Guy: if you take away the subsidy from the executive's Lear jet, what you're doing is harming the flying proletariat in their Piper Cubs. Now, aside from the question whether any proletarians own planes of any kind, that argument would seem to be in conflict with Catch-85, under which the little guy is by definition excluded. The contradiction is more apparent than real. First, there is no requirement that subsidy arguments hold water by any standard. Second, as explained elsewhere, Catch-85 allows a token proletarian or two to be included in any given swindle as long as their presence serves to buttress the position of the 15 per cent.

National Defense: if it is at all possible, find some way in which your subsidy helps hold at bay the foreign hordes. The private airmen see themselves as an informal reserve air force, ready to go into action if the enemy should knock out the major airports, making it impossible for the big planes to fly. Accordingly, as one pilot spokesman explained to the Secretary of Transportation, "it would be a major advantage to the Communist plan to eliminate the vast facilities and National Defense Capabilities of general aviation's fleet of over 110,000 planes." Warding off that major Communist advantage is cheap at $3,500 a plane a year. Others on the subsidy side of the economy have used similar reasoning. The jewel in the crown of the highway lobby, the "highway trust fund," was voted for what originally was named the Interstate and *Defense* Highway System, and the oil import quotas were originally sold as a way to prevent us from getting hooked on foreign suppliers.

Extraordinary Public Benefits: a catchall category essential for those who cannot qualify under national defense, this one requires the subsidy-holders to figure out someone, somewhere, who has cause to care whether their enterprise lives or dies. Imagination is the key. The reader may wish to pause for a moment and try to figure out what public benefit general aviation can claim beyond denying the Communists that major advantage. All right, here it is: "General aviation helps to arrest the decline of sparsely populated regions, thereby conferring benefits . . . for which the society as a whole, rather than the aircraft operators themselves, should be called upon to pay." That argument seems pretty inventive in an admittedly difficult situation.

The creative talent to discover such rationalizations and the energy to pursue them through the corridors of power are supplied by lobbies that are in part financed by the same average man who has just given up part of his booze ration to pay for the fruits of that lobbying. Since 1962, corporate lobbying expenses have been tax-deductible, while public interest lobbying (like, say, Ralph Nader's) is not deductible. The reasoning seems to be that if the rich are entitled to socialism, they should at least be allowed to deduct the expenses they incur in defending what is rightfully theirs. Public interest lobbyists, on the other hand, represent the non-rich, who are private enterprisers; a free ride on a government tax break would be contrary to their ideology. So, if the average man decides to go down to Washington to fight for his shot and a beer, he will pay 48 per cent of his opponents' costs (the value of the corporate lobbying deduction) plus all his own costs; if he chooses to stay home and do nothing, he will be billed only for the 48 per cent.

The other great subsidy by government, exemption and underassessment on the property tax, is quite a different matter. The subject is diffuse and little known. The action is not concentrated in Washington, but scattered through thousands of local tax offices where decisions on who pays how much are made and unmade. Fairly good figures exist on tax exemption, but the other half of the subject, underassessment, is a form of corruption and therefore does not make the statistics; we have only scattered hints about the magnitude of underassessment.

Enough is known to conclude that tax exemption alone is costly to the average non-exempt man. One third of all property in the U.S. is exempt from the property tax. According to a 1966 study, the amount of tax not collected on that property, under that year's rates, was $12.3 billion—an amount that had to be made up by those properties that did pay taxes. That works out to $310 for every family in the nation (not just property owners). Of that $310, $217 went for exemption on publicly owned property, and $93 for private exempt property. That was in 1966, and since then both property taxes and the rate of exemption have been rising. By now, all the above figures would be considerably higher; in particular, the amount that non-government exempt property costs each family must be well over $100 a year. That cost applies to property owners and non-owners alike. Owners pay, of course, through higher taxes on their property to make up for those who are not paying. Non-owners pay indirectly because others' higher tax costs are passed on to them: by the landlord in higher rent, by stores and factories in higher prices. Everyone pays the bill for the tax-exempt.

We can, with these figures, roughly calculate whether we fall in the win or the loss column. Leave aside government property for the moment, and take only that $100 per family for private tax-exempts. This means that any family that does not have an exemption worth $100 in taxes (actual taxes, not assessment) is in the losers' category. Homeowners who get those tax breaks for veterans and the elderly, a reduction in assessment which typically runs around $500, are still net losers unless their lower assessment results in a tax saving of more than $100. That's only the national average; since property taxes are determined locally, the situation will vary greatly from town to town. As for underassessment, each of us has to make his own estimate of how much our fellow residents in the tax district are hustling down at the assessor's office.

Getting on *The Free List* (the title of Alfred Balk's excellent study) means it has been decided that whatever is happening on that property is so worthwhile that other people should pay the taxes on the place. Churches and schools are the biggest and best established of the tax-exempts. Although churches have been getting off on their taxes at least since the time of the pharaohs, there is nothing in the U. S. Constitution that says it has to be, and in fact during the nineteenth century some states taxed church property. President Ulysses S. Grant, not remembered as one of the nineteenth-century's leading anti-clerics, said in his 1875 message to Congress that taxing the churches was a good idea: "I would also call your attention to the importance of correcting an evil that, if permitted to continue, will probably lead to great trouble in our land before the close of the 19th century. It is the accumulation of vast amounts of untaxed church property. . . . By 1900, without check, it is safe to say this property will reach a sum exceeding $3 billion. So vast a sum, receiving all the protection and benefits of government without bearing its proportion of the burdens and expenses of the same, will not be looked upon acquiescently by those who have to pay the taxes."

Grant underestimated the acquiescence of Americans, and by the mid-sixties his "vast sum" had ballooned to $110 billion. (Of that total, $60 billion was Roman Catholic, $40 billion Protestant, and $8–10 billion Jewish.) Even some church leaders have shown signs of worry at getting that far into Caesar's business. Noting that churches enjoy tax exemption for businesses they own as well as their property, Eugene Carson Blake, general secretary of the World Council of Churches, concluded that "it is not unreasonable to prophesy that with reasonably prudent management the churches ought to be able to control the whole economy of the nation within the predictable future." ITT would, of course, disagree.

Churchmen have proved themselves adept at stretching the holy cloth to cover as much as possible of their holdings. In Minnesota, the Oblate Fathers got an exemption on eighty acres of lakefront property on the grounds that it was a "rest area and retreat" for their members, although when the assessor went out to look he found only one priest at play in the fields of the lord. The Catholic Archdiocese of Hartford bought 121.5 acres of land for $23,500; got the land classified as a tax-exempt cemetery; buried a single body there; and later removed the body and sold the land for $607,000. Other residents of that tax district—New Britain, Connecticut—filled in the $200,000 which the archdiocese saved over the years by not paying taxes on its one-man cemetery. One great value of the church exemption is that you do not need to get up on Sunday morning to make your contribution: the system will add it to your taxes while you sleep.

Schools—which in terms of private property means mostly colleges—also range far out of the classroom in their search for tax exemption. In Michigan, the University of Michigan owns, tax-exempt, the Willow Run Airport, and Michigan State owns a department store in Lansing. Back in 1855, Northwestern got itself a charter that specified that "all property of whatever kind or description belonging to or owned by said corporation shall be forever free from taxation for any and all purposes." Armed with that hunting license, the Northwestern Corporation now owns, among other properties, Chicago buildings leased to Pepsi-Cola, Illinois Bell Telephone, and the National Biscuit Co.; a supermarket, a medical center, and a bottling plant built for Pepsi—all tax-free. The Chrysler Building in New York is tax-exempt, because it is owned by Cooper Union University, at a cost to other city taxpayers of $1 million a year. There are limits, however, as New York University discovered when a court ordered it to pay taxes on its spaghetti factory. Under the third-party principle, the average man finds himself an automatic supporter of whatever private education exists in his community. If he lives in Cambridge, Massachusetts, he might as well go to Harvard, since he's helping to subsidize the tuition anyway. Possibly that's what Charles W. Eliot, president of Harvard, meant when he said that tax-exempt institutions are what make a community worth living in.

A whole host of organizations that give off a vague air of benevolence have maneuvered their way on to the free list. A list drawn up by the International Association of Assessing Officers mentions: ". . . the YMCA, YWCA, Elks, Eagles, 4-H, Red Cross, Salvation Army, Knights of Columbus, Masonic lodges, American Legion, VFW, Boy and Girl Scouts, state bar associations, the DAR . . ." Some of the exempt organizations fit Balk's description: "the indigent rich." One example is property owned by the local chamber of commerce, and another is luxurious church-owned retirement homes—one of which charges $23,000 as an "entry fee." When the indigent rich in California were campaigning for a state constitutional amendment broadening access to tax exemption, they combined the small-change and social benefit arguments. While the loss in the tax base would cost the taxpayer a mere one cent per $100 of assessed value, the proponents said, the additional health and welfare services would save the entire exemption cost; the taxpayer was not, of course, to be allowed to choose which health and welfare services he wished to support.

Government-owned property is a special case. At first glance, it would seem that taxing government property would result in chasing one's own tail: tax the property and then raise taxes to pay those taxes. That would be true except for the fact that government property is very unevenly spread out, with cities generally, and capitals especially, carrying more than the average share of freeloading federal and state buildings. In the nation's capital, Washington, more than half of all property is on the free list, and in state capitals the rate runs from one third to half. The effect is to double the tax rate for those properties remaining off the exempt list. The government argument that its properties should be exempt because they bring jobs and business into the community generally finds more favor with government than with the remaining taxpayers. Government officials, like churchmen and educators, have proved skillful at extending the blanket of tax exemption to cover friends in the private sector. One example is the Port of New York Authority, whose statutory purpose, long since forgotten, was to aid transportation in the New York area. The Port Authority has littered the city and its environs with tax-exempt enterprises that include hotels, restaurants, and even a drive-in movie and a miniature golf course. In the late 1960s the Port Authority began building in lower Manhattan two monstrous office buildings whose name, the World Trade Center, provides their only connection with transportation; when the twin towers were completed in the early 1970s, at a cost of $600 million, they seized from the Chrysler Building the title of World's Tallest Tax Exemption. The Pentagon, not surprisingly, has found a way to put tax exemption to work for the benefit of its industrial partners. Over the years the Pentagon has acquired more than $2.5 billion worth of plants, which it leases out to its contractors: both feel that these plants should enjoy the government's right to tax exemption (giving those contractors an edge over competitors who use their own plants). The state of Michigan disagreed, and in a law upheld by the Supreme Court over government-industry objections, it successfully hung taxes on its Pentagon plants. Thereupon, Los Angeles County began collecting taxes from its Pentagon factories, including property leased to the Defense Department's great and good friend General Dynamics. That was too much, said the California Supreme Court, and Los Angeles had to refund the money to General Dynamics. The New York Legislature passed a bill similar to Michigan's, but it was vetoed by a defense industry fan, then Governor Nelson Rockefeller. In most cases, government has been successful in charging the tax burden of its private operations to the rest of the taxpayers.

If tax exemption is little understood, its companion, underassessment, is almost completely unknown. Places on the free list are given under legal cover and appear on the public record—but underassessment is a quiet decision made by the assessor for a worthy special interest. It is extremely difficult to detect, and indeed hardly anyone tries. Here again the average taxpayer tends to be left out. Even if the assessor is his cousin, he will be reluctant to give him a break on his home, because a low assessment on a home shows up too obviously in comparison to higher assessments on similar homes. Low assessments on business properties are much harder to discern, because frequently there are no comparable properties in the district. Who is to say that the assessor put too low a value on the General Motors plant, or the shopping center owned by the county chairman, when those properties are the only ones of their kind in town? The assessor can be pretty sure, in any event, that no one will ask the question. Assessment involves a clear imbalance of power. The assessor, earning a moderate salary, is making a decision worth hundreds of thousands of dollars in tax savings about a multimillion-dollar enterprise. If he assesses the property fairly, the owner will at the very least make him work harder by challenging his figures, and may try to punish him through his political superiors. And the public will not thank him for saving them a few dollars on their own taxes. If, however, he gives the property a good low value, the owners will express their gratitude in tangible form, either to him or to his party—and the public will not punish him for a decision that cost them a few dollars each. The assessor's choice is not hard to predict: some assessors, like some people, are saints, but most are not.

The assessment system is protected by two basic strategies. The first is: underassess everybody, your friends more than the rest. Assessors dislike the notion, occasionally imposed on them by the courts, that they must assess everyone's property at its true market value. They prefer to assess at, say, 50 per cent of market value, 25 per cent for their friends. This permits those who have forgotten their arithmetic to think that everybody is coming out ahead.† It's obvious that the average taxpayer is better off if both he and the county chairman are assessed at 100 per cent, rather than himself at 50 and the county chairman at 25, but that realization does not seem widespread, and general underassessment continues to blanket the extra privileges of the few.

The second strategy, which assessors share with all bu-

---

† The assessment rate makes no difference in one's taxes if it is uniformly applied. Say that your house is worth $20,000 and the county chairman's, $40,000. If everyone is assessed at true value, he'll pay twice as much tax as you do. If everyone is assessed at 50 per cent, you at $10,000 and the chairman at $20,000, both of your taxes remain the same and he'll still pay twice what you pay. (You both won't pay half as much, because that would mean the town's revenue had been cut in half—when the assessment rate is cut in half, the tax rate must be doubled to raise the same revenue.) But suppose you're assessed at 50 per cent and the chairman at 25—now both your houses are assessed for $10,000 and the chairman is paying only half what he would pay under equal assessment. So you and the rest of the taxpayers must pay more to make up for the lower taxes paid by the chairman and others who are underassessed.

reaucrats, is that of secrecy. Assessors take the view that what they do about one property is of no legitimate concern to anyone else. In New York City, until recently, the Tax Commission was able to hear, and decide, applications for lower assessments in secret, on the grounds that the applications contained "trade secrets"; the only reason that arrangement was broken up was that the president of the commission got indicted for fixing not assessments but traffic tickets. The general principle was stated in extreme form in 1973 by Otto Christensen. Christensen is chairman of the Orange County (California) Assessment Appeals Board No. 1, and what prompted his statement was a request from state officials that he review the assessment on the San Clemente property of Richard M. Nixon. Christensen countered that his board could act only if the request came from someone owning a property of comparable value, but, unfortunately, no such person existed, the Nixons' being the highest-priced spread in all of Orange County. The Christensen opinion boils down to the following fine bureaucratic syllogism:

The assessment can be challenged only by a comparable property owner;

There are no comparable property owners;

Therefore, the assessment cannot be challenged.

Assessors follow the policy of secrecy almost as assiduously with respect to tax exemption, even when there is no taint of corruption. During the course of his study, Alfred Balk found that assessors consistently understated, often by wide margins, the value of property on the free list—which has the effect of understating the exemptions' impact on other people's taxes. Some assessors just prefer not to talk about it at all. Balk recounts the following opaque exchange with the Alameda County assessor about the $21.9 million in tax-free church property in his jurisdiction, which includes the city of Oakland:

> "Could you name the five or ten largest church parishes?"
> "I really couldn't name any."
> "Just two or three of the largest downtown."
> "I can't think of any."
> "How long have you lived in Oakland?"
> "About all my life."
> "You've never noticed the larger church buildings?"
> "We don't really have many showpiece buildings, like San Francisco's Grace Church, or Saint Mary's which burned down."
> "Where is the Archbishop's church?"
> "He has a very modest one. It surprises a lot of people. It's really very modest."

Later Balk penetrated the veil, and the assessor told him that when, new on the job, he first looked at the books, he noticed that "about every other parcel seemed to be marked with the initials RCA. I thought, My God, RCA owns a lot of property here. Only later did I find the letters meant Roman Catholic Archdiocese. You won't find the books marked that way now, so it would be hard to run a total valuation."

Sheltered by public indifference as well as secrecy, the burden of tax exemption is growing rapidly as more and more alert citizens hustle their way onto the free list. The percentage of property that is tax exempt has been rising almost everywhere. In Philadelphia, it rose from 13.1 per cent in 1916 to 24.7 per cent in 1969; in Boston from 39 per cent in 1957 to 47 per cent ten years later, and in Buffalo, New York, from 21 per cent in 1951 to 33.6 per cent in 1969. In New York City, the increase in exempt property in one decade, 1957 to 1967, had the effect of doubling the city's tax loss, from $351 million to $777 million.

The frequent outcries about property taxes merely show how successfully the system shelters those on the free list while turning the taxpayers' attention in the wrong direction. Taxpayer "revolts" have a distinctly fishy odor. One senses that a small well-organized group, devoutly wishing to lower its own taxes, has raised the banner of rebellion secure in the knowledge that, if you ask people, they will always agree that taxes are too high. As long as people complain about the amount of taxes, rather than the way they are collected, the system is safe —because most people do not really want to go without the public services paid for by the property tax.

Hardly anyone complains about the injustices in the way the property tax is imposed. (It should be said that, with its warts removed, the tax on property would be one of our fairer taxes: it is, for one thing, the only tax on wealth in this country.) No one is noticeably agitating to put all the freeloaders back on the tax rolls, allowing us really to give to the church or college of our choice, instead of dribbling our pennies into every collection plate and alumni fund in town. No one is arguing that reduced assessments for veteran and elderly homeowners are helping those who need it least, because those who do not own their homes, and presumably are in general worse off, get no help at all in paying their housing costs. No one is campaigning for equalizing the burden on tax-payers of government-owned property. Most important, there is little visible support for the most needed reform of the property tax: making it uniform across entire states. This would remove the inequity in differing local tax rates, and would also eliminate one of the causes of underassessment: the competition among communities to bring in good (that is, non-child-bearing) properties by offering them lower tax rates. Two recent tax reform proposals, in New Jersey and Oregon, included a uniform property tax. Both were defeated, the first in the legislature and the second by referendum, and in both cases the change was opposed by many of the people who would have benefited from it. When, in 1970, a certain Mr. Walz from Staten Island took a case against the church exemption to the Supreme Court, the court ruled against him; Chief Justice Warren Burger managed, in a fourteen-page opinion, to avoid meeting Walz's main contention, that he was being forced to pay higher taxes to support organizations in which he didn't necessarily believe. The case provides, by the way, a good illustration of the power of the fail-to-collect method of subsidy. The courts have repeatedly held that government must not pay out cash to parochial schools, and loud public protest would certainly greet any proposal that government write checks with tax money to all the churches in town. Yet when Mr. Walz argues that essentially the same thing is being done via tax exemption, he can't even get the Supreme Court to answer him.

Federal subsidies, like property tax exemption, come under little public assault these days—the average man continues to acquiesce. Both kinds of subsidies are enveloped in the fog of third-party payment: no one knows just who is getting how much of his tax money. Youtooism colors the property tax system. Not only are God and

School tough institutions to attack, but there is hardly a man now alive who does not have some sort of connection with some kind of tax-exempt property: a church, a college, the Elks, or the Moose. It does not seem to occur to many people that they would be better off if all those properties paid taxes, while they themselves put up an extra ten dollars or so a year for the organizations of their choice.

Most important, perhaps, is the small-change defense. None of these subsidies, taken by itself, is important to the rest of us—while the recipient of course will struggle desperately to maintain his position. As Emory Land said, a prosperous merchant marine only costs a scotch and a beer a year, and the same can be said about each of the other subsidies and each of the tax exemptions. Two drinks is hardly the stuff on which rebellions are made (not, at least, since Alexander Hamilton's booze tax caused the Whisky Rebellion of 1794). Of course, if all the various subsidies imposed on us by government at all levels were added up and presented for payment, the total might be impressive enough to make us fight back. But no one out here is adding up the bill.

13

Government: The Folks from IRS

As APRIL 15 DRAWS NEAR, the average man finds himself thinking about those people who, in their 1973 advertising, called themselves "the folks from IRS." This moment is the surest, and for many Americans the largest, transaction between themselves and their government. As he shuffles through the disorderly records of the past year, the average taxpayer is wondering how much he will have to do for his country this time around—and whether there is any way he can reduce the total.

Rarely will the average taxpayer succeed in making much of a dent in his bill. At best, he may grab a couple of feathers from the tail of a tax loophole through which those above him on the ladder are pushing their money. He may own a few shares of stock; if he sold any of them and came out ahead, or if he sold his home at a profit, he can benefit from the capital gains loophole. If he owns a home, he will get the interest and property tax deductions. He is unlikely to own any tax-free municipal bonds, and still less likely to benefit from the output of what has become known as the "tax shelter industry": those exotic deals in real estate, cattle, or Chinese gooseberries that have the virtue of minimizing the investor's tax bite. Nor does the average taxpayer have a piece of the oil depletion allowance to help him past the fifteenth of the month.

Most taxpayers are aware in varying degree, as they try unsuccessfully to beat their Form 1040, that others are winning while they are losing. Most of us know the truth reported in inverse form by Art Buchwald when he observed that tax loopholes are available to the poor as well as the rich; it's just that the poor choose not to make use of the loopholes. The man making $15,000 may not know that the five biggest oil companies pay taxes at a lower rate than he does—but he gets the general point that oil doesn't pay taxes. By now he surely knows that Richard M. Nixon has been paying less than he does. He may not know the names of the tax escapers from the business world—the J. Paul Gettys and H. Ross Perots— but he doubtless knows that a number of people are achieving the ideal denied him: making a lot of money and not paying taxes on it.

But why J. Paul and not me? Where did the average man go wrong in his preparation for the folks from IRS? The answer lies in one word—*work*. Choosing to get his income by work is the average man's great error. Just as Adam was punished for seeking knowledge by being condemned to work, so his descendants are punished for working by the tax system. It should be noted, however, that tax punishment for working was not included in God's original sentencing of Adam: tax loopholes are articles of a more recent faith, the non-work ethic.

The non-work ethic is evident throughout the tax system. The average man's income earned from work is taxed at twice or more the rate other people pay on income from capital gains, on which the average effective tax rate is 8 per cent, while income from municipal bonds pays no tax at all and, in fact, is not even reported to the Internal Revenue Service. The wealthy understand that earning money by work is a sin, and so they avoid it religiously. Work provides 90 per cent of the income of people in the brackets from $5,000 to $15,000; by $30,000, work drops below half as a source of income, and when you get to the stratosphere, above $1,000,000, the share that comes from work is down to less than 4 per cent. As the rich get richer, they increasingly conform with the principle that it's better to get your money from capital than from work: the share of income from capital gains, only 20 per cent at $100,000, rises to two thirds in the million-a-year category.

On the first page of Form 1040, the taxpayer encounters another punishment for the sin of work. This is line 9, where he attaches his W-2 form, reporting his payments to Social Security. Here the working man is penalized even more heavily than he is by the income tax. The Social Security tax imposed by the federal government is the worst screwing administered to working people—and therefore it is growing rapidly. Widely admired when it was adopted in the 1930s (long after most other industrial nations), Social Security has gradually been transformed from blessing into monster. The original idea, of course, was to secure working people's old age by requiring them and their employers to pay into a government-administered trust fund. Now Social Security is a system that pays today's retirement costs out of the contributions of those now working—and that charges the highest rates to those who earn the least. Because Social Security collects only on income up to $13,200, the highest rate is paid by those who earn that amount or less. If, for example, a person earns $30,000 he pays into Social Security at the rate of 2.5 per cent, while the person earning $10,000, or even $1,000, pays at the rate of 5.85 per cent.

Or so it would seem. In fact, the working man is screwed at up to twice that rate. To get the full impact of Social Security, multiply the amount on the W-2 form by two. This is because anywhere from half to all of the matching amount paid by your employer is ultimately paid by you. To the employer, Social Security is just another labor cost, to be passed on in the form of lower wages. It is like an employer contribution to, say, a pension plan: if the employees had chosen to bargain differently, they could have gotten the cost to the employer of the pension plan in the form of higher wages. So the cost of Social Security to the person earning $10,000 is not $585 a year but more than $1,000, and, of course, there are no deductions at all. At the lower end of the income scale, Social Security becomes a major deterrent to work. It is because of Social Security, not the income tax, that many people on welfare would lose money if they got a job.

Punishment for work pursues the average man right into his old age. If he goes on working after he starts drawing Social Security, his Social Security payments will be reduced by one half the amount he earns—a 50 per cent tax rate; theoretically, he has earned that money, but he will be penalized for the sin of work. If he happens to be between sixty-five and seventy-two, he will both be docked *and* will have to go on paying into Social Security. His work is taxed at more than 50 per cent if he earns more than $2,400. If, instead of working, he has the good sense to collect his money in some other way— *any* other way—he will not be docked a penny by Social

Security no matter how much he takes in. Work, it seems, is an even greater sin after sixty-five than before.

So successful has been the selling of Social Security—so imperceptible its perversion—that most working people continue to believe that Social Security is a good thing. The non-working wealthy, who escape paying anything at all for the support of the elderly, must think that for them Social Security is a very good thing indeed. They are right.

Left out of the big opportunities, oppressed by Social Security, our average taxpayer can only root around for the few small deductions available to him. Here again his take will be paltry compared to that of his betters. The deductions are arranged in an upside-down fashion ensuring that the less you need, the more you will get. This is because of the higher rates on higher incomes. If, for example, your maximum tax rate is 50 per cent, a $10 deduction saves you $5 in taxes, while if your maximum is 20 per cent, that same $10 deduction will only get you $2 off on your tax bill. Stanley Surrey, the former Assistant Secretary of the Treasury, gave this example of the effect of the interest deduction on different classes of homeowners. For a typical couple making $10,000 with a $25,000 home, the interest deduction will be worth about $350 a year; for a couple making $200,000 with a $200,000 home, the deduction is worth around $9,800; and for the couple whose income is so low they do not pay income tax—as is the case with some elderly homeowners—the interest deduction is worth nothing at all. Another calculation showed that the interest deduction is worth an average of $24.49 to people making $7–10,000 and $602.50 to those making over $100,000. If we add the deduction for local taxes, we find that the government through homeowner deductions is financing 70 per cent of the taxes and interest for the rich, 20 per cent for the average man, and zero for the poor.

Our taxpayer will surely remember that $50 he gave to the church building fund in time to claim the deduction, but once more he does less well than the rich. If he makes $10,000 that $50 contribution is worth $12.50 in tax savings. Those in the upper brackets find that charity is worth more than 50 cents on the dollar. Those paintings in the museum were given by the rich not just because only the rich could afford to buy them in the first place; the rich also are the only people who can afford to make such gifts because the government picks up most of the bill. In fact, if he can work out a capital gains angle, the rich man can give the painting to the museum and actually make money on the deal. The medical deduction also most helps those who have the least trouble paying their doctor's bills: for those earning $50,000 and up, that deduction is worth $110–150 a year, but only twenty-three dollars to the average man. Even the personal deduction—seemingly the fairest of deals, since everyone appears to get the same amount—works in favor of the rich. Everyone does not get the same amount from that $750: the average man at $10,000 picks up $187.50 per member of his family, while the family at $100,000 gets $517.50 each.

What strategy can the average man adopt at this unhappy moment?

Assemble enough loot to stop working and start capital-gaining or oil-depleting. Unfortunately the best way to do that is by inheritance, so by the time he hears about April 15 it is far too late for the average man to choose the right parents. Also it is worth noting that, although an individual may climb the loophole ladder, the benefits of the tax system are by definition denied to the average taxpayer as a group. This is because tax loopholes are subject to Catch-85. Under this principle, loopholes are without redeeming financial value unless restricted to no more than 15 per cent of the population. The other 85 per cent must be excluded, since it is their assignment to pay for the 15 per cent inside the loophole. If any great number of the 85 per cent were allowed inside, the value of the loophole would be diluted—a form of watering the stock. So Al Capp's policy—"America wants more tax loopholes, not fewer"—will never reach down to the average man. (Catch-85 was invoked with the U. S. Treasury bills mentioned in chapter 2. When too many people started buying the bills at the minimum of $1,000, the Treasury had to raise the minimum to $10,000 to maintain the integrity of Catch-85.) The figure of 15 per cent included is of course an outer limit. The desire to keep the hole small is in conflict with the need to assemble enough clout to get the hole bored in the first place. Ideally, a loophole should allow just one person through the eye of the needle, and history records congressional acts tailored to the individual tax needs of Louis B. Mayer, the movie man, and Dwight David Eisenhower. Bills are also designed for a single company. Senator Russell B. Long, who occasionally displays a sense of humor about what he does as chairman of the Senate Finance Committee, once managed to record the call letters of the beneficiary, TV station WWL of New Orleans, as an acrostic in the language of the bill itself:

(a) Which consists of . . .
(b) Which is carried on by . . .
(c) Less than 10 percent of the net income of which . . .

Catch-85 is modified somewhat by the principle of youtooism, but there is no real conflict between the two. It is all right for the average man to get an apparent benefit from a loophole, in the interests of youtooism, as long as he remains the overall loser in the transaction. Thus it is acceptable for the average homeowner to get an interest deduction of, say, $500, as long as the 15 per cent are getting huge enough deductions for interest on business loans (Stewart Mott says he takes about $500,000 a year) to guarantee that the average man will pay more taxes than if neither of them had the deduction. The figures on capital gains make the point. People earning $10–15,000 average twenty-four dollars a year in supposed benefits from the capital gains loophole. For those between $100,000 and $500,000 the figure is $22,630 a year, while way up there in the $1,000,000-plus bracket, the average annual tax saving per family is a grand $640,667. It is evident that the average man's twenty-four dollars is in reality a loss: if the capital gains loophole were closed, the rich would pay so much more that the average man's taxes could be reduced by considerably more than twenty-four dollars. Thus the principle of Catch-85 is preserved. (The same principle applies to the other loopholes. For example, people making over $50,000 collect more than half the Treasury's loss on the depletion allowance and no less than 83 per cent of the tax savings on municipal bonds.) These tails on the tax loopholes that give the average man an apparent benefit must be considered as insurance for the system. As such, they are remarkably effective. Most average taxpayers in the lower brackets, as they painfully tally their small shares of the system, seldom are aware that they would be better off if the loopholes existed for no one, themselves included (see page 302). That is the answer to those rich people who may complain about the average man's twenty-four dollars on the grounds that capital gains was designed for the wealthy alone.

Deductions have not gotten our taxpayer very far. Getting rich is both subject to Catch-85 and a long-range strategy at best: hardly a maneuver to be pulled off in the first half of the month of April. What can he do now?

Cheat. As noted earlier in the case of car repairs, cheating is subject to the charge of anachronism in a society where all the best swindles are legal. In the prevailing mythology, Americans do not cheat on their taxes; that's what the French and the Italians do. Still, the IRS man who wrote *The April Game* under the pen name Diogenes quotes estimates of the annual amount of tax evasion that range from $29 billion to $67 billion. Maybe there's a bit in there for the average man.

Unfortunately, the average taxpayer is once more left out of the action. The reasons are imbedded deep in both the tax and the legal systems. It is not so simple as merely saying that IRS goes after some taxpayers and not others. Like any cops, the folks from IRS practice selective law enforcement: many are cheating, few are caught. We are all familiar with this situation from the last time the highway patrol cut us out of a herd of twenty cars that were all speeding too, officer. We have no valid complaint, unless the cop picked us by deliberate design rather than random selection. We learned, after Watergate, that the Administration leaned on IRS to audit its enemies and, according to some reports, not audit its friends—but of course that has nothing to do with the average man, who makes no governmental list of enemies or friends. The average man loses out not because someone has fingered him by name but by the impersonal workings of the system. What matters here is that the IRS man, again like any cop fishing for his quota, catches more easy ones than hard ones, and the average man with his earned income is the easiest fish in the stream. He wears his earnings on his sleeve: a copy of his W-2 form is already in his file at IRS. It takes no effort for the IRS man to catch a working person underreporting his income: all he has to do is compare the return with the IRS copy of the man's W-2. By contrast, capital gains transactions—the main source of income of the very rich —are not reported to IRS. There is no piece of paper comparable to the W-2 available to the IRS man studying a capital-gainer's return; as Diogenes observes, finding the income of the rich is "hunting in the dark." The result, according to Diogenes, is that it is "safe to say that every week day Wall Streeters make at least a million dollars that IRS will never discover." The comparable figure for income earned by salaried work is roughly zero. Similarly, the physician who knows IRS doesn't have the manpower to check all his patients' returns against his own return has a much better chance of understating his income than the unfortunate working man, nailed to his fiscal cross by that W-2 form. Certainly doctors try harder, for they are convicted of tax evasion at four times the rate that prevails in the general population, and that statistic of course measures only the ones that got caught.

The average man could try bribing the IRS man who is closing in on him. Here he is obviously handicapped by lack of means. No one knows how prevalent bribery is in IRS (fairly rare, judging from the few instances that come to light), but clearly the tax evader's chances of success depend at least in part on what he has to offer and how elegantly he can make the offer. Diogenes contrasts the IRS agent who took a high-paying job at a firm he had been auditing, with the agent who was offered $1,000 a year for ten years by a working man he had caught; the second agent felt pity rather than temptation.

Then there is the borderline claim. You put in your dubious deduction—travel for "health" or "education" is a good one—and hope for the best. If IRS doesn't agree that the trip was necessary, the next step is arguing with your auditor; if you lose that debate, you have the option of going to court—if, that is, you can afford it and the amount involved is worth what the case will cost. For the wealthy, the answer to both questions is likely to be "yes": they deal in larger numbers and they can afford lawyers (a thrifty rich man will finesse the cost entirely by using a lawyer on his corporate payroll to do his private legal work). The average man, trying perhaps to make some- thing out of that $199 package tour to Florida, will usu- ally fail on both counts. So he will not contest a case he might have won. "It is very easy for a revenue agent to bully a small taxpayer, forcing him to accept a decision that the taxpayer could dispute if only he had the means," Diogenes observes. Those who can afford lawyers can even get an advance ruling in private from IRS on the tax consequences of a deal they are considering; these private rulings, very few of which are ever made public, result in a drain of tax money which ultimately has to be made up by the average taxpayer. Finally, to round out the picture, the rich man who takes IRS to court can deduct the costs of fighting for his loophole.

Each April is likely to be crueler than the last for the taxpayer, for the screwing of the working man by the tax system has been increasing in recent years. The Social

Security tax, which hits work income hardest of all taxes, has been rising steadily and is now the country's second biggest tax (after personal income). The corporation income tax, which is paid mainly by the wealthy few who own substantial amounts of stock, has been reduced repeatedly; it has dropped to third place among taxes and may soon drop below the property tax. In 1971, Congress voted $6 billion in tax benefits for corporations and those making more than $15,000, and only $1.7 billion for those below $15,000, where the average man is found. Since someone will eventually have to make up the lost revenue from the rich, it is doubtful if most taxpayers below $15,000 gained any lasting benefit from the change. Another big screwing is waiting in the wings—the so-called "value-added tax," which is a variant on the familiar sales tax. This tax is popular with European governments, which find it an easy way to raise large amounts of money without disturbing the rich. The Nixon administration in the early 1970s floated a few trial balloons for value-added; at the time these were shot down on the grounds that value-added would be a bit much even in the present iniquitous system.

(The evolution of the U.S. tax system from bad to worse is further evidence that the trickle-down theory doesn't work. Trickle-down seems to be based on a false analogy between money and food. The idea is that the rich man, sated to capacity, will push back his plate and say: "I can't eat any more of this caviar; give the rest to the servants." Similarly, the loopholer should get so stuffed on tax-free income that he would be willing to give the average man a somewhat fairer shake. But money is more like heroin than like food: the more money one has, the more he needs. Finding one loophole only stimulates the appetite for more. Accordingly, money trickles up, not down.)

It gets worse, at least in part, because there is no effective resistance from the working taxpayers who are being abused. Everyone grumbles about taxes, of course, but popular resentment is never focused on the inequities in the system. This allows officeholders to grandstand about high taxes without disturbing the loopholers who finance them. When tax reform is proposed, the public does not respond. In 1972–73, major tax reforms were defeated in New Jersey and Oregon, in the latter state by referendum, even though the great majority of taxpayers would have benefited from the reforms.

Yet the benefit to the average man of tax reform is not hard to demonstrate. For those interested, here is how to calculate how you would come out under one loophole-closing plan, designed by Joseph A. Pechman and Benjamin A. Okner of the Brookings Institution. Pechman and Okner's point is that the deductions and exemptions are the apotheosis of Catch-85. As more and more income is declared "off limits" to the tax man, the nominal tax rates aren't really a good indication of the tax burden people bear. People making a million dollars a year (before all the funny accounting tricks) should theoretically be paying more than 60 per cent of their total income in taxes, but in fact the actual effective rate is 32 per cent—that is, they get a $280,000 tax savings, down from $600,000 to $320,000.

Consider this alternative: if *all* income were taxable, the government could still take in the same amount of money with much lower tax rates. Loopholes now cost the government about $78 billion a year, which works out to almost $1,000 a year per taxpayer. Pechman and

Okner have a variety of different schemes—imposing a 16 per cent tax on income in all classes, reducing all current rates by 43 per cent, tampering with high and low income tax rates. Almost all the schemes show major reductions for those making between $10,000 and $25,000 a year; the big increases are for those making more than $50,000.

To take one of the proposed schemes, Pechman and Okner would give a $2,000 low-income tax-free allowance and set a ceiling of 44 per cent on marginal tax rates. This would cut actual taxes paid by 10 per cent for those making between $10,000 and $20,000 and raise rates for those in brackets above $25,000. Those interested in knowing whether they are net winners or losers in the present tax system can figure their position from the following chart. Take your total income from all sources, with no deductions or exemptions of any kind.* Figure your tax from the table: just multiply your income by the tax rate for your income bracket. Compare this hypothetical tax to what you paid last time around. If you pay more under the existing system, you are a net loser: you would be better off if all loopholes were abolished.

The average man would also benefit greatly from a change in the way we pay for Social Security. At present the entire cost of Social Security is borne by income from work, and those who earn the least are taxed at the highest rate. Suppose instead that the payroll tax was abolished and the cost of Social Security paid out of general revenue, in effect making other kinds of income bear

---

* If you earn all your income from work and do not itemize your deductions, don't bother doing the table—you're a *sure* loser. What's the matter with you, anyway?

Total Income	Tax Rate
Under $3,000	0.1
$3–5,000	1.7
$5–10,000	5.0
$10–15,000	7.8
$15–20,000	9.9
$20–25,000	11.9
$25–50,000	15.6
$50–100,000	24.9
$100–500,000	33.3
$500–999,000	37.7
$1,000,000 up	40.0

a share of the social cost of old age. Everyone's income tax would go up some, but the burden on work income, especially for those in the lowest brackets, would drop dramatically. Here is how it would affect a family of four that earns its income by one member's work and takes the standard deduction:

Income	Under Present System			Without Payroll Tax	
	INCOME TAX	PAYROLL TAX	TOTAL TAX	ADDITIONAL INCOME TAX	NET BENEFIT
$5,000	$102	$292.50	$394.50	$14.60	$277.90
8,000	573	468	1,041	82.50	385.50
10,000	901	585	1,386	129.74	455.16
13,000	1,391	760.50	2,151.50	230	530.50
15,000	1,820	772.20	2,592.20	262.08	510.12
25,000	4,380	772.20	5,152.20	630.72	141.48

The last column, "net benefit," shows that people whose income is earned by work would get a sizable increase in take-home pay all the way up past $25,000 a year. That's pretty good, but it could be still better with some other changes. The calculations in the table are based on the present income tax system with all its loopholes and also assume that employers will continue to pay their half of the payroll tax. But suppose that abolishing the payroll tax was combined with the kind of loophole-closing on which our earlier do-it-yourself tax reform table was based. The average man would make out still better, because the income that now escapes taxation—the municipal bonds and all the rest—would have to pay its share, thus reducing even more the burden on income earned by work. Now suppose that the employer's share of the payroll tax was also abolished, bearing in mind that, as noted earlier, from half to all of the employer's share is in reality paid by his employees in lower wages. This is what would happen. The cost to the tax system of Social Security would double, so the cost to individuals under the "additional income tax" column would double. But the employer would save much more than that amount. For example, the person at $10,000 would pay an extra $129.74, while his employer would save $585. That leaves a balance of $355.26 up for grabs. Each of us is in his own bargaining position, but most people should in time be able to extract a raise large enough to enable them to share in the employer's savings. For the person at $10,000, a raise of $306.87 would cover his added income tax (to pay the employer's share) and leave both him and his employer ahead by $177.13 each. The man at $5,000 would only need a raise of more than $14.60 to come out ahead.

These figures illustrate the magnitude of the screwing imposed on the average man's wages by the payroll tax.* They are evidence also of the power of the Social Secu-

---

* The figures used here are based on calculations generously supplied by Ms. Sam Senger of Ralph Nader's Public Citizen Tax Reform Research Group.

rity myth, for there is even less popular demand for abolishing the payroll tax than there is for income tax reform.

Assuming that most people know, in general if not in detail, that they are being had on April 15, the lack of widespread resistance is a tribute to the strategies used to protect the tax system. Let us examine these strategies for screwing the average man as they are implemented in the creation and preservation of tax privileges for the rich:

Youtooism: This strategy, one of the great advances in democratic theory, can be seen at its clearest in the tax system. Most of the great tax swindles give the average taxpayer just enough to make him think he's among the takers rather than the taken. Though he loses money on the deal, he is an accomplice in the crime, and so he has the insider's satisfaction, like the man who helped rob the bank even though the others ran off with the loot. His conclusion seems to be that maybe he can do better next time around—not that the crime itself should be eliminated, with the resulting small benefit to him.

Municipal bonds are a special case among the loopholes. They have no youtoo appeal to the average man, for below a certain income municipal bonds are not worth buying even if you have the money. Bonds have a different constituency. Municipals are as popular with state and local officials as with the wealthy people who use them as tax shelters, for bond-financed construction solves the officeholder's dilemma: how to do a lot of building, profitable to his contractor allies, without offending the electorate by raising taxes. By putting off payment via bonds, the officeholder gets the construction while he is in office, leaving the bill to be paid by those who succeed him. Municipal bonds go at an artificially low rate of interest because the interest is tax-exempt; without tax exemption, the interest would rise to the market rate, and officeholders would not be able to issue as many bonds for the same amount of interest. To get around this objection, with its implications for the health of the construction industry, tax reformers usually propose that the federal government directly subsidize local bonds instead of achieving the same effect by tax exemption. This would cut the cost of municipal bonds to the federal tax system in half, since it costs the government two dollars in lost revenue to finance one dollar in lower interest costs. When Senator William Proxmire floated this idea back home in Wisconsin, local officeholders indignantly rejected it. Perhaps it occurred to them that a straight interest subsidy would raise the intolerable question why bonds should be subsidized at all. In any event, local officials are happy with a system in which they can have their construction, charge the bill to tomorrow, and please their wealthy constituents who buy the bonds. Only the average man is left out.

Fail-to-Collect: This principle holds that governments are less likely to attract unfavorable attention if they fail to collect money from their friends, rather than if they actually pay out their favors in cash. Tax loopholes are in the fail-to-collect category, like tax-exempt property and the interest-free deposits governments make in their favorite banks. That $78 billion the government is currently losing through loopholes might cause a stir if it was actually paid out in checks to the beneficiaries: *"Dear Mr. Getty: Enclosed please find . . ."* A variant form is "fail-to-notice": income from municipal bonds, for example, is not reported at all, and therefore does not officially exist as a tax loss to the Treasury.

Third-party Payment: By channeling the money through a third party, the government, the nature of the transaction is made fuzzy and remote. So J. Paul Getty gets $70 million off on his income tax—what's that got to do with me? For one Getty and one taxpayer, the answer is: very little. Suppose, on the other hand, the tax loopholers had to solicit taxpayers directly for their privileges. Getty would have to approach the taxpayer with a message something like this: "If you'll agree to pay just one dollar more on your taxes, you'll be helping to build one of the great American family fortunes." Similar messages would come in from the others, from the Rockefellers to H. Ross Perot. It is doubtful if the average man would respond with any enthusiasm to such appeals. Once the money has been third-partied into a lump sum, however, the taxpayer can no longer tell what it's buying: a share in running the government, a nuclear aircraft carrier, or lower taxes for J. Paul Getty.

Complexity: The tax code gets more complicated each year as it collects its annual crop of special-interest amendments. This IRS prose is not intended to be understood by taxpayers: "For the purposes of paragraph (3), an organization described in paragraph (2) shall be deemed to include an organization described in Section 501(c)(4), (5), or (6), which would be described in Section 501(c)(3)." The need for a guide in finding the treasures hidden in the murky depths of the tax code has caused the number of tax accountants and lawyers to multiply. This follows the general principle that any new screwing by complexity breeds a new category of experts who administer it. Like most experts, the tax guides' services are not available to the average man because his case is not worth what the experts cost. If, however, he does manage to join the wealthy in hiring a tax expert, he will have the pleasure of knowing that the cost of the expert is deductible next year. That seems like a break, unless he happens to reflect that it was the tax code that created the need for the expert in the first place.

Secrecy: Government avoids talking about loopholing and, when evasion is impossible, it muddies the waters. Back in the early seventies the Treasury made studies on the effects of tax subsidies—but it refused to make the results public. The first serious work on tax subsidies came not from the Treasury, nor for that matter from the academics, but from the Joint Economic Committee of the Congress. Occasionally, however, complaints about loopholes reach a level that forces an answer. Then the Treasury comes forward to say that, well, the size of the loopholes has been greatly exaggerated, and besides it's not true that rich people don't pay taxes. This second point is usually demonstrated by trotting out figures showing the effective tax rate paid by the rich on *adjusted* gross income. "Adjusted" simply means that most of the income has already been put through the loopholes; the adjusted income is what's left. While the "adjustment" doesn't mean much to the average taxpayer, it is important to the rich. A few years back, for example, a prominent Californian paid no federal income tax because his income, after adjustment, was zero. But no one took that to mean Ronald Reagan was poor.

Social Utility: Occasionally officials make a rather languid effort to find some redeeming social value in the loopholes. Tax-exempt municipal bonds are needed to keep the public works working out in the provinces; no loophole, no sewer system. Capital gains underpins the American way of life. Without that loophole, we are told, investment would cease, capitalism would wither away, and all our incomes would dry up. The average man's job depends on someone else's capital gains loophole. This argument assumes that the wealthy would not invest if their profits were taxed at the same rate the rest of us pay on money we earn by work. Even granted the sincere aversion of the rich to paying taxes, it hardly seems they would keep their capital out of the market if that were its most profitable use; it still beats working for a living. The idea that the stock market, where capital gains happen, is essential to the economy is a common myth. In reality, as we point out elsewhere, growth is financed mainly by corporate earnings, borrowing from banks and private sales of stock; the market provides only 5 per cent of new capital. If the market closed down, a number of wealthy shirts would be lost, but it would mean little if anything to the rest of the nation. And— but the arguments presented for the loopholes are so perfunctory that it is not worth spending any great effort to refute them.

About the only case that can be made for the loopholes is simply that they are There.

14

In Conclusion: Why

THE QUESTION THAT CRIES OUT from the preceding pages is: why do we let it happen? In a nation where the machinery of democracy is available for our use, why do we not take political arms against those who are taking us to the cleaners?

The question centers on those among us who seem not to be aware that they are losers in the system of net screwing. The position of most other people is pretty clear. The rich, especially those whose wealth was inherited, are obvious winners; a good stock of capital buys immunity from most of the screwings described in earlier chapters, and it cushions the impact of the rest. The poor, as always, are so far out that they need no surveyor to fix their place on the map of privilege. For the majority, who live in between those extremes, there are, as we have seen, a number of ways of figuring their standing in the game, the simplest being the do-it-yourself tax table on page 302. In a broader sense, the arithmetic of Catch-85 tells us that the overwhelming majority of those between the extremes of rich and poor are destined to be net losers.

The failure of most of us to grasp the implications of Catch-85 is one of the keys to the question raised in the title of this chapter. People continue to be screwed because a large number of losers actively support the system that screws them. Throughout history, systems of exploitation have depended not just on the passive obedience of the majority but on the active support of losers who were one step off the bottom; indeed, it is they who usually do the day-to-day work of administering the system, while the beneficiaries play. In ancient Rome, they were the small farmers who joined the legions and fought so that wealthy Romans could acquire enough slaves to man the plantations that put the small farmer out of business. In the American South before the Civil War, they were the house slaves and overseers who managed the plantation while Massa was out boozing or chasing Scarlett. To take the extreme example, in the concentration camps they were the inmates who helped run the camps for the Nazis right up to the moment that they too were shoveled into the gas chambers. In a different sense, the subsidizing of artists by the rulers can be viewed as a way of channeling into safe directions the creative energies of talented people; think, for example, of the revolution that Michelangelo might have conceived and led had he not been on the Pope's payroll and flat on his back under the ceiling of the Sistine Chapel. In all those cases, however, those who administered the system were a small minority compared to the great mass of outright losers. The great accomplishment of modern America is that this minority has been converted into a majority: most of us, that is, apply our skills and labor to working the machinery by which we are exploited. In the terminology of the old South, we have become a nation of house niggers.

We have in earlier chapters explored the strategies that keep the average man sufficiently off balance so he doesn't reach out and smash the roulette wheel that keeps on showing him up as a loser. Third-party payments, with their frills of fail-to-collect and fail-to-notice, make it impossible to locate the croupier who is fixing the wheel or to identify the person who is making off with our chips; you can't fight City Hall if you can't even find the place. As we saw in the case of the forty-five-dollar Blue Cross cat bite, you cannot fight third-party payment systems unless everyone else in the same plight is doing so also. The individual cannot escape third-party screwings, nor can he avoid paying the monopolist's price if he needs his goods or, in the case of the guilds, his services. That does not mean we are entirely helpless as individuals. An attitude of healthy skepticism toward expert claims would enable us to escape at least some swindles. The average man may not be able to put his savings into Treasury bills now that the ante has been raised to $10,-000, but he can avoid being cleaned out in the stock market by staying away. In some areas where real choices exist, like life insurance, an informed person can with a little effort save himself a screwing. Even in those cases, however, people usually need an intermediary—for life insurance, *Consumer Reports,* or Herbert Denenberg—to translate wordnoise into language we can understand. Otherwise, wordnoise drowns out our common sense, and the deliberate complexities of the experts make it too difficult—especially after a day's work—to figure out just how we're being taken. It becomes easier not to try to read the fine print.

It is discouragingly difficult to identify screwings that seem possible to reverse and are also big enough and frequent enough to be worth the effort. The total potentially available for redemption is certainly high enough— so large, indeed, that one can hardly put a price tag on it. Beverly C. Moore, Jr., of the Corporate Accountability Research Group in Washington, took a crack at it a couple of years ago. Moore's total figure for screwings came to an imposing $400 billion a year, and he concluded that, if all those screwings could be eliminated, the average man's income would rise by more than 50 per cent. That kind of increase in the pleasures that money can buy, plus the satisfaction of extracting it from those who are now mining it from us, would seem to be goals well worth fighting for. (Moore's figure may well be incredible, but half that amount will make the point equally well.)

In practice, however, we cannot find a handle on that 50 per cent. Instead, we are confronted with an endless series of swindles that are either small or infrequent, or both, and often third-partied out of our reach. One example is the maritime subsidy, which, as its administrator explained in its defense, costs us each year only a shot and a beer apiece: hardly grounds for an uprising. Another example, closer to home, is the multiple small bites taken out of us by our bankers. It is hard indeed to imagine a mass movement against the 360-day year over which the bank collects the one-year loan on which we pay 365 days' interest. Other swindles are insulated from popular wrath because, like a comet, they come around at rare intervals. Probate is one example. The financial carnage that takes place at a closing is another; the closing industry in general, and title insurance in particular, survive on the fact that the victim does not expect to go through this again soon, if ever, and so has no motive to go out and join an anti-closing movement.

The corrupting influence of youtooism is a more profound reason for our acquiescence. Youtoo is a threat as well as a promise. The promise "we'll take fifty dollars off your taxes, and a million off Rockefeller's," carries with it the unspoken message: "If you don't like that, we'll keep your fifty dollars." Similarly, Massa's message to the house slave was: "You want to be out there chopping cotton, boy, or in here mixing juleps?" The promise of youtoo keeps the average man's eyes directed upwards, to what he might, if he is lucky, attain, and once he identifies, even if only in his dreams, with those above him, he will feel envy rather than resentment at the way they screw people like him (not himself personally, for such third-partied screwings as tax evasion never appear to be directed at anyone in particular). Reformers run into this attitude when they find that working-class people typically are more resentful of welfare than of corporate chiselers. The reformers may hastily conclude that people are just plain ignorant, but it is an insult to the average man's intelligence to suppose that he doesn't realize that the monopolist and Lockheed and the other beneficiaries of socialism for the rich cost him a lot more than those people on welfare in the next neighborhood. Most people are doubtless well aware of that reality; if they don't respond, it is because in some measure they identify with the person doing the screwing: one day they themselves, or if not they, their children, will be defense contractors or tax loopholers or members of professional guilds. Under Catch-85 the odds that the average man will ever make it into the big leagues are remote indeed, but the possibility is there, and envy is no launching pad for revolution.

A more veiled form of the youtoo threat is the practice of directing the average man's attention to comparisons that make his plight look good. This is the you-think-you're-bad-off approach. Union members are told to think about labor's rights in Eastern Europe: so maybe all you've got is Jimmy Hoffa, but over in that Russia unions don't have any rights at all! Women who complain about their status are advised to contemplate Arab societies: why, they have to wear veils every time they go out of the house! In similar vein, Richard M. Nixon once observed that people on welfare here would be considered rich in other countries, although it was not clear whether by welfare he meant socialism for the rich or the cheaper old-fashioned variety. It is true that the average man is better off in Buffalo than in Bombay, but that observation does not seem to explain why he should be screwed in either place. (It should be noted that this line has yet to be extended to more tangible transactions. We do not hear the car dealer say: "You think you got a lemon, you should see the car I sold Jones—didn't even make it to the corner!" Or the surgeon: "You call me a butcher—at least you're alive to complain, which is more than you can say about my last patient.")

The you-think-you're-bad-off approach trades on the principle that we decide how well off we are by comparing our position to that of others, not to some absolute standard of what we ought to have. This makes what others have important, especially those below us; if, under the youtoo principle, the average man envies those above him, he will not resent the fact that people further up the ladder are pulling steadily away from him—that's

where he hopes to be some day. Viewed this way, however, a gain for those below us is a loss for us: so tax reform in New Jersey was defeated by working-class voters
who, though they would have gained by the reform, saw
that the poor would have gained more, narrowing the
gap between them. Taking the idea one step further, if
their gain is our loss, then their loss is our gain. Hence the
cheers that a promise to punish those on welfare can draw
from those one step up the ladder. Thus what appears to
be kicking people when they're down—which, by the way,
is the only safe time to kick them—is an effort to raise our
comparative status by diminishing theirs.

Gookery and its relative, the Menace, also help convince the average man to hold still for the treatment.
Gooks originally were Asians whom our troops felt free
to kill in ways frowned on by the Geneva Convention.
In a broader sense, Gooks are people we don't have to
treat like people: we can abuse them in ways forbidden
by the usual code of behavior. Foreigners are frequently
Gooks; so are those of another color and of a lower class;
women and children are often Gooks; slaves are Gooks
by law. Of course, who is a Gook depends on whose eyes
you're looking through, and one man's Gook is another
man's paisano. In tribal society, the condition of Gook
grows in concentric circles moving out from the individual: the degree of fidelity that you owe decreases as you
move out from family to clan to tribe, until those on the
outermost rim are total Gooks. The lines are clearly
drawn, and the person at the furthest circle knows that
you are as complete a Gook to him as he is to you. In
modern America, the lines are badly confused, for the
reality of gookery is hidden by layers of hypocrisy and
wordnoise proclaiming that in a democratic society no

one is a Gook, that we are all people. This makes it difficult for us to determine whether those in a position to
screw us—the professional guilds, the bankers, the monopolists, the pension plan administrators, and so forth—
whether when they look at us they see Gooks on whom
it's open season or people who are protected by some
kind of domestic Geneva Convention. When he ventured
out on Wall Street, for example, the little guy might well
have asked himself if he was coming on as a Gook.

The question is particularly important when we are
dealing with that rapidly growing army of experts who
ask us to take their mysterious ministrations on faith, for
we have few independent means of checking on whether
they are gooking us. In the old days, we all knew that
you had to sell your goldbrick outside the tribe, but now
we no longer can be sure who is in the tribe and who isn't.
For the average man, the grand illusion is that he has at
last moved up out of Gook status. Two generations ago,
when he was in the working class, the average man knew
he was a Gook to his superiors. Then it seemed, during
that great quarter-century after the Second World War,
that he had climbed to the point where those above him
could distinguish him from those he had left behind, and
therefore treat him better. Now that the pie is no longer
expanding, now that the rich can only fatten their share
at the expense of the average man, that illusion is fading.
Instead, it is increasingly obvious, as the average man
looks up the ladder in the hopes of a sign of friendly
recognition, that those looking down at him see merely—
another Gook.

Gooks are often dressed up as Menaces to distract the
average person from his own Gook status. Jews, for example, served European nations for many centuries as a

peril that took people's minds off the screwing of the average Christian. American Menaces tend to come painted in bright colors to make them more fearsome. Yellow Peril was waved at West Coast workingmen in the late nineteenth century. Black Menace was employed at the turn of the century by Southern aristocrats to secure the votes, and the money, of poor whites; he has recently taken on a similar assignment up North. Today Red Menace stands there like a figure in a shooting gallery to take the blame for the screwing of the average American —though it has never been made clear why the nastiness of the Russians should entitle those who point it out to us to stuff their hands in our pockets. Not long ago columnist Russell Baker reported on the high level concern over the impending retirement of the Great Communist Menace. The leadership was casting about for a successor Menace, but none of those nominated seemed to approach the stature of the incumbent. Baker's column was said to have caused distress bordering on panic in Moscow, where it was feared that the Menace's retirement would force out of office his Russian twin, the Great Imperialist Warmonger. This would have ended many years of fruitful collaboration during which the two brother Menaces had made such mutually profitable arrangements as the sending of submarines to surface off the other fellow's shores—around Florida and Murmansk— about the time the respective defense budgets were being decided upon. The reports of the impending retirements proved to be greatly exaggerated, however, and at this writing the twin Menaces, though a bit creaky with age, are still on display, reassuring the average man in both countries that he is being swindled for his own good.

History suggests that our question—why do we take it?

—can best be answered by the observation that we always have. Around this earth over the endless centuries, we humans have had any number of opportunities to create societies fit for the average man—and the record of failure suggests that the odds against our ever doing it are pretty long. Many a movement has been led for the purported benefit of the average man, and all have come to naught. Some, like the Russian Revolution and the American labor movement, have been betrayed by their leaders, who, once in power, decided that screwing the average Russian or union member wasn't such a bad idea after all. Others were betrayed by the average man himself: Nat Turner's men were gunned down by their fellow slaves, and, a couple of generations later in the same region, the Populists failed when the poor whites were persuaded to turn against their black allies. Still other movements decayed after a brief success, as the French Revolution in less than ten years rotted into Bonapartism. The quick decay of a promising opportunity occurred in the early days of our own West. Matthew Josephson in *The Robber Barons* describes how quickly the average man was subdued in the years after the Gold Rush:

> So in the second decade of the Pacific Slope's terrestrial paradise, the cycle is already completed, the arc defined. Out of the strenuous milling of free frontiersmen, two or three Yankee shopkeepers emerge, a derelict lawyer from the East, a pair of practical Irish miners in collaboration with a pair of Irish saloonkeepers, an English invalid gambler, a land-jobber, a drover and innkeeper from Indiana, these have banded together to form a ruling class, by something equivalent to an imperceptible process of coup d'etat have seized all power, all economic control.

> . . . The human masses of free pioneers who came yes-
> terday plodding over the desert route, with its trail of ox
> and horse skeletons and wrecked wagons, its numerous
> mounds of graves, braving storms, flooded rivers, thirst,
> hunger, heat and Indian raiders—these and their children
> and their children's children are all in subjection to
> princely and dynastic overlords, who rule by "use" and
> "wont," who "own" because they own, and are well seized
> of so much land, forest, mineral deposits, harbor rights,
> and franchises and rights of way because they have
> seized.

The details vary, but the story has been told a thousand
times. That doesn't mean nobody is trying. A look around
the country provides us with ample grounds for hope—
and despair. To name just a sample few: here's Ralph
Nader and a bunch of public interest lawyers fighting an
array of dragons; there's Common Cause, and Consumers
Union has been around for almost forty years. And many,
many others. Each has valuable achievements to its
credit; none has altered the essential lines of the society
in which they operate. They are mortal, and the system
is not.

Exploited human beings evidently find it comforting
to have a faith that assures us it's not our fault but the
way of the world. Organized religion has traditionally
played the role of justifying the social order, explaining
to the average man why it is right that the privileged,
including the priesthood, should eat high on the hog
while he roots for scraps. When Pharaoh's bureaucrats
summoned the common man to work on the pyramid,
they spoke with the authority of the gods of Egypt, and
later gods have continued to countersign the decrees of
those in power. Often the average man is promised in

return for his sacrifice the kind of reward that does not require anyone to put money in the bank. The purest example is the Hindu doctrine of karma, under which the good serf will be rewarded for his obedience and the bad landowner punished for his cruelty—but later, in their next incarnations. It's doubtful that the Indian peasant really believes this; more likely he would seize the opportunity to trade places with the landlord even at the risk of coming back next time around as a cockroach. Still, the peasant is going to be screwed in any case, and karma gives him a rationale for his existence and something to hope for in his more credulous moments. Viewed from the proper angle, it can be seen that the Brahmin is doing the peasant a favor by offering him the consolation of faith.

Faith in modern-day America is more secular than karma. It is a faith, without benefit of the afterlife, in the American system and its products—a kind of brand-name loyalty. Its political form is patriotism—a belief that we are better off being screwed by our own ruling class than by another one—and war calls upon us for its most extreme expression. In a democratic society, this sort of faith has a particularly strong element of self-justification. If we are screwed not because God wills it but because we permit it, we can avoid the implied self-reproach by denying that there is anything wrong—denying, that is, the fact of the screwing. To admit that we're being screwed and could perhaps prevent it would imply hope, which is painful, and the need for action, which is frightening. So we dismiss the problem and renew our faith. We can observe that faith in the example of the two men loyally arguing the respective merits of their cars, while somewhere inside them both are aware that the cars are equally overpriced lemons. Those who are screwed the most are the least willing to admit it—the poor, who are hit by more than the average share of credit frauds, are those who react most angrily when someone points out how they have been taken. Neither they nor anyone else likes to admit that he's been suckered. This self-protecting faith is an asset without price to those in power.

The average man's faith in America has of course eroded spectacularly in recent years. A generation ago, during the years that were fat, that faith was probably at its all-time high. Then the faith began to fade, while the average man was still inching ahead, like one of those mythical stocks that predicts a turning in the market. Religion went first when God died, somewhere in the suburbs, back in the late 1950s. Other institutions followed. Belief in the political order faded, never more noticeably than when American officers in Southeast Asia found themselves unable to force their draftees into dangerous assignments. Finally, skepticism flourished when word began to come down from the top that the growth years were over, that more-is-better was an impossible dream; it was probably true, but the average man could not help observing that those telling him to tighten his belt were the very people who had already lapped up all the heavy cream. Some of society's winners were, it is true, temporarily exempt: a 1973 Harris Poll showed a rising faith in doctors and bankers, from which one might conclude that if you're going to screw people, it's best to do it with dignity. Despite such exceptions, every indicator from polls to simple intuition told us that the average man had suffered a massive loss of faith in the system in which he lived. Instead of the promised Greening of America, or the Graying of America prophesied by some, we are now confronted with what we might call the Souring of America.

This Souring of America is cause for mingled fear and hope among those of us who would like to see an end to the screwing of the average man. The outcome depends on the use we all make of that frighteningly vast quantity of faith that is floating around, like unrequited molecules, in search of an object to which it can attach itself. Those who have lost faith in the existing order can seek new authority, or they can place their faith in themselves. We are in danger of succumbing to whatever messiah can capture all that free-floating faith. To the phony complexities inflicted on us by the experts, the messiah will oppose the false simplicity of his solution. Whatever its specifics, the essence of his message will be: give the power to us, let us run it for you, lay that burden down. If we heed the message, if we lay down the burden of determining our own fates, then all history tells us what will happen next: today's messiah will tomorrow be selling us title insurance, or far worse.

Or we can decide to do it ourselves. Each of the screwings described in this book has its solution—several of them in most cases—but none will come about without the active support of the average man himself. This requires, more than any single policy or platform, a different view of the situation most people find themselves in. More of us must realize that the average man is being screwed, not by accident or by history or for the national defense, but for and by the rich and powerful. We must refuse to let our eyes be lured from the ball by whatever Menace is being brandished about at the moment, or be persuaded that our screwing is justified by the fact that others are more screwed than we. We must see that a fairer society offers the average man a better opportunity than his long shot chance of making it as an individual in the present order.

Beyond that, we must see a vision of a society in which the benefit to the average man will be, not just a rise in income, but the sense that he is no longer being screwed —that when the call to sacrifice is heard, he will not find himself standing alone in line to pay out his money or his life for the benefit of his superiors. That doesn't mean each of us has to figure out the fine print of the experts: we know that's not going to happen. Between the two horns of that dilemma—leave it to messiah or read it ourselves—there is room if we know how to use it. We can have our own experts if we will only learn to recognize them when they raise their heads, and they will continue to be ours if we hold them by the scruff of the neck. That's democracy. If we can make it work, we can beat the house odds.